"Leadership is the
transference of vision".
Best wishes,
Harold W. Reed

The Dynamics of
LEADERSHIP

The
Dynamics of
LEADERSHIP

Open the Door to
Your Leadership Potential

HAROLD W. REED

The Interstate Printers & Publishers, Inc.
Danville, Illinois

CONTENTS

PART I
Fundamentals of Leadership

PART II
Eight Theories of Leadership

PART III
Motivating Forces in Leadership

PART IV
The Heart of the Matter

FOREWORD

For you who seek to be effective leaders, *THE DYNAMICS OF LEADERSHIP* places in your hands a Chart and Compass. It is not just a cerebral or intellectual discussion of leadership but a practical disclosure of all the elements and wisdom of one acknowledged leader's view of leadership, paired with scores of examples of other world class leaders.

I am constantly amazed that so few meaningful books have been compiled on the subject of Leadership. The Author approaches this vital subject in a fresh and challenging way. His work is an exhaustive and complete collection of definition and explanation, yet it is rich with meaningful illustration.

You will especially enjoy Chapter 4 and its exciting characterization of "Seven World Changers," men and women whose colossal leadership shook the pillars of history. Dr. Reed has brought forward information and human example that will live with you for a long time.

Whether your life is centered around business, industry, politics, education, the arts, public or private administration, religion, the military, or the giant corporations, you will discover insights and concepts within this book that will both widen your intellectual horizons and bring you face to face with a number of ideas and values of which you may be instinctively aware, but which you do not implement daily. You will also note some familiar leadership philosophies that will be sharply focused and contrasted.

The ability to define and implement competent and sensitive leadership remains the greatest single need of our nation, indeed of our world. I believe that *THE DYNAMICS OF LEADERSHIP* will stand the test of time. In it, the essence of leadership, and all that it means, is fully illuminated. It is my dream that this high-value book may crystallize our thinking and accelerate our actions in order that we might become the leaders that now we know how to be.

I could not prepare this foreword for *THE DYNAMICS OF LEADERSHIP* without a note about its author. I have known Dr. Harold W. Reed for over 15 years. He remains one of the best living examples of leadership that I know. It is both his capability and his concern in the area of leadership that has brought about this fine work.

—Arthur S. Ward, Jr.

January 9, 1982

PREFACE

Why another book on the subject of "Leadership"? With thousands decrying the lack of leadership in our world, can another voice be heard in this wilderness? What new thrust does *THE DYNAMICS OF LEADERSHIP* have for a leader, or for one who desires a leadership role?

This is not a "HOW TO" manual, nor is it a guide offering "SIX EASY STEPS TO THE TOP." Rather, it is a book that deals with the fundamentals of leadership: WHAT MAKES A LEADER TICK?

This is not a book that deals with "Management," although management in certain areas calls for leadership. MANAGEMENT deals with PARTS—LEADERSHIP deals with the WHOLE.

What are the "Fundamentals of Leadership"? Does one's philosophy of life largely determine the quality of his leadership?

What part did "A Philosophy of Life" play in the leadership of "Seven World Changers"? Why is it important to become acquainted with "Eight Theories of Leadership"? What of the "Motivating Forces in Leadership?" How can a leader come to understand and use these powerful tools? Can "The Impossible Dream" come true? These are the vital issues that are thoroughly explored and fully discussed in a very clear and forceful style.

The Author, Harold W. Reed, is speaking from experience. He has had a long and distinguished career in Administration on the university level, having served as a College President for a period of 30 years. During those exciting and challenging years as an executive, he formulated a theory of leadership that enabled him to succeed at a time when many college and university presidents were "throwing in the towel." This theory enabled him to keep the Institution on a steady course during the turbulent and explosive "Sixties." Although many colleges and universities were closing their doors, his skillful use of the tools of leadership made it possible for him to launch, and to complete, a dramatic expansion program. The erection of 15 major buildings and the expansion of the academic program, along with a sound fiscal policy, brought the Institution into a prestigious standing among the colleges and universities of the Midwest.

President Reed is a graduate of Colorado College and Colorado State University. He received his Doctorate from the University of Southern California and has been the recipient of several honorary degrees as well. He has been active in civic and community affairs. Currently he is serving on the "Foundation Board" of the Riverside Medical Center in Kankakee, Illinois, an Institution that he assisted in the fund raising for its construction and on whose "Board of Directors" he served for eleven years. He has traveled throughout the world and has lectured extensively on the subject of "Leadership."

To him, "Leadership is the ability to get a person to do what you want him to do, when you want it done, in a way you want it done, because he wants to do it." Furthermore, he believes that two of the most important factors in leadership are DECISION MAKING and TIMING.

THE DYNAMICS OF LEADERSHIP states clearly and unequivocally that LEADERS ARE MADE—NOT BORN. Leadership CAN be taught. For the serious student of "Leadership," this is a book that he will want to read, and re-read.

—Maybelle E. Reed

Part I

FUNDAMENTALS OF LEADERSHIP

Leadership arises out of energy, intelligence and character.

Energy is sheer ability to act.

Intelligence is energy engaged in solving problems.

Character is energy and intelligence organized in relation to social situations.

—*Emory S. Bogardus*

1.

An Overview

THE DYNAMICS OF LEADERSHIP is a book that attempts to come to grips with the fundamentals of leadership. We must deal with these fundamentals at some depth if there is to be a logical and complete analysis of this very important subject. There must be a clear-cut view of the following factors:

A Definitive Meaning of Leadership
A Philosophy of Life
A Sense of Mission
Consideration of "Eight Theories of Leadership"
An Understanding of the Factors Involved in "Decision
    Making"
Awareness of the Prime Importance of "Timing"

A Comprehensive Study of the "Motivating Forces in Leadership"

Ability and Willingness to Use the Tools of Goal Setting and Organization

We are fully aware that there are those who have never made a systematic study of the subject of "Leadership,"; and yet, they have excelled in some specific field or specialty. They have been alert to that which "works," and they have been observant of others who have been successful. They have perhaps had natural talents which have been of great assistance to them in attaining a good degree of success. These persons are like the young musician who has a natural ear for music and is able to play the piano with considerable expertise. However, he is limited in his musicianship, so long as he does not have some guidance. Take this same young man, with his natural talent for the piano; place him under the guidance of a great teacher; let him become disciplined in a study of fundamentals of music and let him practice, hour upon hour; then, and only then, will he be able to reach the heights of which he is capable.

In the same manner, those who have high goals in the "Art of Leadership" must study and discipline themselves in the fundamentals of leadership before they can become the Leaders that they are capable of being, and before they can attain the high goals which they have set for themselves. A thorough study of the fundamentals of leadership is a MUST for those who would reach the higher levels of understanding and proficiency in both the science and the art of leadership.

In setting forth a definitive meaning of "Leadership," after a careful perusal of over 100 definitions, we choose to define LEADERSHIP as "The ability to get a person to do what you want him to do, when you want it done, in a way you want it done, because he wants to do it." With this clear-cut definition in our thinking, it is necessary for us to ask the question: What is the best way to develop leadership? Then, it is important to attempt an answer. This question, however, is immediately in opposition to those who believe that leaders are "born leaders"—rather than that they can be made leaders. Thomas Carlyle states that the great men of history were *born to be leaders*. They were "sent" into the world. These are the heroes. To him "The history of the world is the history of great men."[1] If Carylyle's position is correct, it is then futile to attempt to train anyone in the art of leadership. If they are "born leaders," then it is a waste of time to attempt the teaching of "Leadership."

On the other hand, there are many who believe that leaders are "made." Thus, the teaching of leadership qualities, a study of definitions and theories, and an understanding of the motivational forces in leadership, is of real worth and is vastly important for our society, and for all mankind. Not only does the Christian Faith emphasize the intrinsic value of human personality, but it stresses the possibility of personality growth, as well as the potential for the development of leadership. This thought is illustrated in "The Parable of the Talents." This parable deals with three individuals: one who had five talents, one who had two talents, and one who had only one talent. The one with the five talents, through hard work, keen insight, and profitable investments, was able to double his talents. The one with the two talents, likewise, proved his diligence and faithfulness and was able to increase his talents one hundred-fold. However, the one who had received only the one talent became fearful and lost his nerve. He hid his talent and therefore had no increase. For this he was reprimanded; he had utterly failed in his stewardship. This "Parable" harmonizes with real life experiences in Business, in Government, in Religion, in the Arts, and in the various professions.

LEADERS ARE MADE—NOT BORN

Therefore, a study of the "Dynamics of Leadership" is vitally important. Again, we come back to our primary question: "What are the best ways to develop leadership?" In answer to this, we accept the proposition that there are a number of factors with which we must deal if we attempt to study the subject systematically. It is imperative that we begin with A DEFINITIVE MEANING OF LEADERSHIP. We have already listed one very excellent definition, but it is necessary for us to give careful attention to the way in which those who are specialists in this field have defined the term. The serious student of this subject very quickly comes to understand the complexity of the meaning of the word "Leadership." Many times its real meaning seems somewhat allusive. Ordway Tead observed that "The leader is one who knows, with greater than average strength of conviction, what he wants to get done, and where he wants to go. The world stands aside to let pass the man who knows whither he is going."[2]

A second factor in setting forth the fundamentals of leadership is perhaps the most basic fundamental of all. It is the bedrock foundation upon which one builds his leadership; it is HIS PHILOSOPHY OF LIFE. It is worthwhile for the serious student of leadership to

seek out from his acquaintances and friends 10 or 12 whom he believes to have been very successful, and then to spend sufficient time
with them, talking, questioning, and reasoning, until he can clearly
state their philosophy of life. After this mental exercise, let him carefully set forth his own philosophy. Every person should be able to do
this with such force and clarity that it will be a guiding light, and a
tower of strength, for all of the exigencies of life.

While I believe that it is of great import to understand the mean-
ings of leadership and to have clearly delineated one's own
philosophy of life, it is also of great importance that one has a
SENSE OF MISSION—a sense of mission that will enable him to
achieve the goals which have been set forth. There is a driving
power in a "Sense of Mission." Most of the great leaders, both of the
present and of the past, believed that they had a "rendezvous with
destiny." In this connection we want to consider seven great leaders
who we suggest were WORLD CHANGERS. These leaders, each in
their own sphere of action, were imbued with a tremendous sense of
mission. They possessed a well defined philosophy of life. They
were able to seize upon the "motivating forces," which are the very
"tools" of leadership. Because of their dynamic leadership, Com-
munities, States, Nations, and our World were changed.

The leader should give consideration, and careful analysis, to the
various THEORIES OF LEADERSHIP. We have already referred to
the "Great Man Theory" as set forth by Thomas Carlyle. This theory
seemed to have influenced the thinking of most scholars during an
earlier period, and it is still of great import today. However, with the
growing influence of sociology and psychology, there has developed
another theory which is quite pervasive. This new influence emphasizes the strong place of the individual and of the social group.
The "Social Force" thus became, in this theory, more important than
that of the "Great Person." This new philosophy, that focused upon
the "Social Situation" in leadership, exerted a powerful influence in
the colleges and universities, as they attempted to come to grips with
the correct place of theory in leadership.

Another position, which is in striking contrast to the two theories
which we have just mentioned, has to do with "Leadership Through
Followership." When a person becomes greatly interested in an Organization, a Cause, or an Institution, there is a tendency for him to
give generously to it of time, talent, and many times financial support. When this is done, the constituency may come to feel that they
have a potential leader. Thus, it becomes an agency, an opportunity,

or a vehicle for climbing to a place of recognition and possibly of leadership.

For the most part, little attention has been given to the "Creative Artist" as a leader. His leadership may be exerted through the various fields of Art: Literature, Sculpture, Music, Drama, Architecture, and Painting. These creative avenues provide opportunities for the Artist to influence an individual, a community, a nation, and even the world. To those who excel in the "Arts" is granted the privilege of speaking to their generation and to the generations that shall follow. Consider with me, in the field of literature, the influence or leadership of such writers as Tolstoy, Shakespeare, and Solzhenitsyn. These are "Creative Artists" who through their writings have become leaders, let there be no doubt about it.

The "Intimidation" theory of leadership is perhaps a minor theory. However, we should deal with it in order to help to overcome its vicious nature. The actualizing of this theory of leadership has made it possible to destroy potential leaders. On the other hand, recognizing it for what it really is has made possible the full-orbed leadership of some who were about to be ruined by this terrible enemy of true leadership.

There are many who are believers in the "Luck Factor" in leadership. They are of the opinion that one is destined to success, while another is destined to failure. To accept the thesis that one is destined to be a loser is not borne out by those who have made it to the top. This theory may best be observed on the athletic field during a tremendous struggle for victory. Undoubtedly, this theory will be a challenge to the best thinkers on this subject.

It is my considered judgment that the most scholarly presentation of a theory on leadership was given by the late Dr. Clarence Marsh Case of the University of Southern California. His carefully thought-out thesis is known as "The Conjuncture Theory of Leadership." It includes three very important factors: Personality, Social Situation, and Event. These factors, as they converge or flow together, produce leadership or the act of leading. Any leader who fully understands this theory, and who takes advantage of these factors, can greatly enhance the quality of his own leadership.

The eighth theory that we will consider is referred to as "The Reed Theory of Leadership." While this builds upon the classic presentation of Case's "Conjuncture Theory," it goes a step farther and calls for a clear understanding and logical use of "Decision Making," as well as a keen understanding and a careful use of "Timing." As these factors flow together, they will determine whether one's leadership will be at its best or on a much lower level.

Although there are a great many books on the subject of "MOTIVATION," as it is related to leadership, it seems advisable to devote one section of our study to this vital subject. While we endeavor to interpret the primary factors in leadership, which are neglected or misunderstood by so many, we are concerned with the great MOTIVATIONAL FORCES. Although we give more attention to the "Machinery of Leadership" than to the "Motivating Forces" which furnish the driving power, we do consider the six motivating forces in leadership—VISION, IDEAS, GOAL SETTING, ENTHUSIASM, OPTIMISM, and ORGANIZATION. These are power-packed forces that can work for you.

Now, let us begin an exciting journey through the rich fields of growing thought that have to do with LEADERSHIP. These rich fields can ripen into a valuable harvest. *THE DYNAMICS OF LEADERSHIP* can give to you a greater understanding of the *"Fundamentals of Leadership,"* the *"Theories of Leadership,"* and the *"Forces Which Motivate."* IT IS POSSIBLE FOR YOU TO INCREASE THE EFFECTIVENESS OF YOUR LEADERSHIP. YOUR "IMPOSSIBLE DREAM" CAN COME TRUE!

2.

A Definitive Meaning of Leadership

LEADERSHIP IS KNOWN BY THE PERSONALITIES IT EN-
RICHES. LEADERSHIP IS NOT A MATTER OF HYPNOSIS,
BLANDISHMENT OR "SALESMANSHIP." IT IS A MATTER OF
LEADING OUT FROM WITHIN INDIVIDUALS THOSE IM-
PULSES, MOTIVES AND EFFORTS WHICH THEY DISCOVER
TO REPRESENT THEMSELVES MOST TRULY.

—Ordway Tead

There is a great deal being said and written on the subject of
"Leadership." However, there seems to be, for the most part, no pre-
cise meaning given to the term. It is assumed that everyone knows
what is meant by LEADERSHIP, and, consequently, we find both
"fuzzy thinking" and "hazy ideas" on this subject. For instance, most
books on Psychology and Sociology do not bother to define the term;
they launch immediately into a discussion of the subject. Therefore,
we believe that it is essential for us to define with clarity what is
meant by the terms LEADER and LEADERSHIP.

The first view of leadership which we present is one that requires the leader to come to grips with a major crisis. The way in which he performs in a crisis indicates to his fellows whether or not he will be able to pass the test of strength of character and of penetrating understanding of the issues at hand. One of the most perceptive writers on the subject of "Leadership" is John Kenneth Galbraith. In his book, *The Age of Uncertainty*, he goes directly to the heart, or the essence, of the matter.

THE ESSENCE OF LEADERSHIP

Galbraith sees leadership as being willing to confront the major anxieties of the times because of dedication or commitment. "All of the great leaders have had one characteristic in common: it was the willingness to confront unequivocally the major anxiety of their people in their time. This, and not much else, is the essence of leadership."[1] It is true that these leaders were motivated to make the confrontation because of great dedication, or deep commitment, to a cause. The leader, at whatever level of leadership, must be able to confront the anxieties of his day.

One of the best examples of this type of confrontation is that of President Franklin Delano Roosevelt. He was such a leader in the dark days of the "Great Depression." In his inaugural address, and in the legislation of his first one hundred days, he left no one in doubt. All his energies would be committed to the economic miseries of the time. The people's concerns were his concerns. During those frightful days, all of us were inspired and uplifted as we listened to the President, with forceful oratory, proclaim: *"We have nothing to fear but fear itself."* Only a leader who has a deep commitment, which will enable him to confront unequivocally the major anxiety of the time, is worthy of leadership as a statesman.

Galbraith's understanding of the essence of leadership is still more penetrative when he adds to dedication and commitment another element: an instinct for command. "It is certain that John Foster Dulles had an instinct for command. There is a kind of person who, out of the very certainty of his purpose, right or wrong, both assumes leadership and is conceded leadership. No quality so assures public success. Douglas MacArthur was such a man. So was Charles DeGaulle. So, though with slightly less inner certainty, was Winston Churchill. So, we have seen, was Lenin."[2]

The question immediately arises in one's mind: from whence comes this boldness or brashness which causes a person to assume command? Galbraith thinks of it as "an instinct." At this point he comes near to Carlyle's thoughts concerning "the great man." His admiration for this kind of leader is expressed forcefully in an old Scottish saying which celebrates such a leader: "Where MacCrimmon sits is the head of the table." He believes that it is better, by far, to be a "MacCrimmon" than to have brilliance of mind, eloquence of speech, or charm of personality. Thus, commitment, dedication, and instinct for command constitute the very "essence of leadership."

THE PLACE OF INFLUENCE

The leader, in most instances, is thought to have a great deal of influence over others. This, however, is dependent upon the level of his prestige with those he wishes to persuade. In a list of over 100 definitions of the term LEADERSHIP which we have assembled, most of them, by far, see the element of "influence" as being of great import. The *Dictionary of the Social Sceiences* puts it this way: "Leadership denotes the occupany of a status, and the active performance of a role, that mobilizes more or less organized collective and voluntary effort toward the attainment of shared goals and objectives."[3] Terry and Hermanson define leadership as the ability of a person, or leader, to induce followers to work together with confidence and zeal on tasks that the leader sets. Stating it simply, yet solidly: Leadership is the act of one person influencing another, or others.

Another emphasis upon influence sees it in its mildest form, as well as in its extreme and authoritarian form. "Leadership shades, on one side, into other informal types of influence lacking central importance for collective effort. On the other side, leadership shades into domination and formal authority. Any concrete leadership situation will, of course, involve elements of informal influence, emotional dominance, and authority."[4] The central place of influence in the understanding of leadership is set forth in a concise manner in the *International Encyclopedia of the Social Sciences*: "It is an essential feature of the concept of leading that influence is exerted by one individual upon another, or more commonly, that one or a few individuals influence a larger number."[5]

The elected or appointed power of the leader gives considerable influence over the group. This is different from the leadership which one may observe in a voluntary group or association. Paul Pigors thinks that it is advantageous for clarity to utilize the term "headship" in regard to elected or appointed leaders, while reserving the term "leadership" for that which is observed in a voluntary group or association. This voluntary group or association expresses its influence in relative degrees. "Leadership acts influence other persons in a shared direction. The position of leader is then defined in terms of relative degrees of influence."[6]

At the center, or core, of leadership is the leader. He plays the lead part in the scenario. Of course, it is necessary for there to be a follower or followers. The concepts of leading and following define each other in that there can be no following without leading. The leader is "a person who occupies a central role or position of dominance and influence in a group."[7] Dominance, prestige and influence toward group goals are seen as an important role for the leader in meeting his responsibility. Again: "Leadership is the exercise of influence and authority within a social realtionship or group by one or more members. The leadership function is primarily the coordination of group activities toward group goals. The dominance and prestige associated with the leadership role result from its being focus of coordination and unification of activities, information and decisions."[8]

When the term leader is used, there is usually the connotation that this individual is one who has the status which permits him to have sufficient influence over other individuals to exercise a certain degree of power with, or for, his followers. Bernard Bass in his book, *Leadership, Psychological and Organizational Behavior*, takes the position that "influence acts" are at the heart of the definition of leadership. "Leadership has been defined as influence. More specifically, it has been equated with any positive influence act; with behavior required to direct a group and with behavior making a difference among groups."[9] In his defining the leader as an influencer, he refines his emphasis upon influence in yet another direction. "When the goal of the leader is that of changing another member of the group or other members of the group; or when the member's or members' change in behavior will reward the leader or reinforce the leader's behavior, the leader's effort to obtain the goal is leadership."[10]

SOME MISCONCEPTIONS CONCERNING LEADERSHIP

While we have considered commitment, dedication, instinct for command, and influence as positive factors in leadership, there are misconceptions, or negative beliefs, concerning leadership which should be noted. I shall list eight misconceptions, or negative beliefs, set forth by Roger Bellows. Many such views are, at best, only partially true.

The leader is a power.
Leadership stems from the leader per se.
People have inborn capacity for leadership.
Leadership skills are unlearned.
People have power or faculties for managing men.
Some people have great intuition.
Great leaders have singular abilities and powers for sizing
   up people.
People compensate for a leaders's weaknesses.[11]

It was General Eisenhower who declared, in his graphic and forceful style: "You *do not lead* by hitting people over the head. Any fool can do that, but it is usually called 'assault' not leadership." Nor is leadership a process of exploitation of others for extraneous ends.

PERSONALITY TRAITS AND THE SOCIAL SITUATION

Now, let us pick up the positive elements listed by psychologists and sociologists in their analysis of the place where personality traits and the social situation, or environment, come into play. The social situation and personality traits combine in a very significant manner at certain times. The place of personality is a powerful factor in the leadership of any person. Students of leadership find it difficult to decide on which personality traits are a common denominator for leaders; yet all are agreed that the right combination of basic personality traits is of tremendous import.

Kimball Young points out that "Not only do age and sex play a part in social differentiation, but individual variability in mentality must also be taken into account. The dull find the competition for status or occupation severe. Able persons run ahead of their fellows in the race for prestige. The great majority of folks take a mediocre course because their mentality and social status decree it so. Individual variation in mental ability plays its part, together with age and sex in determination of social roles."[12] In this same frame of reference, Pigors defines leadership, in which personality and the social situation are interacting with personality, utilizing the time dimension in pursuit of a common cause. He says: "Leadership is a concept applied to the personality-environment relation to describe the situation when a personality is so placed in the environment that his will, feeling, and insight, direct and control others in the pursuit of a common cause."[13]

One Sociologist, in a study of personality traits, has listed 99 traits, or essential qualities of leadership, which he considers to be important. Leadership may be thought of as an ability to persuade or direct men without use of the prestige of power of formal office or external circumstances; still the fact remains, we cannot ignore personality traits in considering leadership. Where men have to impress other men in face-to-face contact, size and strength are frequently factors of importance in producing prestige and control. It was Shakespeare who said: "All the world's a stage and all the men and women merely players." The "Leader" plays the leading role upon the stage of "Life," passing out at the last scene, leaving the drama in the hands of those who come after him, whether he possessed a strong personality or a weak one. There are ever leaders, good or bad—strong or weak.

EMPHASIS UPON INTERACTION

Another view of leadership considers the fact that there are four very important factors, or basic elements, which should be considered in any serious study of leadership. This view notes that the interaction of these four basic elements furnishes the dynamic situation which the potential leader can exploit for his own benefit and for the cause which he may represent.

The social group is always on the move. The leader is meant to be in the vanguard; hence, there is interaction between the leader and his followers. The "give and take" of these two elements of society determines the strength or weakness of the leader. It also determines the resourcefulness, or lack of it, on the part of the group. Fred Fiedler sees this interplay as initiated by the leader: "Leadership is the initiation of acts which result in a constant pattern of group interaction directed toward the solution of a mutual problem."[14]

A definition which emphasizes the four factors of interaction is given in the *International Encyclopedia of the Social Sciences*: "The definition of the simplest unit of analysis in leadership as 'the act of leading' has led to the identification of four basic elements in the relationship: (1) the *leader*, with his characteristics of ability and personality, and his 'resources' relevant to goal attainment; (2) the *followers*, who also have relevant abilities, personality characteristics, and resources; (3) the *situation* within which the relationship occurs; and (4) the *task* with which the interacting and individuals are confronted. The nature of the leader-influence relationship and the characterization of the act of leading are to be understood in terms of interaction between these four sets of variables."[15]

GOAL ORIENTATION

One may also interpret leadership from the standpoint of "aims or goals." If the leader has an aim or goal which is distinctive, or unusual, he may be able to gather a following and hold his followers; or he may gather together those who have similar interests, aims, and purposes, who are motivated to attain meaningful and worthwhile goals. It is of prime importance that the leader understands the goals which are articulated by the organization or the institution which he serves. "The leader is the individual in the group given the task of directing and coordinating task-relevant group activities or who, in the absence of a designated leader, carries the primary responsibility for performing these functions in the group."[16]

It is also well to emphasize the importance of goal setting in group discussion: "Leadership, in group discussion, is the assumption of the tasks of initiating, organizing, and formulating conclusions; hence, the leader is the person who spends the most time talking to the group, since he carries out most of the verbal tasks."[17] Thus we find that a definition of "goal orientation" as it relates to leadership could be stated, with clarity and brevity, in these words: leadership is the process of influencing group activities toward goal setting and goal achievement.

DYNAMIC ACHIEVEMENT

It is Jerome Davis who offers, in his book *Contemporary Social Movements*, a synthetic definition of leadership from this viewpoint. He states that "a leader is, to be sure, partly the product of biological forces, partly the product of a fiction in the minds of his followers, partly the product of group circumstances and his own distinctive aim, but also that his leadership depends on the achievement he is able to make. . . . Every act which the individual thinks successful is itself a stimulus to further action in the same direction."[18] While this definition is labored, complex, and awkward, at the same time it considers five factors which are relevant.

EMOTIONAL DRIVE

This view recognizes that emotional forcefulness is the driving power which makes possible the accomplishment of the great tasks outlined by the leader himself. "Emotion and feeling may be distinctly important in the development of leadership in the arts. Yet emotional drive seems to be significant in executive leadership. In the latter form of leadership, intellectual cleverness alone often does not succeed in competition with less intellectual ability supported by emotional forcefulness. In any case, leadership seems to call for efficient expenditure of energy on the issue at hand, forceful control of men or materials, emotional drive or persistence, and high intellectual ability."[19] Thus, we see that leadership is represented by emotion and feeling. However, there may be times when it appears that emotional drive even supersedes the intellectual or rational attitude.

Up to this point we have concerned ourselves with seven categories, or definitions, of leadership. We shall limit the remaining categories to only four.

THE ELEMENT OF CRISIS

Without doubt, crisis plays a part in the development of leadership. This element was touched upon while we were considering the "essence of leadership" at the beginning of this chapter. Confronted with a novel situation for which old devices—material or nonmaterial—do not serve, members of the group are subjected to an emotional and intellectual tension. This is the point at which the leader will seek to largely focus the feelings and desires of the group upon a solution.

It is obvious that energetic persons, regardless of other personality traits, are more likely to attempt a leadership role than those less energetically inclined. Moreover, it is also true that persons with strong needs to achieve are more likely to be challenged by a crisis than others who do not feel that need. It is also true that members of a group are tempted to assume leadership as they come to expect more rewards for goal attainment. Still others who are faced with a crisis are primarily attracted to a certain group as a source of status, esteem, and rewards. It is the crisis that launches many possible leaders into actual places of leadership. During emergencies, when members of the group must cope with danger, calamities, and sudden threat, there is a desire for leadership. It is at the time of stress that the emergence of a leader is most welcome. Attempts to lead will be more readily accepted at a time of crisis than they would be if this element were not present.

GROUP IMPACT

It is important to realize the strength or force of the group impact upon the leader, and it is also important to concede the power of a strong leader upon the group. It is the wise leader who understands and utilizes the norms that the group values most highly. Fiedler deals with the group impact in the following manner: "The leader is the man who comes closest to realizing the norms the group values highest; this conformity gives him his high rank, which attracts people and implies the right to assume control of the group."[20]

STREAM OF EVENTS

It is indeed difficult for the leader to swim upstream against a powerful current. An unusually strong leader may be able to accomplish great feats of strength even against a riptide. However, the wise leader, if he understands the currents, many times is able to take advantage of the stream of events and mold a program of his own design. Yet is does seem quite clear that no matter how unusual a given leader may seem to his contemporaries, the stream of events is usually more powerful than an outstanding individual. "This is not to belittle the leader, but to free us from the bias that he can control events without reference to societal organizations and culture."[21]

LEADERSHIP IS ACTIONS

It is possible for one member of a group to be persuasive with another member if he has been able to demonstrate effectively that he has the ability to solve the problems of individuals and of the group. By his actions he is able to prove that he is a leader. It is not his "high and mighty" theories which are most meaningful, but, rather, it is his success in the arena of positive actions.

It was Machiavelli who said: "There is nothing more difficult to take in hand, more perilous to conduct, or more uncertain in its success, than to take the lead in the introduction of a new order of things."[22] This view of leadership implies that leadership involves a re-ordering or organizing of a new way of action. Further, it implies that there is a genuine need to overcome resistance to change. Thus, the view of some is that leadership is actions. Leaders are known by the leadership acts which they perform. A person may have a long list of the attributes or traits of a leader, but if he never takes leadership action, he is not (yet) a leader.

DISTINCTIVES OF LEADERSHIP
AND MANAGEMENT

There is a distinction between the leader and the executive manager. There is a definite distinction between leadership and managership. Leadership is asking the fundamental questions, while management is implementing the answers. As an illustration of this distinction, Robert McNamara shifted from being a leader to that of a manager when he stopped asking his probing questions about the validity of the Viet Nam War and started concentrating on the most efficient manner for getting the troops to Southeast Asia.

Intelligence, imagination, and knowledge are important resources in both leadership and management; but only effectiveness may convert them into worthwhile results. Peter Drucker in his book, *The Effective Executive*, stresses the fact that effectiveness can be learned. "Whether he works in a business or in a hospital, in a

Government agency or in a labor union, in a University or in the army, the executive is, first of all, expected to *get the right things done*. This simply means that he is expected to be effective."[23]

While we have concerned ourselves with the analyzing of leadership from many angles, it is altogether proper that we should compare and contrast leadership with managership. Leadership is concerned with bringing people together in a way that they can work together for a common goal, effectively and happily. Managership directs organizations and, in so doing, subordinates individuals in working toward organized ends. The leader guides and develops individuals so they may better share in the realization of group accomplishments. Thus, it becomes increasingly clear that leadership and managership embody entirely different traits. One seeks to inspire men; the other seeks compromise and consensus to conserve resources. Olan Hendrix has given us the following list of the distinctives which we have been considering:

1. Leadership is a quality:
   Managment is a science and an art.

2. Leadership provides vision:
   Management supplies realistic perspectives.

3. Leadership deals with concepts;
   Management relates to functions.

4. Leadership exercises faith;
   Management has to do with fact.

5. Leadership seeks for effectiveness;
   Management strives for efficiency.

6. Leadership is an influence for good among potential resources;
   Management is the coordination of available resources organized for maximum accomplishments.

7. Leadership provides direction;
   Management is concerned about control.

8. Leadership thrives on finding opportunity;
   Management succeeds on accomplishment.[24]

It is evident that there are certain functional similarities between the leader and the executive manager. However, at the same time, there are indeed shades of distinction which we have just noted in the foregoing list of comparisons and contrasts. It is management that deals with *parts*, while leadership deals with *wholes*. Management deals with things, while leadership deals with people.

AN INCISIVE DEFINITION

In our attempt to explore carefully and fully the meaning of leadership, we have noted that there is a broad spectrum of leaders.

The professional person is a leader.
The business executive is a leader.
The knowledge worker is a leader.
The creative artist is a leader.
The statesman or politician is a leader.
The military commander is a leader.
The administrator is a leader.
The pioneer is a leader.
The scientific inventor is a leader.

It is true that these leaders may be effective or they may be ineffective. They may be successful or they may be downright failures. They may lift the level of the cause they serve or they may allow it to decline. They may shine brilliantly or they may pale and fade away. They may grow and improve themselves, becoming stalwart persons of integrity and effectiveness.

But what do all leaders have in common? What is the common denominator? What is the fundamental meaning of leadership and what can be considered an incisive definition of this important term? To me, leadership in its generic sense is like the late President, Dwight D. Eisenhower, once said: "Leadership is the ability to get a person to do what you want him to do, when you want it done, in a way you want it done, because he wants to do it." This formula may also be stated in this way: Leadership, or the act of leading, is the ability to get a person, or persons, to do that which you want them to do, at a time when you want it done, and in the way that you want them to do it, because they desire to do it.

This definition is all-inclusive; it cuts through the gray areas and goes immediately to the heart of the matter.

It implies COMMITMENT.

It implies an INSTINCT FOR COMMAND.
It implies INFLUENCE.
It implies PERSONALITY TRAITS.
It implies EMOTIONAL DRIVE.
It implies SUCCESSFUL USE OF CRISIS.
It implies GOAL ORIENTATION.
It implies DECISION MAKING.
It implies GROUP IMPACT.
It implies UTILIZATION OF THE STREAM OF EVENTS.
It implies SUCCESS, WHICH LEADS TO OTHER SUC-
CESSES.
It implies ACTIONS.

Again, the definitive meaning of leadership with incisiveness is: LEADERSHIP IS THE ABILITY TO GET A PERSON TO DO WHAT YOU WANT HIM TO DO, WHEN YOU WANT IT DONE, IN A WAY YOU WANT IT DONE, BECAUSE HE WANTS TO DO IT.

THIS IS THE HEART OF THE MATTER

3.

A Philosophy of Life

IF A MAN DOES NOT KEEP PACE WITH HIS COMPANIONS,
PERHAPS IT IS BECAUSE HE HEARS A DIFFERENT DRUM-
MER. LET HIM STEP TO THE MUSIC WHICH HE HEARS,
HOWEVER MEASURED OR FAR AWAY.

—*Henry D. Thoreau*

You may think that a philosophy of life is irrelevant to the best in leadership, but I would strongly disagree. Your philosophy of life colors the type of leadership which you embrace. If your philosophy is to win at all costs, there is a grave possibility that your leadership will be tainted with dishonesty and that your leadership will be of an inferior quality. We are told that Abraham Lincoln held as a part of his life's philosophy: "Honesty is the best policy." This basic concept became a part of all his activities and decisions. It gave guidance and meaning to his philosophy of leadership. THE QUALITY OF YOUR LEADERSHIP IS LARGELY DETERMINED BY YOUR PHILOSOPHY OF LIFE. Your philosophy of life gives color, gives tone, gives direction to your leadership.

When Louis Goldblatt, a Chicago business leader, was honored by the Lincoln Academy of Illinois, in May of 1976, he spoke of his philosophy of life:

LET LIFE BE WASTE-FREE

As a great merchandiser, he suggested that: "The frame, and brain, and soul of man is tuned to service. Let life be waste free! Free of time waste above all else. Therein lies the key to good health, happiness, and fruitful long life. Time, and all you do with it, is an investment in the future. And the future is where you spend the rest of your life. Nothing is spontaneous, not even an accident. Everything happens because . . ."

During a seminar on "The Dynamics of Leadership" at the Reed Institute for the Advanced Study of Leadership, Mervyn L. Goins, a college administrator, shared with us his philosophy of life. He had spent time in formulating this philosophy, and expressed it in this way:

ACCEPT LIFE'S SITUATIONS CREATIVELY, AND THEY BECOME BUILDING STONES IN THE DEVELOPMENT OF A GREATER FUTURE

He further stated: "I believe that life has eternal worth. Life is a search for identity and self knowledge, and that identity can only be fully realized when one experiences total commitment to God. Integrity is the ideal goal regardless of one's stature in life. I believe that happiness comes through service to others with no expectation of reward. True love of life is to give, and to share, and to make a meaningful contribution."

How very different was the philosophy of a boyhood friend of mine. At an early age he adopted a very popular philosophy of life. It is expressed in these words:

LIFE IS A BOWL OF CHERRIES. LET'S LIVE IT UP!

In his attempt to extract only the luscious nectar from life, having a life of pleasure as his goal, he soon found himself "among the pits." He died in a drunken brawl before he was 40 years of age.

Another friend of my youth had a "Midas" touch. He was able to make money with seeming ease on projects large and small. His "golden touch" soon brought him from poverty to millions. His philosophy of life was:

THE ALMIGHTY DOLLAR FOR ME

Money had first place in his life. He now lives in a beautiful mid-western city in which he has vast holdings. However, it is doubtful if his philosophy of life has brought him happiness or fulfillment. His family life has suffered, and he is now living with his third wife.

Let us now consider the philosophy of one whose leadership affected the entire world, Adolph Hitler. The rapid rise of this leader to supreme power in Germany is inexplicable to us; however, it is a cruel fact that cannot be forgotten. By the sheer force of his will he conquered greater territories than either Alexander the Great or Napoleon Bonaparte. His philosophy of life is most difficult to comprehend. We find it couched in one of his statements made during World War II:

*THE VICTOR WILL NOT BE ASKED, LATER ON,
WHETHER HE TOLD THE TRUTH OR NOT. IN
STARTING AND WAGING A WAR, IT IS NOT RIGHT
THAT MATTERS BUT VICTORY. HAVE NO PITY.*

Robert Payne says of Hitler: "He erupted like a force of nature, a tornado or a hurricane, destroying everything in his path. There was madness in him almost from the beginning. His mind was a distorted mirror in which he saw himself as a vast imperial executioner, the destined master who had come to cleanse the world of its iniquities. Because he lived, forty million people died, most of them in agony, and as though this were not enough, he spent his last days giving orders for the destruction of Germany, devoutly hoping that no Germans would be left alive to mourn over their defeats. 'They are not worthy of me,' he said. Such was his ultimate verdict on the people who had obeyed him as blindly as the children obeyed the 'Pied Piper' of Hamelin."[1]

Now, let us contrast the ruthless philosophy of Adolph Hitler with that of one of the great leaders from the distant past, Shah Jahan, Mogul Emperor of the seventeenth century. His philosophy of life can be stated in five words:

WE BUILD FOR THE AGES

During his reign, he was known as "King of the World." Upon the death of his wife, Mumtaz, he determined to build history's finest monument to the love of a man for a woman. Thus was conceived the idea of the "Taj Mahal," a seventeenth-century love poem in marble, written by an Emperor for his Empress. The monument was to be of such perfect proportions, and of such purity, that all who beheld its beauty would be overwhelmed by the eternal wonder of the power of love and the inevitability of death.

According to legend, some 20,000 men and women worked for some 22 years to give form and beauty to the Emperor's majestic vision. It has been my privilege to see this loveliest of all created monuments, one of the "Seven Wonders of the World." Today our world is enriched through the philosophy of Shah Jahan; truly HE BUILT FOR THE AGES.

There is yet another great leader to whom I would call your attention, Cecil John Rhodes of Great Britain. He took three years to decide upon his philosophy of life. During that time, and after his pattern of life and his objectives had crystallized, he reached his great goals, through hard work, imagination, and determination. In fact, he molded a continent to the form of his dreams. His whole life is summed up in a phrase from his first "Will," which seems to very clearly express his philosophy of life:

TO RENDER MYSELF USEFUL TO MY COUNTRY

His towering objective was to build a great empire in Africa for Great Britain. To do this, he realized that there were three all-important steps necessary: Education—Wealth—Power. This could only come about through his developing a capacity for hard work. J. G. McDonald, his biographer, wrote: "The width and immensity of his dreams were limitless and reached out into the far distant future. They were not bounded by the span of the creator's life, but extended forward and moved onward down the further avenues of human progress."[2] Included in his dreams were a railroad from Capetown to Cairo and a telegraph communications system from Capetown to Cairo. The former he did not achieve, but the latter was accomplished. He spent many years as a member of Parliament in Capetown and amassed great wealth both in gold and in diamonds.

His commitment to education continues through the "Rhode's Scholarship" to Oxford for American scholars.

When Rhodes died at the age of 48, Mark Twain said of him: "When he stood on the Cape Peninsula (the southern tip of Africa) his shadow fell on the Zambesi (a river near the equator)." Propelled by his philosophy of life, he literally made his dreams come true. His final words: "SO MUCH TO DO—SO LITTLE DONE—MY LEGACY TO THE EMPIRE."

Each of the "Life Philosophies" that we have considered should help us to see more clearly the very close relationship that exists between one's leadership and one's philosophy of life. Let me say it again: "The quality of your leadership is largely determined by your philosophy of life."

YOUR PHILOSOPHY OF LIFE IS THE FOUNDATION STONE OF YOUR LEADERSHIP.
YOUR PHILOSOPHY OF LIFE DETERMINES YOUR GOALS IN LIFE.
YOUR GOALS IN LIFE DETERMINE THE BOUNDARIES AND THE HORIZONS OF YOUR FUTURE.

We shall now pursue this important fundamental of leadership further as we turn to a study of the leadership of "SEVEN WORLD CHANGERS." These men and women portray for us leadership which extends over a period of five centuries. They represent a wide range of activities and services. As we view them closely, we shall find that their lives and leadership verify the validity of the premise that: THE QUALITY OF ONE'S LEADERSHIP IS LARGELY DETERMINED BY HIS PHILOSOPHY OF LIFE.

4.

Seven World Changers

THE QUALITY OF YOUR LEADERSHIP
IS LARGELY DETERMINED
BY YOUR PHILOSOPHY OF LIFE.

| MY PHILOSOPHY OF LEADERSHIP |
| MY DEFINITION OF LEADERSHIP |
| MY PHILOSOPHY OF LIFE |

YOUR "PHILOSOPHY OF LIFE"
IS
THE FOUNDATION STONE OF YOUR LEADERSHIP.

GOLDA MEIR

Pioneer and Politician

DON'T BECOME CYNICAL. DON'T GIVE UP HOPE....
THERE IS IDEALISM IN THIS WORLD. THERE IS HUMAN
BROTHERHOOD.

—Golda Meir

Golda, as a young girl in Milwaukee, Wisconsin, seemed to be possessed with child's idle talk, and her mother spoke of her as a star gazer. But Golda was determined that her dreams should come true.

In those early years her philosophy of life was already well set. She had lived fully and thought deeply. She expressed her philosophy of life with great clarity:

> *ONLY THOSE WHO DARE,*
> *WHO HAVE THE COURAGE TO DREAM,*
> *CAN REALLY ACCOMPLISH SOMETHING.*

She confided further to her close friend, Regina, while in high school: "People who are forever asking themselves, 'Is it realistic?

Can it be accomplished? Is it worth trying?' accomplish nothing that is really worthwhile or imaginative. What's realistic? a stone? something that is already in existence? That's not realism. That's death. It's stagnation."[1] For Golda Meir, realism included the ability and the courage to dream and then the will and determination to do what was necessary in order for the dreams to come true.

When Golda graduated from high school she gave the Valedictorian address. She declared that "preparation for living a life that was intellectually and socially useful was the highest purpose of education and . . . to fulfill one's greatest potential in both these respects was the best way of giving thanks for the wonderful opportunity a free education in America offered."[2]

Golda Meir was born in Russia. She emigrated, with her parents, to the United States and settled with them in Milwaukee, Wisconsin, when she was a small girl of eight years. Thus, she grew to womanhood in America. At the age of seventeen Golda "dedicated herself to a vision of a reborn people in a reborn land, and she felt her life would be meaningful only in the measure that she helped to realize that vision."[3]

Her fiancee, Moshe Myerson, responded with great caution to her deep commitment to emigrate to Palestine. He was aware of the hardships, privations, and difficulties involved. Finally, he gave his approval for their emigration together to Palestine. Golda was desirous of being a good wife and homemaker, but she also had a driving ambition to be a doer, an activist. These twin desires could possibly be realized on one of the collective farms. In fact, "even before leaving America, she had selected Merhavia as the Kibbutz she and Moshe would ask to join," for other American Jews were a part of this settlement. The total membership of this Kibbutz was 32, and only 8 were women. Both men and women worked to produce income for the group. The main source of income was the money that each one received from the Jewish National Fund for planting trees. It was hard work, and Golda reported later that at the close of the first day she could scarcely move a finger.

In the Kibbutz Golda gave leadership. She taught the girls lessons in the preparation of food. She insisted upon serving hot cooked cereal for breakfast. She insisted that the herring must be peeled. She learned the art of breadmaking and insisted that the food be prepared with the same thoughtfulness as one prepares food for one's family.

A little later she was sent to a nearby settlement to learn modern methods of poultry-raising. After completing her study, she was put in charge of the poultry enterprise. Chicken houses were built, and a 500-egg incubator was purchased. This project proved very successful and very worthwhile for the Kibbutz family.

Golda's ideals, intelligence, determination, and character, along with her ability to influence crowds, assemblies, and conferences, quickly gave her a place of leadership. When the United Nations, on November 29, 1947, created a new Jewish state, it was a miracle. Golda watched the cheering, screaming crowds surge through the streets. Tears streamed down her cheeks as she watched stranger embrace stranger. It was actually happening! After all the centuries of dispersion and persecution, Jews were once again going to have their homeland. As head of the Political Department of the Jewish Agency in Jerusalem, she spoke with simplicity and with feeling. Her appeal was to the Arabs of Palestine and to the Arabs of other nations. Her message had strength and warmth: "Our hand is offered to you in peace and friendship."[4] However, within a few hours the first victims of an Arab attack were buried.

On May 14, 1948, Golda Myerson sat in the Tel Aviv Art Museum, along with 38 men and women, for the purpose of signing the "Proclamation of Independence" of the new State of Israel. As she wrote her name, she could barely see, for her eyes were filled with tears as she wept openly. Now she was a representative of the new State of Israel.

Three days later she was asked to leave for America on a money-raising trip. She was the first official of the new State to arrive in the United States of America. Fund raising was relatively easy for her. The American Jews responded with liberality and with joy, for after 1,878 years there was once again a Jewish Nation.

The new challenge was great. The young nation was immediately involved in a war in which seven Arab nations vowed to drive the Jews into the sea. Moreover, at the same time, thousands of Jewish refugees were arriving in the New State each day; and tens of thousands were on their way. To fight this war on these two battlefronts required courage, determination, and finance. The Israelis had the first two in abundance, and Golda was securing the finance that was so desperately needed. Her idealism now fused with realism:

Don't become cynical. Don't give up hope. ... There is idealism in this world. There is human brotherhood.[5]

When Golda left Russia at the age of 8, she never dreamed that she would be returning in 42 years as the Minister to Russia, representing the new State of Israel. Her service in that position was brought to an abrupt close when Prime Minister Ben-Gurion announced his Cabinet appointments. There would be one woman and her name was Golda Myerson; she would be the nation's first Minister of Labor and Development. On April 20, 1949, she left Russia, after only eight months, to assume her new position.

Golda's new position was a most difficult one. "They came from different civilizations, different cultures, different centuries. They spoke a babel of different languages. They came from seventy-two different lands. And they kept on coming at the rate of a thousand a day. 'Sound the great trumpet for our freedom, raise the banner for gathering our exiles, and gather us together from the four corners of the earth into our land.'"[6] This prayer had been prayed three times daily by Jews for over 2,000 years. And now, their prayer was being answered.

The new task that rested on Golda's shoulders was threefold. She needed to present a program. She needed to put it into operation, and she needed to finance it as an ongoing proposition. (Note the progressive steps of leadership.) She presented to Parliament a project for 30,000 one-room houses to be built by the end of the first year. Parliament approved the plan, but there was no money appropriated. Nevertheless, "the 30,000 units were built, as were hundreds of thousands more under what was called 'the Myerson plan.' Indeed, by the end of Golda's seven-year 'reign' as Minister of Labor and Development, there was not one single new immigrant family in Israel still living in a tent. Over 200,000 attractive, balconied, low-income apartments had been built."[7]

Once, when Golda Meir was asked, "What makes a great man?" she replied without hesitation: "You have to have an ideal. There is a difference between someone who has great financial success, or academic success, and a great man. The great men gave their lives to an ideal which everyone thought crazy, and which became a reality."[8] Golda had an ideal, a dream, and now it was becoming a reality.

Once again, in June of 1956, Mr. Ben-Gurion, recognizing the tremendous leadership of Golda Meir, asked her to accept the position of Foreign Minister of Israel. This was not only the second most important post in the Government, but whoever had heard of a woman serving as Foreign Minister? Many people asked Ben-Gurion this question. His answer was simple: "She's the best man in my Cabinet."

After a short retirement period, Golda, at 70, was called upon to assume the most important, and the most responsible, position in her nation. She was elected Prime Minister with 40 votes in favor and none against. As Prime Minister she had great skill in negotiation. She seemed to know how to make her decisions, and she was skilled in the art of timing. She was a leader.

On October 18, 1970, Golda traveled to the United States. She came because the United Nations were celebrating their twenty-fifth anniversary. She came, moreover, because Israel was the first country that the United Nations had voted into existence. Therefore, it was appropriate that Israel's Prime Minister be present and address the United Nations.

Max Lerner, American correspondent, expressed the thoughts of many when he wrote: "Who would have foreseen a quarter-century ago when the U.N. was founded that at its 25th anniversary meetings the focus would be, not the representatives of the great powers with all their fanfare and panoply, but the woman Prime Minister of a tiny nation, with a tiny territory of only 8,000 square miles, and a population of scarcely 3,000,000. . . . Israel's Prime Minister was the center of attention because what happens to Israel holds the key to what may happen in resolving the global power struggle. Also, it should be added, because of the kind of person Golda Meir is."

When the Prime Minister addressed this great assembly, she spoke with firmness. Her philosophy of life shone through with clarity and strength:

> *ONLY THOSE WHO DARE,*
> *WHO HAVE THE COURAGE TO DREAM,*
> *CAN REALLY ACCOMPLISH SOMETHING.*

Her voice was strong as she affirmed in conclusion: "For each of us to attain the best for his people, cooperation with his neighbors in the solution of regional problems is essential. *Our borders not only separate us but are bridges between us. No people is an island.* We are bound to each other by the problems of our region, our world. We can make of these ties a curse or a blessing. Each nation, each land must decide."

She was an idealist. She never sought power or fame, but rather purpose and duty. IDEALS, DETERMINATION, INTELLIGENCE, CHARACTER, the ABILITY TO INFLUENCE—these were the qualities of greatness that she possessed.

THOMAS ALVA EDISON

Inventor and Scientist

MORE POWERFUL THAN THE SHATTERING OF AN ATOM
IS THE PENETRATION OF THE HUMAN MIND. FOR IT IS
WITHIN THE HUMAN MIND THAT IDEAS ARE BORN,
GROW, AND FINALLY BURST FORTH, THROUGH COM-
MUNICATIONS, TO THE BETTERMENT OF THE WORLD.

Thomas Alva Edison, the Wizard of Menlo Park, was born on
February 11, 1847, in the little town of Milan, Ohio. Al, as he was
known to family and friends, was a born optimist. The many failures
and reverses during his illustrious career never caused him to lose
this strong characteristic. He firmly believed that failure was never
final. On one such occasion he declared: "I'll never give up, for I
may have a streak of luck before I die." A vital part of his philosophy
of life was:

LOOK ON THE BRIGHT SIDE OF EVERYTHING

Since he was history's most prolific inventor and one of the nation's
most honored men, there were certain factors and events that caused
him to be at one time the best-known American in the world.

Thomas Alva was the son of Samuel and Nancy Edison. As a child he was delicate in health and was able to attend school for only a few months. His teachers felt that he had a dull mind and was unable to do standard work. However, his mother perceived that this was not true, and she assumed the responsibility of directing most of his education. Very early he developed a desire for knowledge. He spent much of his time reading and was especially interested in history and science, particularly chemistry. At the age of nine his parents gave him *Parker's Natural and Experimental Philosophy*. This was an elementary text on Science. With his absorbent mind, he soon came to read very well, and, as a result, reading became his life-long favorite enjoyment.

As a lad of 11 he assembled a laboratory in the basement of his home. He was able to pay for this scientific equipment through getting a job on the "Grand Trunk Railroad" selling newspapers. Since this run took him into Detroit, he would spend his spare time there in the Detroit Public Library. Chemicals and pharmaceuticals were among Detroit's chief products, and Al, from his meager income, purchased a collection. Soon he had a shelf full of chemicals stashed away in the baggage car and began experimenting with them. One of these chemicals was phosphorus. Al forgot to keep it covered with water, and one day the chemical caught fire and fell off the shelf, spreading flames over the floor of the baggage car. Fortunately, the baggageman was able to extinguish the fire, but not until he was burned severely. In anger he boxed young Edison's ears and proceeded to throw out his whole collection of chemicals.

By the time he was 16 he felt that it was time for him to begin learning a trade. A friend of the family, James MacKenzie, offered to teach him telegraphy. He proved to be a very apt pupil. In order to practice his trade, he converted a cave in his backyard into his telegraphic office. From there he stretched stovepipe wire through the trees to a friend's home some one mile distant. Organizing his friends into a "Telegraphic Corps," he taught them what he himself had learned from MacKenzie. Here we see coming into focus another facet of his philosophy of life:

WORK—BRINGING OUT THE SECRETS OF NATURE
AND
APPLYING THEM FOR THE HAPPINESS OF MAN

Within the year he had secured a job as a telegrapher at the Stratford, Ontario, station and was now a man on his own.

For several years he moved about the country, from one side to the other. During these travels he met a man in Boston by the name of Sam Ropes, who was also a telegrapher. Together they attempted to invent a telegraphic printer. Ropes put up the money and Edison furnished the concept. Upon the successful completion of the invention, young Edison was to receive the small sum of $250. Now, for the first time, his imagination and mechanical skills had hope of being rewarded. His interests lay primarily in the mechanical and electrical aspects of telegraphy. One of his prized possessions was a second-hand induction coil which transformed the current from a battery into high voltage. Taking with him a friend, he went to the railroad roundhouse and there connected his coil to a long wash trough. Quietly they went up onto the roof to watch the fun and to see what would happen. Soon an unsuspecting fellow worker came to wash his hands in the trough. The electrical shock caused his hands to shoot upward as his arms were nearly wrenched from their sockets. This sense of humor was unique, and, while enjoyed by some, it was not appreciated by most.

Having received his first money from an invention, he became supremely confident. He was highly imaginative, and his zeal seemed boundless. Now he would make his living in the position of a deviser and seller of telegraphic equipment. At this point in his life he had an overriding goal of making money. However, from this time, and for several years, one thing after another went wrong. It was at this juncture that he exclaimed: "I'LL NEVER GIVE UP—for I may have a streak of luck before I die." Edison, along with other great world leaders, was deeply committed to the "work ethic." This factor, together with his eternal optimism, caused him to press on.

The "Streak of Luck" for which Edison longed started to come his way as the inventor in him began to come of age. It was now that "the truly remarkable powers of his mind, which multiplied devices from a single idea like a dividing amoeba and then compartmentalized the creations and endeavors, were being tested to the limit. Still in his middle twenties, he was a one man conglomerate, spanning the entire field of telegraphic development. In addition to his work in the multiplexing of wires, he was the leading inventor of printing telegraph devices used in the stock-ticker network and private telegrpahy. On the night of February 3, 1874, he successfully tested a one-wire Roman-letter telegraph. One month later he perfected the instruments for a police fire-alarm and messenger system to the point that Tracy Edson of the Gold and Stock Company agreed to raise $20,000 for the formation of a Domestic Telegraph Company of which Edison was to be President."[9]

Yet the overriding goal of the young inventor was to make money. This became a driving force in his experimentation as a young man and continued throughout his life. His inventive genius seemed to know no limits. During the summer of 1876, with a small group of helpers, he worked on the electromotograph, the acoustic telegraph, the autographic telegraph, the speaking telegraph, the electric pen, and the mimeograph. He also proposed electric shears, a revolving display case, and many other inventions. However, his most important proposed invention was to be an electric sewing machine. This mechanism was able to drive a sewing machine at the rate of 82 stitches per minute through six layers of cloth.

In 1877 there was a continuation of his explosion of creativity. It was during the latter half of the year that he experienced one of his great "break-throughs,"—the "talking machine," to become known as the phonograph. This invention can be traced in his laboratory notebooks during the last half of 1877. The "Wizard of Menlo Park" was capable of dealing with several possible inventions at the same time. While working on an autographic copying press and an autographic telegraph, as well as trying to perfect a speaker for the telephone, on July 18 he attached a stylus from an embossing telegraph to a telephone speaker and shouted into it while running a band of paraffined paper rapidly beneath. So it was, on August 18, that he named his new invention—the Phonograph. He had set down plans on paper for a new machine, and in some 30 hours "a talking machine" was in operation. Also, other related mechanisms were brought nearer together in the mind of the inventor. As a result, a "mental flash" ensued, combining certain features of each mechanism. Bogardus, commenting on this phenomenon, has this to say: "Flashes of insight are transitory, if not captured on the spot. Who has not had a bright idea only to let it slip away from him as quickly as it came, and to lose it, sometimes never to return? Who has not learned to make a tangible notation even at great inconvenience in order to capture a fleeting idea or glimpse of the new? TO CONSERVE FLASHES OF INSIGHT IS BASIC TO LEADERSHIP."[10]

The phonograph was Edison's first invention which stirred great public interest. This instrument was able to produce sound. It was suggested to him while he was developing a machine to repeat Morse characters. Through this new instrument he was able to magnify sound until a voice was heard in its original strength.

Soon after this, Edison began working on his greatest invention, the incandescent electric light bulb. This was undoubtedly his greatest challenge, inasmuch as other great scientists had attempted the task and had failed. The inventor believed that the electric light would be his greatest opportunity for commercial exploitation.

To achieve this goal he gave of his time and talent lavishly. Some 100 persons were employed to utilize the process of eliminating negative possibilities and to experiment with the positive possibilities. He was able to secure some definite results in a little over a year. During that time he and his staff had tested and eliminated around 6,000 substances before a suitable means of producing a carbonized filament was discovered. At the time that he began his work of experimentation in 1878, he organized the "Edison Electric Light Company" for the purpose of financing the project.

On October 21, 1879, he was able to successfully test the electric light bulb. Two months later, on December 31, Edison was ready to publicly demonstrate his system at Menlo Park. Thousands of visitors were brought to this location by special trains to witness this "MIRACLE OF LIGHT." In the hushed darkness they waited!

WILL IT LIGHT?
WILL IT BURN?

A breathless pause—"Ladies and Gentlemen—IT LIGHTS!" There were hundreds of small lights burning brilliantly in the buildings and on the streets. All of these lights were fed by current from underground circuits. Truly the "Wizard of Menlo Park" had turned DARKNESS INTO DAY.

From Edison's fertile mind inventions poured forth year after year. We are told that he filed more than 1,500 applications for United States Patents and for an equal number of foreign patents. "On these applications he was granted 1,093 patents in the United States, not counting re-issues, and 1,239 foreign patents. This is the greatest number ever accredited to one man."[11]

There were few fields of human activity which escaped his penetrating mind, and none which did not profit immensely by his achievements. A belief in his own mystique as a "Wizard" caused him to believe that his mind could conquer matter. He believed that by concentration he could think a big pendulum into movement. We have no record of his accomplishing this impossible feat. However, at times his audacity seemed to border on folly. Nevertheless, he did conceive unbelievably bold and original ideas. Robert Conot has said that "When Edison's imagination latched on to a concept, ideas tumbled through his head and he was unable to sleep. He emptied his mind as if it were a barrel of apples." We are told that while working on a problem, he saw, heard, and did practically nothing that would interfere with his thought concentration. On one occasion he did not leave his laboratory for two weeks. For five days and five nights he worked continuously with no rest and with very little food.

While he was a great lone inventor, he saw the value of organizing for inventive productivity. He envisioned the laboratory as a mill that would transform ideas into articles of commerce. New products would flow from the mill in an endless stream. He would operate, in effect, a factory of creativity. At one time he compiled a list of more than 100 projects, some old, some borrowed, some new. Some of those included on the list were: a cotton picker, an apparatus for deaf people, an improved battery, artificial silk, artificial ivory, an artificial Mother-of-Pearl, a cheap India ink, an ink for the blind, an electric piano, heat-activated photography, a miner's lamp, rubber derived from many different sources, and scores more. Certainly Edison believed that "man was designed for accomplishments, engineered for success, and endowed with the seeds of greatness."[12]

Sometimes there is an assumption that this great genius was indeed a wizard and that his inventions, by and large, were underived. However, the facts show that he had an excellent reference library at Menlo Park for himself and for his staff and that he leaned heavily upon book learning. He once made the statement that "Aside from special research, for which I have collected and studied vast quantities of printed matter, I have also constantly read in such favorite subjects as astronomy, biology, mechanics, metaphysics, music, physics (including, of course, electricity) and political economy."[13] In addition to this, he kept himself fully in touch, through scientific journals and proceedings of scientific bodies, with new developments in science.

Moreover, he had a genuine interest in literature. He expressed his special liking for Victor Hugo. We have already noted that as a boy, while working on the train, he would spend his spare time at the Detroit Public Library. Here he would read his way from one section to another. He was interested in what he called "true poetry," in such writings as "Evangeline," "Enoch Arden," and, more particularly, in the writings of Shakespeare. "That's where you get the ideas! Ah, Shakespeare! My, but that man did have ideas! He would have been an inventor, a wonderful inventor, if he had turned his mind to it. He seemed to see the inside of everything."[14]

Because of Edison's remarkable achievements and his striking personality, he became a sort of folk hero and was accorded great respect, admiration, and affection by the American people. Although he was not a man of "Letters," many honorary degrees were conferred upon him by some of the great universities. He was, also, the recipient of many "Awards" and "Medals." One such medal was from the United States Congress: "For the development and application of inventions that have revolutionized civilization during the last century."

Thomas Alva Edison succeeded because he was an eternal optimist. He would not let himself or those about him accept the possibility of failure. The quality of his leadership had certainly been derived from his philosophy of life and of service. On his seventy-seventh birthday he was asked to state his philosophy of life. He answered this request in writing:

WORK
BRINGING OUT THE SECRETS OF NATURE AND
APPLYING THEM FOR THE HAPPINESS OF MAN.
LOOKING ON THE BRIGHT SIDE OF EVERYTHING.

Growing out of this philosophy of persistent work was his classic definition of "Genius." He declared that "Genius is one per cent inspiration and ninety-nine per cent perspiration." Every room in his laboratory contained the quotation from Sir Joshua Reynolds: "There is no expedient to which a man will not resort to avoid the real labor of thinking."

By taking Edison and his works *OUT* of the world, we engender the keenest appreciation of Edison *IN* the world. He was the possessor of a unique conjunction of talent, ambition, and opportunity. The ingredients of his success included imagination, dedication, and persistence. Our world still needs the Inventor who is both DREAMER and MAN OF ACTION.

MAO TSE-TUNG

Revolutionary

I HAVE LONG ASPIRED TO REACH THE CLOUDS . . .
NOTHING IS IMPOSSIBLE,
IF YOU DARE TO SCALE THE HEIGHTS.

—Mao Tse-tung

It was on December 26, 1893, that a little boy was born in a small village called Shao Shan, in the Central Chinese Province of Hunan. His name was Mao Tse-tung. He was the eldest of four children, with two brothers and one sister. His father owned a farm of three and one-half acres. From its produce of rice and vegetables they were able to secure a modest peasant's living.

When Mao was 7 years of age, he was sent to school, and by the time he was 13 he was taken from school and given the task of managing the accounts of the family's little farm. This lasted for a short time, and then he ran away from home. He went to a little Chinese school where he studied the Classics and read many contemporary articles and a few books. A little later young Mao reports: "I had first heard of America in an article which told of the American Revolution and contained a sentence like this: 'After eight years of difficult war, Washington won victory and built up his nation.' In a book called *Great Heroes of the World*, I read also of Napoleon, Catherine of Russia, Peter the Great, Wellington, Gladstone, Rousseau, Montesquieu, and Lincoln."[15] Mao had a great hunger for knowledge. By the time he was 18 he had developed not only a love for learning, but a great sense of duty toward the poor peasants. He decided to be a teacher and to improve their lives.

During his youth, over 90 per cent of China's people lived in the country. Their lives were burdened with backbreaking work, with famines, and with great suffering. They were victimized by natural disasters like floods, drought, and crop failure. In addition, the population was growing at a rapid rate, with ever-increasing numbers to be fed. The Landlords treated the peasants unfairly and took advantage of them; and, finally, the peasants were crushed by unfair taxation. Hugh Purcell observes that "The Chinese peasant is not passive; he is not a coward. He will fight when he is given a method, an organization, leadership, a workable programme, hope—and arms. The Chinese peasants were ripe for rebellion, and were only waiting for a leader. Although they did not know it, they were waiting for Mao Tse-tung."[16] Mao was preparing himself to be that leader.

Very early, Mao became a follower of Sun Yat-sen, who was a Christian revolutionary. At least that was true as far as it was summarized in *Three People's Principles*. These "principles" were:

Democracy (which meant overthrowing the Emperors and introducing a democratic political system);
Socialism (which meant taking the land from the landlords and giving it to the peasants); and
Nationalism (which meant freeing China from all foreign control).

By 1918 Mao was in Peking where he worked at Peking National University as a Library Assistant. While there he eagerly read the works of Karl Marx and became a dedicated Communist. In 1925 Sun Yat-sen died, and the Kuomintang was under the new leadership of Chiang Kai-shek. The Communists were now unwelcome in the Kuomintang. Chiang Kai-shek declared that Communist members would be punished by death. One of those to be put to death was the wife of Mao Tse-tung. Now that the Communist Party was freed from the Kuomintang, "Mao was convinced that any communist revolution should start in the countryside. One day he predicted: 'Several hundred million peasants will rise like a tornado-force so extraordinarily swift and violent that no power, however great, will be able to suppress it.'"[17]

Somewhere, during this time, Mao's philosophy of life became crystallized. It is best stated, or expressed, in his poem from *"Chinhiang Mountain."*

I HAVE LONG ASPIRED TO REACH THE CLOUDS . . .
NOTHING IS IMPOSSIBLE,
IF YOU DARE TO SCALE THE HEIGHTS.

As a young man he had wandered through the mountains of Hunan and Kiangsi; he knew that they were excellent grounds for guerilla warfare. he now determined to withdraw into the base areas and win peasant support by improving their lives. He would also train them into Red Armies. Of the six separate base areas set up, the largest was Kiangsi, and Mao was its Chairman. He set up four rules of tactics:

1. When the enemy advances, we retreat.
2. When he escapes, we harass.
3. When he retreats, we pursue.
4. When he is tired, we attack.

However, the Red Army was too small to defeat Chiang at this juncture. These base areas were surrounded, and slowly the circles were tightened, until Mao made a momentous decision. He would make a "do-or-die" attempt to break out of this ring of destruction. It was in October of 1934 that Mao Tse-tung, along with ninety thousand men and thirty-five women of the Red Army, started on the epic "Long March." "One may compare the 'Long March' with Hannibal's journey across the Alps and say smugly that the Chinese did better, or with Napoleon's retreat from Moscow and say coldly that the Chinese did worse. But it must be admitted that man has never seen the equal of it before or since. It was a flight in panic, yet it was also an epic of human endurance. In 370 days from 16 October 1934 to 20 October 1935 the 1st Front Army under Mao Tse-tung walked on and on to cover a distance of 6,000 miles."[18]

In the town of Yenan in Shensi Province, Mao chose to set up his headquarters. He established a Cave City in the cliff face of a deep gorge formed by the river. Some 20,000 people would live here, and here he would establish hospitals and a Military University. According to Edgar Snow, this university was "probably the world's only seat of higher learning whose classrooms were caves, with chairs and desks of stone and brick, whose blackboards were walls of limestone and clay, whose buildings were completely bombproof. In this underground city, deep in the heart of friendly Shensi, Mao was able to nurse his weary followers back to health, safe from the Kuomintang."[19]

Mao was an avid reader, and he said that he considered the day wasted if he had not fought a battle or read "sixty pages." Hugh Purcell evaluates Mao Tse-tung as a leader in this way: "Mao was a peasant leader, an expert guerrilla, a self taught Communist and a fine poet. But behind these roles lay a complex personality which Edgar Snow, who knew Mao over a period of thirty years, described as a mixture of peasant cunning and intellectual depth. It was this mixture that appealed to the Chinese people. As a peasant, he was one of them. As a tough soldier, he was always in the front line. As a teacher, he was able to inspire. As a politician, he was able to lead. These qualities enabled him to pull the Chinese people through a quarter-century of war and to push them through a further quarter-century of Revolution."[20]

The historian A. L. Rowse wrote in 1975, one year before the death of Mao, that "he was probably the greatest man of this century."[21] While he did exert tremendous power and a strength of leadership that is not often equalled, we have called attention to his leadership because it so vividly illustrates the strong relationship between a "philosophy of life" and the accomplishments of a leader, rather than to extol his leadership. The author is in strong disagreement with the philosophy of Communism and its ruthlessness in achieving its goals.

As the Red Army and the Kuomintang drove out the Japanese with the aid of America in her attack on their Empire, the Red Army then drove out Chiang Kai-shek and the Kuomintang. By October 1, 1949, the new Communist Government was in full control of all of China and the Chairman of the New Central Government was Mao Tse-tung. The Country with the largest population was now a Communist State, and Mao declared: "The Chinese people, one quarter of the human race, have now stood up."[22]

Mao was the great conqueror. He was the revered leader. His philosophy of life was transcendent here:

I HAVE LONG ASPIRED TO REACH THE CLOUDS . . .
NOTHING IS IMPOSSIBLE,
IF YOU DARE TO SCALE THE HEIGHTS.

These are his indelible thoughts. This was his philosophy of life that was reflected in his leadership. He firmly believed that this IMPOSSIBLE task had to be accomplished in his lifetime. His tornadic drive is reflected in another facet of his philosophy of life:

TEN THOUSAND YEARS IS TOO LONG—
SEIZE THE DAY!
SEIZE THE HOUR!!!

ALBERT SCHWEITZER

Humanitarian and Theologian

IDEALS THAT HAVE ENDURING WORTH WILL ADAPT
THEMSELVES TO CHANGING CIRCUMSTANCES AND
GROW DEEPER AND STRONGER IN THE PROCESS.

—*Albert Schweitzer*

Albert Schweitzer was a man whose life embraced at least four full careers. He was professor and lecturer; musician and organ builder; theologian and author; physician and humanitarian. Many persons have given lavishly to the service of humanity, but scarcely any have given so much as he, simply because they did not have so much to give. He has been described as a man whose countenance showed vast power and purpose. His face, both lean and strong, portrayed expressiveness and sensitivity. "His eyes, set wide apart, were like steel lanterns in the rugged landscape of his face."[23]

This extraordinary person was born in the little town of Kaysersberg, in upper Alsace, in the year 1875. This meant that he was a German citizen as well as of German stock. Very soon after his birth his family moved to the village of Gunsbach, where his father became pastor of a small evangelical congregation. Here young Albert spent a happy childhood with his three sisters and one brother. It was here that his illustrious music career began. Not only his father and mother, but his grandfather also, were lovers of music. His father began giving him piano lessons at the age of five. When he was nine he played the organ at a service in his father's church. Thus began his study of music, and of the organ, which later led to his being considered one of history's greatest interpreters of Bach. He possessed a detailed understanding of the life and meaning of this great composer. He gave organ recitals in London, in Paris, and Berlin, and could fill any concert hall in the world.

However, it was during his very early years that he came to view "all life" with a deep concern. Even as a child, while fishing with a rod and line, he decided that this sport was not for him. The treatment of the worms that were put on the hook for bait and the wrenching of the mouths of the fish that were caught made this sport impossible for him to enjoy. He grew up with "an unshakable conviction that we have no right to inflict suffering and death on another living creature unless there is some unavoidable necessity for it, and that we ought, all of us, to feel what a horrible thing it is to cause suffering and death out of mere thoughtlessness."[24]

From this time on it was quite apparent that young Albert had a sensitive mind and heart for all life. This reverence for life was at the very heart of his thinking. His own youth was filled with great happiness, so much so that he felt he must not accept it as a matter of course but must give something in return for it. As he pursued his academic training, he came to believe deeply in the sacredness of man and began to develop his own philosophy of life:

REVERENCE FOR ALL LIFE
AND
SERVICE TO ALL MANKIND

In 1893, he entered Strassburg University. This ancient seat of learning was then at the height of its reputation, with a faculty composed of some of the greatest minds in resurgent Germany. At Strassburg he completed his Doctorate in Philosophy and later, at the University of Berlin, he completed his Doctorate in Theology. During this time he continued his study of the organ. Once, while giving a concert in cooperation with a choir and orchestra, he exclaimed: "For the first time I knew the joy of letting the organ send the flood of its own special tones to mingle with the clanging music of choir and orchestra."[25]

At the age of 30, Albert Schweitzer was famous as a musician, philosopher, and theologian. He had been made principal of the Theological College at Strassburg. Already, he had made major contributions as teacher and author in philosophy, theology, and history. It appeared that he had laid a solid foundation for a lifelong career in these fields. Every opportunity that he wanted seemed open to him now. However, as a philosopher he held to the firm belief that he must deal not only with the techniques of reason, or with matter and space and stars, but with people. He believed that *ideals which have enduring worth will adapt themselves to changing circumstances and grow deeper and stronger in the process*. He believed in REVERENCE FOR ALL LIFE and in SERVICE TO ALL MANKIND. Thus, in the light of his philosophy of life, he must re-evaluate his present circumstances.

Then, on October 13, 1905, an inner urge, unknown to others, caused him to make what seemed an incredible decision. He would renounce his brilliant career in Europe and would prepare himself as a medical doctor in order that he might serve those who were in such desperate need in equatorial Africa. To do this he would need to spend seven years in preparation. This seemed like a very long time, but when he was inclined to feel that the years he would be sacrificing were too long, he reminded himself that Hannibal prepared for his march on Rome by the slow and tedious quest of Spain.

So it was that in 1913, Doctor Schweitzer, and his bride of one year, embarked for the long voyage down the west coast of Africa to the equator. From that point they continued inland by river boat through dense jungle for a distance of 200 miles. The Ogowe River carried them to Lambarene in French Equatorial Africa. When word spread that a doctor had come to this primitive hospital at the edge of the primeval jungle, an unending procession of the sick came, through the jungle paths and by the Ogowe River, in canoes hollowed out of tree trunks.

He entered into his work with great enthusiasm. Soon the jungle was being pushed back and new buildings were being erected, much of this by his own labor. As the years slipped by, while working under the most exhausting circumstances, he refused *to give up his enthusiasm* or *his reverence for life*. This led him to exclaim: "What we are usually invited to contemplate as 'ripeness' in a man is the resigning of ourselves to an almost exclusive use of reason. One acquires it by copying others and getting rid, one by one, of the convictions which were dear in the days of one's youth."[26] To maintain his enthusiasm, he was ever on guard.

It has been said that when Dr. Schweitzer walked through the grounds at Lambarene, it seemed to make everything right, even though it was so primitive and inadequate that it would startle the casual observer. Each night he caused a lamp to be lighted on the wharf by the Ogowe River, a light which carried into the African darkness this message: "Here, at whatever hour you come, you will find light and help and human kindness."[27] His ministry reached out to all mankind, including the children. For them he wrote a philosophy that he entitled: "For Children Only."

> *Seek quietly to deepen The Inner Reverence.*
> *Reverence all Holy Writ and The Life it reveals.*
> *Reverence the Holy Day and keep it as a day of renewal.*
> *Hold fast to thine own sincerity: seek always for the higher*
>   *motive in others.*
> *Honour thy parents: be kindly affectioned to thy kindred.*
> *Be kind to all animals: do not thoughtlessly hurt any bird or*
>   *wayside flower.*
> *Give heed to the natural laws of health.*
> *Hold sacred the life creating power.*
> *Do not strive for sudden wealth: there is truer happiness in*
>   *higher affection.*
> *Finally, it is required of thee, as in a spirit of pure adora-*
>   *tion, to work for God uninfluenced by fear of punish-*
>   *ment or hope of reward.*[28]

The influence of this most capable and versatile leader upon our world is incalculable. The power of his life and thought is unending. While Hitler wrote, *"My Fight,"* poisoning the arteries of Europe and massacring thousands, Schweitzer wrote, *"Civilization and Ethics,"* urging a deep concern for the natural rights and the safety of the human community on earth. Many have considered Albert Schweitzer to be "the conscience of the age," as he probed some of the deepest problems of modern civilization.

Dr. Albert Schweitzer of Lambarene gave his life in fruitful service both to the cultured West and to the deprived people of Equatorial Africa. He did so because of his abiding philosophy of life: "ALL OF LIFE IS SACRED."

J. PAUL GETTY

Businessman and Industrialist

TO MY WAY OF THINKING, BEING IN BUSINESS WAS
WORTHWHILE AND CHALLENGING—ONLY—IF ONE
VIEWED IT AS A FORM OF CREATIVE WORK.

—*J. Paul Getty*

One of the greatest financial leaders of this century was the late
J. Paul Getty. He was born in 1892 and became an active businessman at the age of 22. He believed that he lived and worked
through the most exciting and exhilarating, the most turbulent and
terrible, eight decades of human history. Some referred to him as a
billionaire. Some have suggested that he was the richest man in
America. Still others, amazed at his wealth, have said that he was the
richest man in the world. Mr. Getty responded to these grand-
iloquent titles by saying that he did not know, or could not know, the
extent of his wealth. However, he believed that anyone could make a
million dollars in our day IF he would follow the 10 fundamental
rules which Getty had laid down. As far as he was concerned, the
door to the "Million Dollar Club" was not locked. He asserted that
"Over and over, we have illustrations of alert, imaginative, and re-

sourceful young persons who have made their millions in various business endeavors."

His college education was begun at the University of California in Berkeley, but he decided to complete his college work at Oxford. He found that there was infinitely more emphasis placed upon the "Humanities" at Oxford and that he was encouraged to read widely, far beyond the limits of any specialty or major. In speaking of his college education, he says: "My studies, especially at Oxford, served me in excellent stead throughout my business career. I learned much, and I have often applied the knowledge I gained to good advantage. But my studies in the "Humanities," subjects that expanded my cultural horizons, were of the greatest value. It was from these studies that I gained understanding and insight into the structure and development, the functioning and the dynamics, of our world and our society. At the same time, I developed interests that have provided me with great pleasure and gratification throughout my life. They helped me be a better man and a better businessman. My exposure to a wide variety of liberal-arts subjects made my mind more flexible, more receptive to new ideas, more readily aware of changing circumstances, and, at the same time, more convinced of what constitutes real and lasting values."[29]

It is worthwhile to note Getty's evaluation of present-day education as it relates to the aspiring young leader. He observes: "While I am gratified that today's young executive is extremely well educated professionally and that he has the knowledge necessary to do his job well, I deplore the narrowness of his formal education and of his interests. I cannot help but feel that an education that fails to broaden one's outlook is an inadequate education. Neglect of the "Humanities," which give a student cultural interests and at least some understanding of people, the world and its institutions, can have no beneficial effect."[30]

In seeking out J. Paul Getty's philosophy of life, the philosophy that was his guiding light through eight decades, I found it set forth in his book: *How to Be a Successful Business Executive*. He states it in this way:

TO MY WAY OF THINKING, BEING IN BUSINESS WAS WORTHWHILE AND CHALLENGING—ONLY—IF ONE VIEWED IT AS A FORM OF CREATIVE WORK.

He firmly believed that he was a creative businessman. Because of his vision and his dreams, he was able to see the great opportunities in the domestic oil markets of the United States. His creative urge enabled him to see the bright horizons in oil as they related to the field of International Trade. He believed that in spite of confiscatory taxes, high labor costs, unfair foreign competition, and creeping Socialism, the American "Free Enterprise System" was still workable. That was, if a person is open-minded, far-sighted, and progressive and views his business as creative work. To him, industry was an "Elysian Field" awaiting the young person who was about to embark on a career or launch a business of his own. In a magazine article entitled, "You Can Make a Million," which was directed toward an audience in the 21 to 40 age group, he wrote: "I envy your chances. I wish I could take them for you. It would be fun to do it all over again."

Already, we have observed that Getty believed there were fundamental rules which the creative business person should apply to all business ventures. These 10 fundamentals acted as a bulwark, strengthening his philosophy of life. Now, let us note the correlation between these fundamentals and his philosophy:

1. Go into business for yourself.
2. Never lose sight of the central aim of business, which is the production of more and better goods; or provide more and better services at lower costs.
3. A sense of thrift is essential for success in business.
4. Be on the alert for legitimate opportunities for expansion. But be aware of possible over expansion.
5. The businessman must run his own business. He must maintain careful supervision.
6. One must be constantly alert for new ways to improve products and services.
7. The businessman must be willing to take risks when, in his judgment, the risks are justified.
8. One must constantly be alert to new horizons and untapped, or under-exploited, markets. This includes foreign markets for the shrewd businessman.
9. One should have a reputation for honesty. He must be willing to stand behind his work or products. Guarantees should always be honored.
10. One must maintain a stewardship of wealth. For wealth must be a means for improving living conditions everywhere. He has responsibilities toward his associates, employees, stockholders, and the public.[31]

These fundamentals served as the guidelines, or basic tools, with which he built his "Empire." To the potential business leader he further suggests that there are limitless opportunities for the one who is able to creatively recognize them, who will apply these 10 fundamentals, and who is willing to work hard. "In fact, ALL THAT GLITTERS truly CAN BE GOLD."

At all times, this business genius was an exponent of the "well-rounded" man. He believed that the "Liberal Arts" contributed to a person of taste, discernment, creativity, understanding, and intellectual versatility, thus, increasing his chances of reaching the TOP, and of his enjoying life, and himself, much more in the process. He was an avid student of the "Arts" and during his life acquired one of the world's great art collections. Much of this magnificent collection is now being shared with art lovers at the J. PAUL GETTY ART MUSEUM, beautifully situated in California over-looking the Pacific Ocean. Speaking of art, he very penetratingly observes: "To me, my works of art are all vividly alive. They are the embodiment of whoever created them—a mirror of their creator's hopes, dreams and frustrations. They have led eventful lives—pampered by the aristocracy and pillaged by revolution, courted with ardour and cold-bloodedly abandoned. They have been honoured by drawing rooms and humbled by attics. So many worlds in their life-span, yet all were transitory. Their worlds have long since disintegrated, yet they live on—and, for the most part, they are as beautiful as ever."[32]

A study of the philosophy of this multi-faceted multi-billionaire is indeed stimulating. Much of his philosophy is revealed in his book: *How to Be Rich*. Scanning the chapter titles one learns a great deal about this giant business leader, a Goliath among his peers. In this book he writes on "The Art of Individuality," "The IMP of the Impossible," "The Art of Investment," and "The Millionaire Mentality." Getty is very convincing when he states that ANYONE can become a millionaire; that is, with luck, knowledge, and hard work—especially hard work. But, above all, he asserts that one must have what he calls "the millionaire mentality," that vitally aware state of mind which harnesses all of an individual's skills and intelligence to the tasks and goals of his business.

And yet, *MILLIONS* and *BILLIONS* ARE ONLY WORTHWHILE AND CHALLENGING *IF* THEY ARE VIEWED AS A FORM OF CREATIVE WORK.

MICHELANGELO

Sculptor, Painter, and Architect

HOW CAN IT BE?
THAT WHICH ALL MEN LEARN BY LONG EXPERIENCE—
SHAPES THAT SEEM ALIVE,
WROUGHT IN HARD MOUNTAIN MARBLE,
WILL SURVIVE THEIR MAKER,
WHOM THE YEARS TO DUST RETURN!

—Michelangelo Buonarroti

"As touching Michelangelo, there is no name in the whole of ART more exalted than his." He was born on March 6, 1475, the son of Buonarroti, Mayor of Caprese, Italy. Inevitably, he was destined for great accomplishments as Sculptor, Painter, and Architect. Moreover, he was to be an engineer, a poet, and a patriot. With all of his vast talents, in manhood he was somewhat timid, due to his great sensitivity. But there was "iron" in his soul, whether as a small boy opposing his father, or as the artisan confronting the Pope. In him, there was a courageous sense of destiny which was most unusual.

His name, Michelangelo, is interpreted to mean "Angel Michel."

Although he came from peasant stock and experienced poverty during his youth, he was one of the best educated men of his day. It was in the city of Florence, explosive with ideas, and in the most powerful State in Italy, that Michelangelo came to manhood. He was highly educated in philosophy and theology, and was one of the best educated men of his day. He was well acquainted with the most brilliant of his contemporaries, and as a young man of 15, he conversed with the educated men of the city. They seemed to sense the fire that flamed within his mind and heart. No doubt the effect of this upon his work witnesses to the decisive influence exercised by these outstanding "Thinkers" and "Poets." These men had been greatly influenced by the great philosopher Plato, as well as by the fiery sermons of a Dominican Monk, Savanarola, who was later burned at the stake in Florence and his ashes strewn upon the Arno River.

As a youth, Michelangelo committed himself to a philosophy which he embraced throughout life:

A CLEAR UNDERSTANDING OF DIVINE THINGS IS MADE POSSIBLE ONLY THROUGH A SEIZURE OF THE SOUL, THE FUROR DIVINUS. THE SPIRIT OF GOD THEN TAKES COMPLETE POSSESSION OF THE BODY, ELEVATING THE SOUL AND THE SPIRIT TO A KNOWLEDGE OF THE SUPERNATURAL.[33]

As he came to maturity, he accepted a basic belief in the unity of "Art." This belief is stated in these words: "Design, which by another man is called drawing, and consists of it, is the fount and body of painting and sculpture and architecture and of every other kind of painting, and the root of all the sciences."[34]

At the age of 22, Michelangelo received a commission for a "Pieta" in Saint Peter's Basilica in Rome. For him, Rome was a new world. It would mean the imbibing of the new spirit of the Renaissance. In Rome he would discover monumental classical sculpture, and here he would attempt to emulate it. During this period, he would produce two of his most magnificent sculptures, "Bacchus" and the "Pieta." When he received the commission for the "Pieta," he made a journey to Carrara to quarry the finest marble possible. He was certain that his "Pieta" would be the most beautiful marble statue in Rome. This expectation, while very high, was to be amply fulfilled. The perfection of this sculpture made Michelangelo the most distinguished and celebrated sculptor in Christendom.

The Holy Virgin is seated on a rock as she holds the dead body of her son, Jesus Christ. Her right arm encircles and sustains him, while the gesture of her left arm signifies her sadness and her helplessness. Rolf Schott, in writing concerning the "Pieta," states: "The master had chosen a theme found less often in 15th century Italy than in the Gothic North. He re-created and raised it to heights of naturalistic and spiritual perfection not since surpassed—unless it be by himself, although in an entirely different and marvelously muted key."[35]

Another of Michelangelo's most celebrated sculptures is "David." David, an adolescent youth, powerfully built, is of gigantic proportions. He is totally nude and holds in his hand a sling which is largely concealed behind his back. The position of his head and limbs, and the contrasted movement of the arms in opposite directions, reveals something of the permanent features of David's character and his present mood. Again, the finest of white marble was selected for this superb statue. We have here a revelation, or incarnation, of ethical, moral, and spiritual strength.

Charles De Tolnay says in commenting on this masterpiece: "This slender, muscular body reveals no slackening of energy but rather an alertness, a dynamism of potential power. Outwardly he seems to be self-possessed and calm; inwardly he is taut and ready for action. Anger and heroic scorn are written on his noble face. Under the thick shock of hair—like tongues of flame—and the stormy furrows of a brow frowning in indignation, we encounter the fire of a glance full of pride and disdain. The eyelids are contracted, the nostrils pinched with rage, the lips swollen with anger. He is the embodiment of force and anger."[36]

The impact of his philosophy upon his work is indicated in much that has been written about him. Vasari, a contemporary scholar and biographer, refers to his friend as a spirit with universal ability in every art. He believed that Michelangelo was sent down from heaven so that he might be able to reveal the perfection of design in lines, contours, and highlights, thereby giving relief to the works of painting; also, that he might reveal correct judgment in sculpture and that he might be able in architecture to render works healthy, cheerful, rich with varied ornaments, and well proportioned. From this we learn something of the acclaim that was accorded to this Master who was to bring about great change in the "World of Art."

The demands of an untamed vital force are magnified in every one of his figures. In each gesture they permeate the whole creation. The head of David, like that of his other creations, is full of thought; the hands are large and strong; the palm is very large, which makes it possible to fight or to create. Imagine the creator of these giants as he walked in the marble quarries in the Alps, dreaming of modeling these white hills into sculptures: the PIETA, BACCHUS, DAVID, his TITANS, and his MOSES. Irving Stone said of him: "He placed his chisel on the block, struck the first blow with his hammer. This was where he belonged. He, the marble, the hammer and chisel, were one. Soon his chisels were singing through the white marble like plows through the spring earth."[37]

Again, his friend and admirer, Vasari, writes with enthusiasm concerning Michelangelo's statue of "Moses." "Never will any modern work approach the beauty of this statue. Nay, one might with equal justice affirm, that of the ancient statues none is equal to this. Seated in an attitude of imposing dignity, the lawgiver rests one arm on the 'TABLES' and with the other restrains the flowing beard. . . . The countenance is of the most sublime beauty, and may be described as that of a truly sacred and most mighty Prince; but to say nothing of this, while you look at it, you would almost believe the figure to be on the point of demanding a veil wherewith to conceal that face, the beaming splendour of which is so dazzling to mortal gaze. So well has the artist rendered the divinity which the Almighty had imparted to the most holy countenance of that great Lawgiver."[38] We are told that on one occasion Michelangelo threw his sculptor's hammer against this life-like statue because Moses refused to speak.

Once during a visit to Italy, we spent many days in the city of Florence and in the city of Rome. While in Rome we visited most of the usual points of interest: the Roman Forum, the great Colosseum, the Arch of Constantine, the magnificent Cathedrals, and the beautiful Fountains. However, it was Michelangelo's creations that caused other wonderful works to pale. In Vatican City we visited Saint Peter's Basilica, which is the largest Cathedral in the world. This ancient church, with its vast wealth of art treasures, great paintings, tapestry galleries, libraries, and costly Mosaics, seems to overwhelm the visitor.

Here, in the Sistine Chapel, we were completely overwhelmed by the magnitude and grandeur of its awe-inspiring ceiling. Words are totally inadequate to describe all that this masterpiece of art portrays. Kenneth Clark states perceptively that: "The Sistine Ceiling passionately asserts the unity of man's body, mind and spirit. You can admire it from the point of view of the body—as nineteenth-century critics used to do, who looked first at the so-called athletes, or from the point of view of the mind, as one does when one looks at those great embodiments of intellectual energy, the Prophets and the Sibyls. But when one looks at the sequence of stories from Genesis, I think one feels that Michelangelo was chiefly concerned with the Spirit."[39] It would seem that truly the Spirit of God had completely possessed him, *ELEVATING THE SOUL AND THE SPIRIT TO A KNOWLEDGE OF THE SUPERNATURAL.*

Without Michelangelo there would be no "Sistine Ceiling," with the entire panorama of Bible history portrayed superbly and in detail. Imagine this creative genius painting this immense panorama from the position of lying upon his back! This special fresco demanded the utmost in patience, understanding, and consummate skill. As he came to the time of completing his sketches for the vault, "they called for three hundred men, women and children, all imbued with the potency of life, displacing space as three-dimensional as those who walked the earth. The force to create them must come from within himself. It would take days, weeks, months of demonical energy to imbue each individual character with an authentic anatomy, mind, spirit and soul, an irradiation of strength so monumental and outpouring that few men on the earth below could match them for power. Each one had to be pushed out of his artistic womb, pushed out by his own articulate frenzied force. He must gather within himself his galvanic might, his burgeoning seed must be generated each day anew within his vitals, hurtled into space, projected onto the ceiling, given life everlasting."[40] Thus, in a four-year period, the greatest painting ever created by man was completed despite the fact that he did not even have an assistant to help him mix his paints or an apprentice to grind the colors. He ate little when he was working, many times only a piece of bread which he put in his pocket before climbing onto the scaffolding. When the fever of creation was upon him, he slept in his clothes with his boots on his feet. During this time he remained alone in the loneliness of his visions. However, "in moments of unforeseen emergencies he was capable of tremendous exertion. Thus he built by daily exertions a gigantic world of superhuman ambitions, of superhuman artistic and moral power."[41] Toward the completion of this vast commission, Michelangelo wrote a letter to a friend stating: "I work harder than anyone who ever lived. I'm not well and am worn out with this stupendous labor and yet I'm patient in order to achieve the desired end."

This creative genius of the sixteenth century is acclaimed throughout the world as Sculptor, Painter, and Architect. His talents seemed to know no boundaries. The thrust of his dedicated personality influences the world today. He was, and is, a world leader in the "Arts." A personal and sociological equation which best fits him may be stated in this way:

COMPLETE CONSECRATION OF TIME,
TALENT, AND ENERGY

PLUS

COMPLETE CONCENTRATION OF TIME,
TALENT, AND EFFORT

EQUALS

A DYNAMIC THRUST OF PERSONALITY
FOR ANY CAUSE

For Michelangelo the *CAUSE* was *ART* in its various forms. This is true in his sculpturing, in his painting, and in his architecture.

The ancient city of Rome, like most European cities, is oriented in the past.

Its glory is that of the "Caesars."
It is that of the great "Roman Empire."
It is that of the early "Christian Church."
It is that of the surging "Renaissance."
It is that of the great "Artists." [42]

And yet today, when in Rome, we feel the dynamic thrust of Michelangelo's personality. He, who was the Master or leader in the Arts, lives on:

He lives in the adorable *Pieta*.
He lives in the fearless statue of *David*.
He lives in the sublime beauty of the lawgiver, *Moses*.
He lives in the inspiring frescoes of the *Sistine Chapel Ceiling*.
He lives in the grandeur of the *Basilica of Saint Peter's*.
He lives in scores of other works of *Art*.
He lives in Rome today, as he has for the past four centuries.

One can feel his presence. The impact of his genius is felt throughout the world. His personality is stamped upon his creative art. It has been said that "Art has a magic quality: the more minds that digest it, the longer it lives."[43]

Michelangelo believed that man was created in the image of God, and because of that, man longs to be creative. He believed that God was the creative force and, therefore, the "Absolute Artist." This gives credence to his vibrant philosophy of life, which was indeed the foundation stone of his illustrious career.

DOUGLAS MacARTHUR

Patriot and Military Commander

DUTY, HONOR, COUNTRY: THOSE THREE HALLOWED
WORDS REVERENTLY DICTATE WHAT YOU OUGHT TO BE,
WHAT YOU CAN BE, WHAT YOU WILL BE. THEY ARE YOUR
RALLYING POINT TO BUILD COURAGE WHEN COURAGE
SEEMS TO FAIL, TO REGAIN FAITH WHEN THERE SEEMS
TO BE LITTLE CAUSE FOR FAITH, TO CREATE HOPE
WHEN HOPE BECOMES FORLORN.

—Douglas MacArthur

As a young man of 18, Douglas MacArthur prepared to take his examinations for entrance to West Point Academy. His mother, Pinky, urged him to be self-confident, to be self-reliant, and to do his best. This he did, and in so doing learned a lesson that he would never forget: "Preparedness is the key to success and victory." He was endowed with great personal charm, a will of iron, and a soaring intellect. Some believe that he was the most gifted man-at-arms this nation has produced.

But now let us view this rising young leader. In 1915 he was promoted to the rank of Major, and in 1917, as Colonel, he was assigned to the "Rainbow Division" as Chief of Staff. In 1918, while fighting in World War I, he was decorated nine times for heroism and in the same year was promoted to General. In 1919 he became Superintendent of West Point, where he served with distinction.

In his early years, Douglas MacArthur adopted the "Academy Motto" as his philosophy of life and service:

DUTY—HONOR—COUNTRY

He was vitally interested in physical exercise, including football and baseball, at West Point. In the autumn of 1927, when the President of the American Olympic Committee died suddenly, the Committee, knowing of the General's strong support of athletics at the Academy, offered him the position, which he accepted immediately. His charge to the American athletes at the Olympic games was typical: "Americans never quit! We are here to represent the greatest country on earth. We did not come here to lose gracefully. We came here to win—and win decisively."[44] After this speech the Americans set 17 records and won more victories than the next two countries combined. Again, it was—DUTY—HONOR—COUNTRY.

After MacArthur had completed his three years as Superintendent of West Point, and after he had presided over the ninth Olympic competition in Amsterdam, he challenged America: "We must build athletically, not only for health, but for character. In learning how to play we learn how to live."[45]

In 1930, Douglas MacArthur was appointed "Chief of Staff" by President Hoover. It was an appointment which carried very heavy responsibility. He was sworn in as the eighth American in history to hold that exalted title. During the five years which he served as Chief of Staff, he attempted to strengthen the military defenses of the nation, to enlarge West Point, and to predict the manner in which World War II would be fought.

In 1936, he was appointed by Manuel Quezon, President-elect of the Commonwealth of the Philippines, as military advisor to the President of the Commonwealth. While serving in this position he drew up a 10-year development plan of defense. This plan would be operative with defense capability by 1946, this being the time established for their complete independence from the United States of America. It was clear to the General that the Philippines could be defended. However, there were those who did not believe that it could be done. The Japanese, on the other hand, were strongly opposed to its defense, for reasons soon to be made obvious.

The growing threat of a war with Japan in the Pacific led to MacArthur's recall to active duty and to his assignment as Commanding General of the U.S. Army Forces in the Far East. The invasion of the Philippines came too soon for the young and untested Philippine army facing the Japanese veterans. Luzon was lost after a brave stand except for Corregidor and the Bataan Peninsula. General MacArthur led the defense until he was ordered to Australia as Supreme Commander of the Southwest Pacific area. His famous words, "I shall return," were most meaningful to those in the Philippines.

During the busy war years in Australia, one night after supper he wrote a prayer for his son Arthur:

Build me a son, O Lord, who will be strong enough to know when he is weak, and brave enough to face himself when he is afraid; one who will be proud and unbending in honest defeat, and humble and gentle in victory.

Build me a son whose wishes will not take the place of deeds; a son who will know Thee—and that to know himself is the foundation stone of knowledge.

Lead him, I pray, not in the path of ease and comfort, but under the stress and spur of difficulties and challenge. Here let him learn to stand up in the storm; here let him learn compassion for those who fail.

Build me a son whose heart will be clear, whose goal will be high; a son who will master himself before he seeks to master other men; one who will reach into the future, yet never forget the past.

And after all these things are his, add, I pray, enough of a sense of humor, so that he may always be serious, yet never take himself too seriously. Give him humility, so that he may always remember the simplicity of true greatness, the open mind of true wisdom, and the weakness of true strength.

Then I, his father, will dare to whisper, "I have not lived in vain."[46]

On June 18, 1942, the National Father's Day Committee selected

Douglas MacArthur as "Father of the Year." His pride in his little four-year-old son, with his boyish enthusiasm, is reflected in his response: "Nothing has touched me more deeply than the action of the National Father's Day Committee. By profession I am a soldier, and take pride in that fact, but I am prouder, infinitely prouder, to be a father. A soldier destroys in order to build; the father only builds, never destroys. The one has the potentialities of death; the other embodies creation and life. And while the hordes of death are mighty, the battalions of life are mightier still. It is my hope that my son, when I am gone, will remember me not from the battle but in the home repeating with him our simple daily prayer: 'Our Father who art in Heaven.'"[47] MacArthur, as General and as Father, had in his philosophy of life an underlying bulwark of faith and confidence: Duty—Honor—Country.

By October 1944 the long-awaited return to the Philippines was accomplished. Listen as he proclaims: "The hour of your redemption is here. . . . Let the indomitable spirit of Bataan and Corregidor lead on. As the lines of battle roll forward to bring you within the zone of operations, rise and strike. Strike at every favorable opportunity. For your homes and hearths, strike! In the name of your sacred dead, strike! Let no heart faint. Let every arm be steeled. The guidance of a divine God points the way. Follow in His Name to the Holy Grail of righteous victory."[48] On March 2, 1945, at the flag-raising ceremonies on Corregidor, the General recalled that it was from its South Dock that he had boarded the PT boat which took him to Australia. Now, he had returned and had retaken the Island by parachute and amphibious assault. His promise to return had been fulfilled.

By September 2, 1945, the terrible war was over, and MacArthur stood on the deck of the USS Missouri in Tokyo Bay for the purpose of obtaining the complete surrender of Japan. When the formal surrender ceremonies were completed, once again the General spoke: "Today the guns are silent. A great tragedy has ended. A great victory has been won. The skies no longer rain death—the seas bear only commerce—men everywhere walk upright in the sunlight. The entire world lies quietly at peace. The holy mission has been completed."[49]

From the battlefield MacArthur turned to the task of rebuilding, and to the pursuit of long-range peace. It was to be built on the solid foundation of Duty—Honor—Country. As Supreme Allied Commander he was the executive authority for the United Nations. He was assisted by an advisory body called the Allied Council for Japan. However, he made it crystal clear that the Council's function was advisory only. Thereby, he checked the Soviet members from the very beginning. He also outlined to the Council and to the World that his general philosophy would be based upon rebuilding Japan and upon the securing of the peace. Of course, the primary policy of the Far Eastern Commission, and of MacArthur, was to insure the world that Japan did not pose a military threat to the free nations of the world. He realized that reorientation of the entire nation was vitally important if there was to be a long-time peace. The 11 nations that fought against Japan adopted a liberal policy for Japanese reconstruction and thereby laid the groundwork for an enduring peace.

While the General was busily engaged in winning the peace by creating a peaceful Japan, the Communist Government of North Korea launched a full-scale invasion of South Korea on June 25, 1950. The United Nations accepted the challenge, with the United States bearing the brunt of the thrust. MacArthur was designated as Commanding General of the United Nations Command. He immediately transferred to Korea major elements of the Eighth Army, which were at his command in Japan. By late July the situation had been largely stabilized. The Eighth Army was doing a holding action in the Pusan perimeter. At the same time, the General landed two Divisions at Inchon and was thus able to cut the North Korean Army's supply line from the north. This attack, plus a simultaneous attack from Pusan, led to the disintegration of the North Korean forces. Consequently, MacArthur was able to liberate Seoul, the Capital.

For a time it looked as if there would be an early victory. But, on November 28, 1950, a massive Red Chinese counteroffensive developed, which split the United Nations Forces and caused a rapid withdrawal. The Red Chinese were able in time to drive beyond Seoul before their forward movement was stopped. Early in February of 1951 the United Nations Forces were approaching Seoul and were pushing the Red Chinese Army and the North Korean Army back from whence they came. Then seven weeks later came the shattering words: "General MacArthur is relieved from his Command by President Harry S. Truman."

Upon his return to his homeland, Douglas MacArthur spoke in the City Hall of San Francisco on April 18, 1951. With deep feeling he said: "I cannot tell you what it means to be home—how I have longed for it, dreamed of it, through the dreary years of absence abroad. My emotions almost defy description as I find myself once more among my own people—once more under the spell of the great American home which breeds such magnificent men as I have just left fighting the battle in Korea."[50]

The following day he addressed both Houses of Congress. It was his report to a nation concerning the current situation in the Far East. It was his report concerning his own stewardship of Duty— Honor—Country. He concluded this address with words from an old ballad: "Old Soldiers Never Die. They Just Fade Away."

One of his last great speeches was delivered to the United States Military Academy at West Point. At this time he was awarded the distinguished "Thayer Award." The title of his address was: "DUTY—HONOR—COUNTRY." These three dynamic words were the "Motto of the Academy"; moreover, they were the very words that he had taken as his philosophy of life. The entire Corps of Cadets were present for this very special occasion. His words were especially for them: "Duty, Honor, Country: Those three hallowed words reverently dictate what you ought to be, what you can be, what you will be. They are your rallying point to build courage when courage seems to fail, to regain faith when there seems to be little cause for faith, to create hope when hope becomes forlorn."[51]

The grand "Old Soldier" was aware that for him the shadows were lengthening. He knew that time was running out, and that the dreams of youth were long past. However, he concluded this eloquent address by stating: "In my dreams I hear again the crash of guns, the rattle of musketry, the strange, mournful mutter of the battlefield. But in the evening of my memory always I come back to West Point. Always there echoes and re-echoes: *DUTY— HONOR—COUNTRY.*"

YOUR PHILOSOPHY OF LIFE
IS
THE FOUNDATION STONE OF YOUR LEADERSHIP

Part II

EIGHT THEORIES OF LEADERSHIP

The concept of leadership should be understood as encompassing a wide range of activities.

It applies to the running of small groups and to the governing of nations.

It may concern the relatively diffuse process of influence in establishing norms of style or opinion—or it may involve specific orders in a chain of command.

It includes supervision and statesmanship, routine administration and organization building.

—Arnold S. Tannenbaum

5.

The Great Man Theory

THE GREAT MAN THEORY GIVES TO ITS HEROES AN AL-
MOST SUPERHUMAN CONTROL OVER THE FATE OF THEIR
GENERATION. WHETHER THEY HAPPENED TO BE
EVENT-SHAPERS OR EVENT-MAKERS, IT HAS BEEN AR-
GUED THAT GREAT MEN HAVE CHANGED THE COURSE
OF HISTORY. WHETHER THEY HAVE GRASPED DEEPER
AND LARGER FORCES IN HISTORY AND SHAPED THEM OR
WHETHER THEY HAVE CONTROLLED EVENTS AND
TURNED HISTORY IN A CERTAIN DIRECTION, THEIR
PRESENCE WAS CRUCIAL TO THE WAY THE FUTURE
EVOLVED.

—Sidney Hook

This theory or philosophy of leadership has to do with the great
issue: What are the moving forces of history? This is a question
which has often been asked and is one of great significance. Thomas
Carlyle believed that "the history of the world is the history of great

men." Ralph Emerson believed that "great men exist that there may
be greater men." The intellectual giants of every age have struggled
with the idea. The answers given by the great minds of the past, and
of the present, are varied and challenge our best thoughts.

For instance, for Hegel it was a moving battleground of economic forces, ideas, and spiritual elements. It was the thesis battling
with the antithesis until the synthesis was formed. The new thesis
for Hegel was then the former synthesis. This in turn brought out a
new antithesis and, as the battle between the thesis and the antithesis was waged, it produced another synthesis. Thus, ideas
proved to be the dynamic force of change and of movement.

For Marx, the moving forces of history were economic forces. He
accepted the philosophic framework of Hegel's dialectic; but he sub-
stituted, or limited, economic forces for the forces that propelled men
and nations. For Marx, it was a battleground of economic forces
struggling to reach the Utopia of the classless society. The thesis was
feudalism. The antithesis was capitalism and, as these great economic forces battled each other, there emerged the synthesis which
was socialism or communism. It is a bit ironic that for Marx the
Utopia or end of the struggle was the classless society. This synthesis
did not become a new thesis. Rather, the classless society was the
end of the road. The moving force of society would no longer move.

Tolstoy also dealt with the momentous issue, "What are the moving forces of society?" He was especially interested in the relationship of the men who command with the men who are commanded.
This seemed to be that which constituted "the essence of the conception called power." Tolstoy attempts an answer, directly and posi-
tively, to two essential questions of universal history:

"What is power?"
"What force produces the movement of the nations?"

His answer to the proposition: What is power?: "Power is the
relation of a given person to other individuals, in which the more this
person expressed opinions, predictions, and justifications of the collective action that is performed, the less is his participation in that
action."

His answer to the proposition, What force produces the movement of the nations?: "The movement of nations is caused not by
power, nor by intellectual activity, nor even by a combination of the
two as historians have supposed, but by the activity of all the people

who participate in the events, and who always combine in such a way that those taking the largest direct share in the event take on themselves the least responsibility and vice versa." He further states: "Morally the wielder of power appears to cause the event; physically it is those who submit to the power. But as the moral activity is inconceivable without the physical, the cause of the event is neither in the one nor in the other but in the union of the two."[1] This view of the forces which move men and nations causes Tolstoy to come to grips with luck, genius, Great Men, and freedom of the will. He was strongly opposed to the "Great Man" theory of leadership. Perhaps his fear and hate for Napoleon was a factor in his thinking, as well as his philosophical differences in understanding those forces which move men and nations.

It was Thomas Carlyle who came to a very different theory or point of view from those presented by Hegel, Marx, and Tolstoy. Carlyle's answer to the controversy, "What are the moving forces of history," is very different. He sees the dynamic and constructive forces moving history as Great Men and Heroes. Carlyle put it this way: "For as I take it, universal history, the history of what man has accomplished in this world, is at bottom the history of the great men who have worked here. They are the leaders of men, these great ones; the modelers, patterns, and in a wide sense creators, of whatsoever the general mass of men contrived to do or to attain; all things that we see standing accomplished in the world are properly the outer material result, the practical realization and embodiment of thoughts that dwelt in the great men sent into the world: the soul of the whole world's history, it may justly be considered, were the history of these."[2]

In this theory the focus is upon the personality of the leader. He has certain innate characteristics and qualities. He is a man of distinctive stamp. He is predestined by his unusual capacity to become a leader, controlling events, and molding situations. He is destined to have an impact upon the lives of men and nations. "The history of the world is the history of great men."

In Carlyle's book entitled *Heroes and Hero Worship*, he deals with the great men who have fashioned the society and the world in which we live. They are endowed with superior intellect and powers to lead. They are born leaders; they have not been made leaders. In six of the lectures given in the book, he considers The Hero as Divinity, The Hero as Prophet, The Hero as Poet, The Hero as Priest,

The Hero as Man of Letters, and The Hero as King. Now, let us consider these categories as listed:

The Hero as Divinity

In this discourse the author is concerned with the coming into the world of these great leaders—their manner of appearance and the way in which they have appeared among men. He is concerned with their ideas, plans, and work. The first lecture deals with the Hero as Divinity, a brief study of Odin, Paganism, and Scandinavian Mythology. In all of paganism, in its varied forms, nature is divine. "Out of many roots: every admiration, adoration of a star or natural object, was a root or fiber of a root: but hero-worship is the deepest root of all; the tap-root, from which in a great degree all the rest were nourished and grown. And now if worship even of a star had some meaning in it, how much more might that of a hero! Worship of a hero is transcendent admiration of a Great Man. I say great men are still admirable. I say there is, at bottom, nothing else admirable!"[3]

There were opponents to this view of "Heroes and Hero-Worship." There were those who denied the existence of these great men. They would account for Luther as a creature of the times; for in their thinking it was the time that called him forth. But had not needful times called others who did not come forth? For, said Carlyle: "All this I liken to dry dead fuel, waiting for the lightning out of Heaven that shall kindle it. The great man (Luther) with his free force direct out of God's own hand is the lightning. . . . In all epochs of the world's history, we shall find the Great Man to have been the indispensable savior of his epoch; —the lightning, without which the fuel never would have burnt. The History of the World, I said already, was the Biography of Great Men."[4] Thus, as we conclude our examination of this lecture, we are informed that the "Hero as Divinity" is the oldest form of "Heroism."

The Hero as Prophet

This lecture gives consideration to the prophet of Mohammedanism. Mahomet is regarded as the prophet of God. There is a change from nature worship to that of what is regarded as a God-inspired prophet. It is interesting to note the various ways and methods the world has of recognizing its Great Ones. "For at bottom the Great Man, as he comes from the hand of nature, is ever the same kind of thing: Odin, Luther, Johnson, Burns; I hope to make it appear that these are all originally of one stuff; that only by the world's reception of them, and the shapes they assume, are they so immeasurably diverse."[5]

But all of these great men are deeply in earnest. There is a sincerity and genuineness about them. The "inspiration of the Almighty giveth him understanding." This genuine sincerity is a characteristic which is in reality heroic. "The great Fact of Existence is great to him. Fly as he will, he cannot get out of the awful presence of this Reality. His mind is so made; he is great by that, first of all. Fearful and wonderful, real as life, real as death, is this universe to him. At all moments the Flame-image glares in upon him; undeniable, there, there! I wish you to take this as my primary definition of a Great Man." This is the hallmark of the Great Man: "Such a man is what we call an *original* man."[6]

Mahomet was one of those original men. He was brought up deep down in the wilderness. It is said that his companions called him, "The Faithful." His reputation was that of truth and fidelity in what he spoke and in what he did. He was 40 before he talked of any mission from heaven. "In his fortieth year he went to Mount Hara, near Mecca, for a month of prayer and meditation on the great issues of life and religion. His wife Kadijah and household were near him." He reported that "by the unspeakable special favour of Heaven he had now found it all out; he was in doubt and darkness no longer but saw it all; . . . that there was one God in and over all . . . that God is great; and that there is nothing else great! He is the Reality . . . He made us first, sustains us yet; we and all things are but the shadow of him; a transitory garment veiling the Eternal Splendour."[7]

Mahomet was a leader in Arabia. His influence was like a spark fallen on his world. Yes, "These Arabs, the man Mahomet, and that one century—is it not as if a spark had fallen, one spark, on a world of what seemed black unnoticeable sand; but lo, the sand proves explosive powder, blazes heaven-high from Delhi to Granada! Yes, the Great Man was always a lightning out of Heaven; the rest of men waited for him like fuel, and then they too would flame."[8]

In the pre-scientific period it was natural that the hero would include Divinity and the Hero as Prophet. He would be either a God or one speaking for God.

The Hero as Poet

Now, we consider the Great One as Poet. The Poet belongs to all ages. But there is a likeness on the part of the Prophet and that of the Poet. They both penetrate into the great mysteries of life and living. They are men sent here to enlighten. "He is the living light-fountain, which it is good and pleasant to be near. The light which enlightens, which has enlightened the darkness of the world; and this not as a kindred lamp only, but rather as a natural luminary shining by the gift of Heaven; a flowing light fountain, as I say, of native original insight, or manhood and heroic nobleness."[9]

While Dante and Shakespeare are not deified, they are like the prophet in that they are inspired, perhaps even God-inspired. There was verse and song in their poetry; and for the author, poetry was musical thought. "'A musical thought is one spoken by a mind that has penetrated into the inmost heart of the thing; detected the inmost mystery of it, namely the melody that lies hidden in it; the inward harmony of coherence which is its soul, whereby it exists, and has a right to be, here in this world. All deep things are song.' Music is a kind of inarticulate unfathomable speech, which leads us to the edge of the Infinite, and lets us for moments gaze into that!"[10]

It would, therefore, seem very proper for both Dante and Shakespeare to qualify as two of the great or universal poets of all time. Especially is this true of Shakespeare. He is without peer of all the poets and possessed of the greatest intellect of them all. "Two fit men: Dante, deep, fierce, as the central fire of the world; Shakespeare, wide, placid, far-seeing, as the sun, the upper light of the world."[11]

The Hero as Priest

Now, shall we consider two other great ones who have been sent into the world: Luther and the Reformation; Knox and Puritanism. These great men are considered as priests. We are to remember that all of these heroes are made of the same material.

The are all possessed of a great soul.
They are all open to the Divine Significance of Life.
They are all possessed of a sense of mission.
They are all prepared to "sing of this, to fight and work for

this, in a great, victorious, enduring manner; there is given a hero—the outward shape of whom will depend on the time and the environment he finds himself in. The Priest too, as I understand it, is a kind of Prophet; in him too, there is required to be a light of inspiration."[12]

While Luther and Knox fall in the grouping of priests, they were, moreover, reformers. Here the great light of the poet becomes the "fierce lightning of the reformer."

They were sincere men.
They were original men.
They were men of integrity.
They were men who were genuine.
They were men of truth.

Luther and Knox were hero-teachers. For them there was a powerful message to the people of their day. "Luther's message was despotism and abolition to all false Popes and Potentates, but life and strength, though afar off, to new genuine ones."[13] Any complete study of the Reformers reveals their great sincerity and dedication to their task. They were truly Heroes of the Reformation.

The Hero as Man of Letters

The fifth lecture has to do with a study of great men of Letters, such as Johnson, Rousseau, and Burns. Perhaps they are inferior to Shakespeare, to Goethe, or to Milton. However, there is in all great literature a love and worship of the true and of the beautiful. There is "the sphere-harmony of a Shakespeare, of a Goethe; the cathedral-music of a Milton."

The Man of Letters, like every hero, is inspired with his task. He is sincere, original, and he penetrates the inward sphere of things. For in the true Literary Man, or Man of Letters, there is a sense of the sacred. He is a light in the world. He is the world's priest; he guides it, "like a sacred Pillar of Fire, in its dark pilgrimage through the waste of time."[14]

These three literary heroes were considered to be genuine men, and faithful men, even though they lived under difficult circumstances. All three, Johnson, Rousseau, and Burns, knew the galling conditions of poverty. These Men of Letters "were men of such magnitude that they could not live on unrealities—clouds, froth and all inanity gave way under them. . . . To a certain extent, they were Sons of Nature once more in an age of Artifice; once more, original men."[15]

The Hero as Man of Letters discharges a vital function. He is an inspired soul and breathes forth his message for all to hear and see by act or speech. "The Hero is he who lives in the inward sphere of things, in the True, Divine and Eternal, which exists always. . . . His life is a piece of the everlasting heart of Nature herself."[16]

The Man of Letters, as is the case with every other Hero, is sent to proclaim or teach. In a very real sense He is like the Prophet or Priest, unfolding God or the God-like to man.

The Hero as King

In this, the last lecture of Carlyle on Heroes and Hero-Worship, we consider Cromwell and Napoleon as examples of the Hero as King. Both men were living in revolutionary times. Both men were actively engaged in revolutionary activity. Both men were elevated, or elevated themselves, to the status of Kings. The trapping was Protectorship or Emperor. War of the Puritans or French Revolution; it was a time of tempest and struggle. "In rebellious ages, when Kingship itself seems dead and abolished, Cromwell, Napoleon step forth again as Kings."[17]

The position is taken that Hero-Worship is an important or precious fact, for it symbolizes the universal hope one has for the management of our world. These Kings are in reality Able-Men sent into the world. Consequently, we have a responsibility to give loyalty and reverence. This necessity "shines like a polestar through smoke clouds, dust clouds, and all manner of down-rushing and conflagration. . . . We cannot do without great men! . . . Hero-worship exists forever and everywhere."[18]

The successes of Cromwell seem quite natural. He had his enemies, and they were many and they were strong. However, he had the keenness to hear, to see, and to do. By whatever name you may give to him, he was "the acknowledged Strongest Man in England, virtually the King of England."[19]

It was 101 years after Puritanism that there broke out a great burst or explosion which is known as the French Revolution. This Revolution, like the one in England, got for itself a King. Thus, Napoleon comes upon the field of action. At first, Napoleon was a democrat in philosophy, but was strong on authority and discipline, as would be any great military genius. Consequently, he attempts "to bridle-in the great devouring, self-devouring French Revolution; to tame it so that its intrinsic purpose can be made good, that it may become organic, and be able to live among other organisms and formed things, not as a wasting destruction alone. Is not this still what he partly aimed at, as the true purport of his life; nay, what he actually managed to do? . . . There was an eye to see in this man, a soul to dare and do."[20] Napoleon saw with clear eyes. He saw with strength and decisiveness. He saw with vision. He was in truth a Hero. Then pride and selfishness led him down the road of destruction, both for himself and for great multitudes. "Having once parted with Reality, he tumbles helpless in vacuity, no rescue for him. He had to sink there, mournfully as man seldom did; and break his great heart, and die—this poor Napoleon: a great implement too soon wasted, till it was useless: our last great man."[21]

THE GREAT MAN *IS ONE OF GENUINE SINCERITY.*
THE GREAT MAN *IS AN ORIGINAL MAN.*
THE GREAT MAN *SENSES THE AWFUL PRESENCE*
   OF REALITY.
THE GREAT MAN *PENETRATES THE INWARD SPHERE*
   OF THINGS.
THE GREAT MAN *POSSESSES THE HEROIC QUALITY.*
THE GREAT MAN *BELIEVES WITH HIS WHOLE MIND.*
THE GREAT MAN *IS HERO FOR THE MANY.*

   The HERO as DIVINITY
   The HERO as PROPHET
   The HERO as POET
   The HERO as PRIEST
   The HERO as MAN of LETTERS
   The HERO as KING

These six classes of "Heroes" are typical of many countries and of many centuries. They lift the curtain for us and allow us a penetrating glimpse into the very marrow of the world's history.

This philosophy of "The History of the World," and this "Philosophy of Leadership," leaves us with many thoughts to ponder. Without doubt, we have in Thomas Carlyle a thinker and one of great literary talent. However, to fully comprehend *LEADERSHIP*, there are other theories and philosophies which we should consider most carefully.

6.

The Follower Theory

EXECUTIVE POSTS ARE LEADERSHIP OPPORTUNITIES.
THE OPPORTUNITY TO BE A PRESIDENT, MANAGER, SU-
PERINTENDENT, EXECUTIVE SECRETARY, DEPARTMENT
HEAD, TEACHER, TEAM CAPTAIN, SUPERVISOR, FOREMAN
OR GANG BOSS IS THUS AN OPPORTUNITY TO BE A
LEADER. EVERY DIRECTIVE POST OVER PEOPLE IS PO-
TENTIALLY A LEADERSHIP POST.

—Ordway Tead

The concepts of "leading" and "following" tend to define each
other; there can be no leading without followers, and there can be no
following without leaders. LEADERSHIP THROUGH FOLLOW-
ERSHIP. Our observations will show that the most active followers
initiate acts of leading. The "Great Man" theory of leadership de-
clares that the "Great One" (the leader) is sent into the world. In a
very real sense he is a gift to his people and his age. He appeared
upon the horizon and gave leadership to his day, which was truly
heroic. For him, leadership was caught and not taught.

According to the "Follower Theory of Leadership," the leader is trained in a variety of ways for a position of leadership. The alert follower becomes the leader. The expectations of the followers stimulate the leader and draw upon his, or her, leadership resources. In this theory, the path to leadership is through the open door of followership. To illustrate: within the group, or the organization, the faithful and intelligent follower is elected to a position of responsibility:

It may be that of Secretary.
It may be that of Treasurer.
It may be that of a Trustee.
It may be that of Vice-President.
It may be that of the more exalted post of President.

Through these avenues, the follower-leader is on the way to bigger and better things, because he excelled as a follower. Thus, the alert follower may become the top leader; the mediocre follower may become a mediocre leader; the careless follower exhibits little potential for leadership, and it is quite probable that the careless follower will never become a leader.

The thesis of this philosophy is that the only road to leadership is through the gateway of followership. While this theory is a broad one, it carefully considers various *patterns*. First, let us consider the academic path. This is the pattern in which the leader instructs or inspires the follower until he is adequately prepared for leadership, whether it be in a vocation, a profession, or a calling.

The University-trained Pattern

The business neophyte is a student in the field of business education. (This same pattern pertains, whether the neophyte is a man or a woman.) He studies diligently until he is able to understand the theories of economics. He is instructed in accounting until he can balance the books for his uncle's store.

He is given a modicum of instruction on the computer.
He spends several months studying the monetary system.
He studies banking and other related subjects.
His professors are the leaders.
He is the follower.

He graduates with honors and then goes on to graduate school.

Let us suppose that he goes to the Harvard School of Business. There he has the great privilege of studying under several master teachers. These master teachers are the leaders. He is still the follower, but a follower with sharp tools for his task. He has a Baccalaureate degree, with honors, and now he has his Master's degree. Academically, he is as well prepared as a follower can be. Perhaps he has spent the summer months in the business department of some corporation. Thus, this follower has not only training that is academic, but training that is experiential. He is now in the position of transferring from the status of "Follower" to that of "Business Executive." In time, he may become a leader in business.

The same process is usually followed in becoming an educator. The neophyte educator, or student of education, decides upon the level of academics through which he wishes to prepare himself. He may desire to be an Elementary Instructor, or he may have in mind secondary education. Moreover, he may desire to teach at the college level or may aspire to faculty status on the university level. At any rate, his master teachers are his leaders; he is a follower through all these years of preparation. Somewhere along the way in his preparation there is student teaching; he is the learning teacher under the leadership of the supervising professor. In time, he may become a leader in education.

For the young person who desires to go into the ministry there is similar preparation. There is the desire, or Divine call, to serve needy humanity, but with a call to service there comes an awareness that there must be preparation. Those under whom this preparation is made are the leaders. A followership role continues for whatever length of time this may be: college, seminary, university, or postgraduate studies. Along with this academic preparation there is a period of apprenticeship in the ministerial field. The student has learned about the seven tools of worship in ministerial classes, and now, in the laboratory of the parish church, under the leadership of a senior minister, these seven tools are put into use. At the conclusion of these many years of study, and at the conclusion of an apprenticeship under many leaders, the young minister is now ready to transfer from the status of follower to that of leader.

The same situation prevails for the neophyte or student lawyer. College work is completed, including required courses in law, as well as courses in history, political science, and perhaps sociology. Graduation from "Law School" is achieved. The professors have been the leaders. The student has been the follower. The faculty-leaders prepare the student-follower for his bar examinations. He studies faithfully, prepares himself intelligently, and is rewarded by passing the bar examination. For several months he has been an apprentice in a prestigious law firm, where the lawyers were the leaders and he was the follower. Now he is ready to join this prestigious law firm, no longer as the follower, but as a leader. He is the Junior Partner in this law firm.

In addition, the young person who aspires to Medicine must undergo many years as a follower. The faculty in the Medical School are the leaders. The course work is rigorous. In possibly four years he is graduated from Medical School. The next step in preparation is that of internship. With the completion of this intensive training, the young doctor is ready to assume the privileges and responsibilities of leadership as a doctor; it may be as a Surgeon or as a Specialist in a specific field of medicine. Careful and studious followership has brought the young doctor to a new dimension of leadership.

Thus far we have considered the academic role, or the University-trained pattern, which has led the follower to a place of leadership in his chosen field. This new status of leader begins at a low level but through diligence and wisdom it can ascend. Now let us turn to:

The Great Corporation Pattern

For the purpose of our study—the place of leadership which the great corporation imposes upon the new employee—the corporation becomes the new teacher (leader), and the new employee is again the student (follower). However, the new employee is better prepared to follow the corporation pattern. He is prepared to be an apt student and to adapt to its ideals. Here again we have the follower attempting to follow the pattern laid out by the corporate leader. Let us consider the pattern of corporate leadership.

The essence of the leader's task. He is to plan for production and to supervise all those who are under his direction. He is to understand the long-range and the short-range objectives which have been worked out by experts, by Boards, and by Commissions. These goals which have been adopted by the Board of Directors need implementation, and only the Chief Executive is in a position to carry them out with courage and with strength.

The leader must be able to analyze and arrive at workable conclusions. The topmost leader is in a position to have a tremendous array of facts before him. He is in a position to have charts prepared which tell the story of annual production and annual sales. He has the audits with the bottom line in Red or in Black. He knows the history of successes and of failures. In the light of this he is able to evaluate the moves which should be made at a particular time. The higher one rises in a corporation, the more important becomes the ability to analyze problems. It is at the top levels that the most important and far-reaching decisions are made, beginning with the first fundamental decision about objectives.

Moreover, it is important to have *an organization which functions with maximum efficiency.* The top business executive again bears the greatest responsibility for structure and functional ability of the organization. He bears the responsibility also of securing the kind of people who are adequately trained for the tasks. These people must understand the objectives, ideals, and decisions of higher management. "Leadership is interested in how people can be brought together to work together for a common end, effectively and happily. There is a difference between command and leadership. Commanders direct organizations and, in so doing, subordinate individuals in working toward organized ends; leaders guide and develop individuals so that they may better share in realizing group accomplishments."[1]

Perhaps it would be well for us, at this juncture, to paraphrase our definition of "Leadership," as stated earlier. "Leadership is the activity of influencing people to do what the leader has in mind, because the people find that it is desirable and worthwhile for all concerned." However, the fact remains that "even with good organization, we can never achieve the strongest group cooperation unless someone makes it all appealing. Someone must make the group loyal to the purpose. Someone must be able to show people how they are benefited by joining and how they are benefited by the purpose. That someone is the leader."[2]

We may well ask ourselves the question: What are the qualifications of leadership? We are desirous to know the qualifications which are necessary for the Business Executive or the important qualifications for leadership in general. In the following list of eight qualifications I believe that this question is answered quite satisfactorily.

1. *Ability to inspire confidence in people.* To be a leader, one must have the confidence of the people he is to lead. In order for one to inspire confidence it is necessary to have knowledge competency in their field of operation. There must be honesty and there must be enthusiasm for the task.

2. *Persistence in driving toward the goal.* The leader must believe firmly in what he is striving to accomplish. He must have the persistence and perseverance to look for methods to attain the goal, trying many different ones if necessary, until the right one is reached.

3. *Ability to communicate without misunderstanding.* The leader must have the ability to explain the desired goal to others and make it appealing to them. It is an ability that can be acquired.

4. *Willingness to listen receptively.* This attribute often distinguishes the leader from the commander. There is a difference between listening with a closed mind and listening with a sincere desire to understand and make the best use of the other person's point of view.

5. *Genuine interest in people.* All leaders must have a genuine interest in the welfare of the people under their leadership. Such an interest cannot be simulated; a lack of genuineness will sooner or later betray itself.

6. *Understanding of people and their reactions.* A leader must understand people and know why they act as they do. This knowledge may be an intuitive understanding or it may be that the leader is well acquainted with those on the staff and knows quite well what their reactions will be. This understanding often comes through communication with the individual from time to time.

7. *Objectivity.* A leader must be careful to be objective and not allow the sentiments of other people to act upon his feelings. Objectivity is not always easy; in fact, it may be a very difficult assignment. One way to practice objectivity is to ask yourself "Why?," "Why does he say this?," and "Why does she feel the way she does?"

8. *Forthrightness.* The leader must be out in the open, not one to hedge or vacilate. Forthrightness builds self-confidence and self-

assurance. In this forthrightness, the leader must maintain a strong sense of fair play. This also necessitates being generous and dependable.

Along with the eight characteristics already listed is one that must be present in each of these, and without which no leader can succeed. This all-important characteristic, or qualification, is *IN-TEGRITY*. Integrity will greatly assist the leader in avoiding, or overcoming, the habit of worrying.

The follower-leader should strive to emulate all of these characteristics as he strives to rise from Junior leadership to Senior leadership. We shall list six more tools of leadership which will be needed in this climb:

1. Having close and frequent contacts with people.
2. Keeping all interested parties fully informed.
3. Making sure that all employees receive fair, impartial, and considerate treatment.
4. Knowing what is going on.
5. Assuming full responsibility for directing one's work.
6. Utilizing teamwork.

Teamwork means that one has the ability to think in terms of others. It has been said that the most important five words are *"I am proud of you,"* the next four are *"What is your opinion?,"* the next three are *"If you please,"* the next two, *"Thank you,"* and the smallest word in the world is the pronoun, *"I."*

Having been a member of Rotary International for many years, I have observed a pattern that graphically illustrates this theory of LEADERSHIP THROUGH FOLLOWERSHIP. Let us consider this through:

The Rotary Club Pattern

We turn now from the *University Trained Pattern* and the *Great Corporation Pattern* to a more simple group organization; namely, the *Rotary Club Pattern*. The Service Club Organizations are well designed for our study of the follower theory of leadership.

Rotary International is a meaningful service organization which has four major objectives as are set forth in the "Four-Way Test" of what we think, say, and do.

Is it the truth?
Is it fair to all concerned?
Will it build goodwill and better friendships?
Will it be beneficial to all concerned?

The new member is a representative of a certain business or professional group. He is interested in boosting his Club and his community. He may enter the Club for a number of other reasons. He enjoys the fellowship of his fellow Rotarians. He feels that Rotary is a prestigious organization. The weekly meeting furnishes a pleasing atmosphere in which to have his noonday lunch. He is definitely a follower.

Through the coming year he spends as much time as possible with the Club and eagerly accepts assignments given to him. His faithfulness in serving on committees and in personal work for the Club make him a very valuable and helpful member for the next two years. Then, because of his great interest and faithful and able work, he is moved up to a position on the Rotary Board of Directors. In another year he is elected vice-president. This will put him in line for possibly becoming president of the Club. He has been an excellent follower, and through the open door of followership he is now a leader. Through this same pattern, it is possible for the follower to move up to a place of service and leadership on the National and International level.

Thus, we find that a very important theory, or philosophy, of leadership is one that is brought about through "followership." It is a growing leadership that is brought about through various patterns of intelligent followership. THE ALERT FOLLOWER BECOMES THE LEADER.

7.

The Situationist Theory

SOCIAL SITUATIONS ARE NEVER STATIC. THEY ARE EVER
CHANGING; THE IDEA OF PROCESS IS IMPLICIT. SOCIAL
SITUATIONS CALL NOW FOR ONE SET OF LEADERSHIP
QUALITIES BUT TOMORROW PERHAPS FOR ANOTHER SET
OF TRAITS. A LEADER, HENCE, MUST MANIFEST AT LEAST
A MINIMUM DEGREE OF VERSATILITY AS A RESULT OF
THE PROCESS ELEMENT IN SOCIAL SITUATIONS.

—Emory S. Bogardus

In the social situation, the leader is buffeted by his environment.
Certain environmental factors work to his advantage, while in other
instances the environmental factors greatly restrict what he is able to
accomplish. The situationist leader is thus limited by social institutions and by external forces.

John W. Gardner puts it this way: "Most leaders are hedged
around by constraints—tradition, constitutional limitations, the
realities of the external situation, rights and privileges of followers,

the requirements of teamwork, and most of all the inexorable demands of large-scale organization, which does not operate on capriciousness."[1]

The "situational theory" is largely an environmentalist approach. More specifically, it attributes leadership to a specific historical period. A leader, from this point of view, can emerge only if THE TIMES are such as to permit him to use whatever skills and ambitions he might possess. The "Great Man" theory stresses the thought that leadership is mostly, if not wholly, attributed to the "Great One" who has been sent into the world. He is able to arise out of the environment in which he is placed. This includes the social environment and also the physical environment around him. In the "Great Man" theory, the leader is independent of, or superior to, the group which he heads, while in the "Situationist" theory, he is dependent upon, or is in the grip of, external social forces over which he has little or no effective control.

Those who accept the situationist view of leadership point out with telling effect that some of the greatest men of history would not be able to perform so successfully if they were alive in this, our day. They were the "Great Ones" because of the social and physical forces which combined in such a way as to permit their skills and talents to function when they exerted great leadership in their time. But let us take them out of their environment and place them in our complex environment, and things might turn out in a radically different way. Here are some pointed questions that forcefully illustrate this thought:

> Would Napoleon Bonaparte be able to become a great military genius if he were living in present-day France?
> Would George Washington be able to become the President of the United States of America if he lived in present-day Virginia?
> Would Thomas Edison or Henry Ford be able to achieve greatness if they had been born in the seventeenth century?
> Would Socrates be as effective in asking questions and teaching in present-day Athens if he were alive today?

The answer to all of these questions is a definite "NO." Then it would seem to follow that environmental forces combined to make possible the successes of these great ones. It also seems to follow that even in the case of the "Great Ones," they could be severely limited by these external and internal social forces until their leadership would be greatly reduced in another historic period. The social, cultural, historic, economic, geographical, religious, political, and scientific environment places the origin of events outside of the person rather than within, as is the case with the "Great Man" theory.

There is a weakness in the "Social Situation Theory" in that it presumes to have the power to generate social change of and by itself. But it obviously does not have this power apart from personality or personalities. It is the leader-person or group, or both, who has this power. However, the environmental forces of social, cultural, historic, economic, political, religious, and scientific factors unite to determine the direction to which the social change is oriented.

It is not easy to define the "social situationist" theory of leadership to the satisfaction of all concerned. Perhaps it is best for us to consider the limiting factors which work against positive leadership.

Limiting Physical Factors

It was in my freshman year of high school that a boy we called "Big Charles" joined our class. He was 6 feet 3 inches tall. He weighed 200 pounds. He wore a bright, bulky, red sweater. He possessed an infectious smile. One day he was asked to make a speech at the assembly period. He smiled, fidgeted, and patted himself gently as he spoke. It was a *very ordinary speech*, but the magnetism of his personality sent an electric charge through the entire student body. It was the physical factor that largely gave "Big Charles" his charm or charisma. Let us note: "Physical factors inevitably crop up in studies of leadership. A number of investigations suggest a positive relationship between leadership and such traits as height, weight and energy output. Leaders tend to be taller, heavier, and more energetic than non-leaders. Group-dynamics studies would suggest, however, that the relation of these traits to leadership probably varies with the type of leadership activity performed. It is certainly possible that tall, heavy, and energetic persons impress people more than short, slight and sluggish individuals; and yet it is a fact that some world famous leaders were conspicuously devoid of the former characteristics."[2] Thus, it would seem as if the physical factors are a part of the social situation which reflects, one way or another, in determining leadership.

Limiting Leadership Styles

The "Situationist" approach apparently first emerged out of a polemic with the "Great Man" theory of leadership. In short, the latter was a theory that considered that the great one was a person of distinguished stamp. He was a person sent into the world, and one predestined by his possession of special talents to lead events and mold situations.

In contrast, and antithetical to this point of view, is the theory of the situationist. For the situationist, leadership is molded and determined by the social situation. Thus, the center of gravity shifts from the "Great Person" leader to the group or to the social situation. The social situation has a determining effect upon the leader, and the leader in turn attempts to shift and turn in such a way as to take advantage of as many of the limiting factors as is possible. For instance, he may choose between three or more different styles of leadership in an attempt to find the most acceptable style possible to reach his objective or objectives at a given time. It may be helpful for us to consider a comparison of leadership styles.[3]

COMPARISON OF LEADERSHIP STYLES

Directive	Participative	Free Rein
Leader makes most of the decisions	Subordinates are involved in decisions	Subordinates make decisions
Leader uses power and discipline	Leader tries to persuade, not force	Reliance is on self-control
Leader utilizes one-way communication	Leader encourages two-way communication	Communication is free and open
Leader stays aloof from group	Leader is involved in group	Leader is not identifiable in group
Leader takes full responsibility	Leader shares power and responsibility	The individual is responsible
Employee orientation is obedience	Employee orientation is cooperation	Orientation is individual performance
Psychological result is dependence	Psychological result is participation	Psychological result is independence

Here we have the preference of the leader because of his own personality in choosing his leadership style, but also he chooses the style that he believes will be most successful in reaching the goals or objectives which he has set. The social pressure of the groups with which he has to deal will be, moreover, strong factors in his decision.

Limiting Economic Situations

We have, on a number of occasions, attempted to distinguish between Management on the one hand and Leadership on the other. It is our contention that management is a form of leadership, but it is a limited and mechanistic form of leadership. While leadership encompasses the full-orbed and creative style which goes far beyond mere routine, the social situation in any study of the economic factor must include measurements of economics as a force. This would include perhaps a study of the gross national product, with special concern zeroing in on the growth factor in the business enterprise under study. It should include the personal income level of the community and also the average income of the same sampling. It should show figures of employment as well as unemployment over a period of time. It should present facts concerning sales, profits, and markets. Further, other factors such as competitors, suppliers, customers, pulse of business activity in community, and kind of community in which to live are salient factors in an analysis of positive and negative forces with which one must come to grips.

Again we refer to Carlisle, who made a study of environmental factors in plant location.[4] This study was made by a group of creative specialists. Here are the checklists which were given.

1. Labor considerations:
    Availability of labor supply
    Types of skills available
    Wage rates in the region
    Productivity of the labor
    Extent of Unionism
    Existence of right-to-work laws

2. Support services:
    Energy sources (electricity, oil, natural gas, fuels)
    Transportation (rail, air, truck, water)
    Communication systems
    Financial services (banks, investment firms, etc.)
    Skilled contractors (construction, machinery, research)
    Water supply—amount and cost

Sewage disposal
Insurance

3. Market locations:
Proximity to raw materials
Proximity to subcontractors and suppliers of components
Proximity to customers
Types of industries in the area

4. Tax structure:
Property tax rates
State income, sales, and other taxes
Community taxes
Existence of free-port laws

5. Land:
Prices
Availability
Opportunities for future expansion

6. Climate:
Rainfall
Humidity
Temperature extremes
Unusual conditions (fog, hurricanes, etc.)

7. Community services:
Schools
Churches
Recreation
Hospitals and medical services
Hotels, motels, and convention centers
Roads, highways, and transportation systems
Housing availability and rental rates
Income and indebtedness of community
Attitude of community officials
Community acceptance
City ordinances and zoning regulations
Cost of living

The leaders weigh these factors of location and finally reach a decision to establish their plant in a certain community. *They are creative leaders.* The managers have the skills and know-how to run the plant after it is once set in motion.

The creative leaders are studying ways of strengthening their ties to the community, while the managers are attempting to increase productivity. The creative leaders set up a short-range and long-range planning commission, while the managers are concerned with the day-to-day operation of the plant.

Moreover, the environmental factors, from within and without, have a strong bearing on the direction to which the business enterprise orients itself. Both leadership and management are thereby influenced by the social situation.

We have considered in some detail the impact of internal and external forces upon an economic institution. This same kind of impact is present in a study of other institutions in our society.

It is true concerning political forces and institutions.
It is true of socio-cultural forces and their institutions.
It is true concerning technical and scientific institutions.
It is true concerning educational and religious institutions.
It is, moreover, true concerning the legal profession.

Thus, it is plain to see that the leadership of an institution is constantly dealing with important environmental forces, and a central thesis of leadership must be that these environmental forces are continually shifting and changing. The social situation is constantly on the move and either threatens or thrills the leader.

A leader faces these multiple social situations and attempts his solution. Another leader, facing the same set of circumstances, would possibly have an altogether different solution. In fact, if a score of capable and creative leaders were to give serious thought to the same set of problems, they would probably go about the task in 20 different ways.

There is no one best way to handle the important problem.
There is no one best way to plan an institution's future.
There is no one best way to meet the situational challenge.
There is no one best way to lead.

"In situational analysis the objective is to identify each key factor in the situation by evaluating the dimensions of the factor. Once the situation is mapped, the question becomes that of the course of action or leadership styles that will be effective. In relation to leadership the objective is to identify the dimensions and variables that affect leadership patterns."[5]

The situation in which a group operates definitely influences the kind of leadership which is given. Does the impact of the group determine leadership, and does it tend to mold the leader? Does the external environment give change and momentum to leadership? In other words, does the social situation press leadership, partially at least, into its mold?

The situationist theory of leadership is very much aware of the dynamic nature of society. It is ever-changing and as a result has much to do with leadership. The social situation is most inclusive and, as a result, challenges the leader from hour to hour and from day to day. Here are some factors which are constantly changing:

The mood of the day or the climate of the group
The economic situation
The historical background
The political situation
The educational theories of the time
The attitude toward science
The religious mood
The attitude toward today's institutions
The questions about inflation which may determine optimism or pessimism
The geographical factor
The population traits and trends
The place of communication, conflict, and cooperation
The nature of public opinion

"Situational Leadership," as suggested in this chapter, is not advanced as the fundamental theory of leadership. However, it is a popular view of many sociologists. We consider it as only one of the eight correlative theories which is necessary in order to fully explain leadership.

8.

The Creative Artist Theory

THE ARTIST ... SPEAKS TO OUR CAPACITY FOR DELIGHT
    AND WONDER,
TO THE SENSE OF MYSTERY SURROUNDING OUR LIVES;
TO OUR SENSE OF PITY, AND BEAUTY, AND PAIN;
TO THE LATENT FEELING OF FELLOWSHIP WITH ALL
    CREATION,
TO THE SUBTLE BUT INVINCIBLE CONVICTION OF SOL-
    IDARITY
THAT KNITS TOGETHER THE LONELINESS OF INNUMER-
    ABLE HEARTS,
TO THE SOLIDARITY IN DREAMS, IN JOY, IN SORROW,
IN ASPIRATIONS, IN ILLUSIONS, IN HOPE, IN FEAR,
WHICH BINDS MEN TO EACH OTHER, WHICH BINDS TO-
    GETHER
ALL HUMANITY—THE DEAD TO THE LIVING AND THE
    LIVING
TO THE UNBORN.

—Joseph Conrad

THE ARTIST AS LEADER and THE LEADER AS ARTIST. There is much in common between the rational thinker, the scientist, and the artist. They are all committed to seeking for the truth.

The thinker is engrossed in ideas.
The scientist deals with a myriad of facts.
The artist, poet, or architect penetrates reality and speaks to
    our capacity for wonder and beauty.

The work in which the artist is involved may be as varied as that of any other leader. It may deal with material ends, spiritual ends, economic considerations, or political considerations; or it may have to do with religious, moral, or aesthetic ends. It may be that the artist is involved in an attempt to enrich or alter the existing stock of values in the possession of a society by gaining acceptance for an innovation freshly created by the leader or, if the innovation has been borrowed from another culture, by diffusing it in the new era.

The creative artist works mostly alone. He is usually highly talented, trained, and dedicated. All of the world's great artists fall within this category: Michelangelo, Beethoven, Shakespeare, Tolstoy, Liszt, Rubens, Sir Christopher Wren, John Bunyan, Jonathan Edwards, Charles Wesley, Leonardo da Vinci, Bach, and a myriad more. "The importance of great writers, composers, painters, sculptors, architects, film directors and the full range of artists is acknowledged, but they are seldom thought of as leaders. Leadership is not the exclusive province of any particular area of human activity. Leaders must be measured by their total impact:

How many people are influenced.
How much they are influenced.
How long they are influenced.

Compare the continuing significance of Michelangelo with Pope Julius II. Why do we even remember Pope Julius II? Who were the important German statesmen during Bach's lifetime? Have you read any of their political writings lately? How many business tycoons can you name who were contemporaries of Shakespeare?"[1]

The "matter-of-fact" world is accustomed to the rational and gives great reverence to the thinker and to the leaders in scientific discovery. However, the ordinary person on the street is a bit baffled by the artist leader who deals with things more intangible. The work of the scientist and the thinker may be preserved for many generations, but the same is true, if not more so, of the artist, the writer, the musician, the sculptor, and the architect.

The great men of literature of the nineteenth century and on into the twentieth century were concerned with art and its influence upon their nation and the world. This was especially true of the great writers, such as Joseph Conrad, Henry James, William Faulkner, Leo Tolstoy, and Alexander Solzhenitsyn. The literary artist was a leader of a distinct type.

It was Solzhenitsyn whose life was filled with unthinkable suffering and loneliness. He was nourished by the wellspring of his own artistry of writing and creative thoughts. It was this person who had lived through such unbearable suffering who wrote about the soul enrichment of art. He speaks forcefully of art. "Art praises and nourishes life, art hates death. This is what we mean when we say recognize power in the work of art. The life forces in us are encouraged."[2]

The literary artist leaves an indelible mark upon society. Likewise, the painter, the sculptor, the architect, and the musician all deeply influence the culture of their time and across the centuries. The creative artist is a leader.

At this point it would be well to attempt a definition of art. It is important for us to have as clear and decisive an understanding as possible of the term. It emphasizes feeling rather than the rational and logical. Art may be defined as "a single-minded attempt to render the highest kind of justice to the visible universe by bringing to light the truth, manifold and one, underlying its every aspect. It is an attempt to find in its forms, in its colors, in its light, in its shadows, in the aspects of matter and in the facts of life, what of each is fundamental, what is enduring and essential—their one illuminating and convincing quality—the very truth of their existence."[3]

All creative activities, the conscious and the unconscious processes underlying artistic originality, scientific discovery, and comic inspiration, have a basic pattern in common, which Arthur Koestler defines as "'bisociative thinking'—a word he coined to distinguish the various routines of associative thinking from *the creative leap* which connects previously unconnected frames of reference and makes us experience reality on several planes at once."[4]

Koestler considers that there are two ways of escaping from the routine of associative thinking. One way is to plunge into dreams or dreamland, where the rational gives way to a world of fantasy or vision. The other is also an escape—from boredom, stagnation, intellectual predicaments, and emotional frustrations—but it is an escape in the opposite direction; it is signalled by the "spontaneous flash" which shows a familiar situation or event in a new light.

It is my reasoned judgment that the true leader, whether he be prophet, priest, or king, business executive or one in the arts or professions, needs to give attention to the idea of "bisociative" thinking.

> It is the *"act of creation."*
> It is the *"creative leap."*
> It is the *"spontaneous flash of insight."*
> It is the *"intuitive flash."*

All of the great leaders of the past and of the present have experienced this "creative leap," which has placed them on a higher level of understanding and has prepared them for new and important breakthroughs.

We are greatly concerned with the triggering of the intuitive flashes which are necessary for successful progress. It seems to be somewhat of a mystery as to how the act of creation takes place. It may be through cumulative or associative thinking, or by "bisociative thinking." If it is by the latter process, it may be somewhat like this: "Often in the history of ideas we find two opposite methods at work, *the downward approach* from the complex to the elementary, from the whole to its component parts, and *the upward approach* from part to whole. The emphasis on either of these methods may alternate according to philosophical fashion until they meet and merge in a new synthesis."[5] This new synthesis is something brand new. It may come gradually with greater clarity until the creative act is fully formed, or the synthesis may come as a bolt of lightning, as the "creative leap" or the "spontaneous flash."

"When a creative scientist struggles with a problem and sees no solution, frustration is inevitable. This is what makes us hard to live with sometimes. It is often desirable to push the problem back into the subconscious where memory is better. The vast majority of creative people have had the experience of going to sleep with a problem in mind and waking up with the solution.

"We have hardly begun to grasp the capabilities of the subconscious mind. In the brief second of falling out of a dream will occur that which may require five minutes to tell. The importance of this is that it proves that not even the most creative person has even come close to realizing his potential rate of productivity.

"The flash of insight, when a possible solution to a difficult problem occurs, is one of the most satisfying of all human experiences. Thought is so rapid that many people have the feeling of being simply an amanuensis for another personality."[6] It was George Handel who, during the composition of his immortal Oratorio THE MESSIAH, experienced a prolonged "intuitive flash."

The process of creativity is so important that it has been analyzed in various ways. Eliot Hutchinson, a thoroughly trained psychologist, has made a study of creative thinking and considers that it could be presented in four main steps:

Preparation
Frustration
Insight
Verification

In emphasizing these leaps of creativity, we do not discount the routines of associative thinking. Newton, as a scientist, understood that we are deeply in debt to those who have preceded us. He put it this way: "If I have been able to see farther than others, it was because I stood on the shoulders of giants."

One such giant who speaks to us on the subject of "Art" is Leo Tolstoy. His book on *Art* was written soon after his conversion. It was published in the year of 1896. He first gives consideration to the activity of art: "To evoke in oneself a feeling one has once experienced and having evoked it in oneself then by means of movements, lives, colours, sounds, or forms expressed in words, so to transmit that feeling that others experience the same feeling—this is the activity of art." From his thoughts on the activity of art, he proceeds to his definition of art: "Art is a human activity consisting in this, that one man consciously by means of certain external signs, hands on to others feelings he has lived through, and that others are infected by these feelings and also experience them."[7]

It is also most important to remember that creativeness is linked to freedom. According to Berdyaev, *creativity is inseparable from freedom*. For, "only he who is free creates. Out of necessity can be born only evolution; creativity is born of liberty." Furthermore, "creativeness does not move along a flat surface in endless time, but ascends toward eternity." God is the ultimate source of love; He is the ultimate source of liberty; and He is the ultimate source of creativity.

Moreover, there is a strong link between creativity and imagination. Richard Wolff makes a point of this close relationship: "The ability to imagine is the ability to create in advance, in one's own mind, a new plan, a new line of action. Creative imagination is the ability to conceive of that which is merely seen in fragments or on the surface as a complete, perfected, integral whole. It is not fantasy nor fantastic, but constructive and creative."[8]

Imagination is of prime importance if there is to be creativity. All of us have known men who knew many Facts, yet they were not creative persons. Facts are vitally important, but there must be the ability and willingness to go beyond the facts. Creative leaders must have this extraordinary sensitivity to their surroundings and the ability to see things to which the average person is blind. To combine the images of past sensations into fresh groups for purposes of their own, to use these images to symbolize abstract ideas, this is the power of imagination at work. The skill to go beyond the obvious limitations of a problem, the capacity to discover new dimensions to the problem, the willingness to deviate from established norms— these are some of the characteristics of the creative leader.

We have dealt largely with THE ARTIST AS LEADER, but we wish to consider, in this same frame of thought, THE LEADER AS ARTIST. Ordway Tead has addressed this theory of leadership most forcefully: "The leader is an artist—an artist working in a medium which is at once complex and universal. His material is people. And just as the task of the artist is one of organization of ideas or materials if any work of art is to be achieved, so with leadership the bringing of human desire and energy into organized relations becomes a work of high artistry.

"Indeed, this is more than a verbal analogy. The technical deftness, the new insight, the devotion to a vision, the effort at communication—these are all attributes of the artist which the leader should have. His task of influencing others—looking at the problem first from his point of view—should be gone at with artistic economy, precision and skill."[9]

The flash of intuitive insight which occurs in an attempted solution to a very difficult problem is one of the most satisfying of all human experiences. Along with that "spontaneous flash," that "creative leap," there comes an overwhelming assurance that the right solution has been found. For the creative leader who possesses "imagination" and "freedom," this is a "creative act." "Creative leadership envisions opportunities and moves ahead to capture the moment, mold it, and make it great."[10]

The price of creative leadership is selling one's ideas to people. Herein lies the challenge. "A sizeable portion of indifference to 20th-century artists as leaders has been earned. Excessive concern with technique and experimental form has tended to detract artists from their traditional exploration of truth and beauty. Freedom has not been disciplined by the nature of the medium. Doing something new has been emphasized at the expense of doing something well. Time, the most reliable art critic, continues to make clear that representations of what is REAL and what is PERFECT are the enduring attraction of art and the legitimate basis of the artist's claim to leadership."[11]

9.

The Intimidation Theory

A GREAT MAN SHOWS HIS GREATNESS BY THE WAY HE
TREATS A LESSER MAN.

—*Rex Schoaf*

The "Intimidation" theory of leadership is that desired ends may
be achieved through influence, fear, power, threats, agitation, warnings, persuasion, and in some instances even by raw force itself. This
theory, or philosophy, of leadership calls for a technique calculated
to evoke fear in the mind of the individual or group that is expected
to act or perform in a certain manner. Intimidation is a powerful instrument in the hands of those who are in control at the present moment.

We note that "Intimidation as a practice is not limited to parties
in the opposition who do not share in the privilege of operating, controlling or directly influencing the machinery of government and the
administration of law. The resort to intimidation is also practiced by
persons, groups and institutions of functioning authority as an extra-

legal means of achieving desired political, economic, fiscal or other pecuniary ends."[1] Intimidation of one sort or another is a way of life for many leaders. It is used quite naturally by some and is honed to a sharp edge of proficiency by others. Let us consider how intimidation is used by the rich, the powerful, or the influential.

The Slave Owner

In other years, when slavery was practiced in this country, Uncle Tom was assigned to work in the cotton field from early morning until sunset. He was granted a cottage in which to live. He was granted food, shelter, and clothing. These essentials of life belonged to him. But he was a slave and not free to leave the plantation. He was constantly under the surveillance of the great master who owned him and all the chattel. The owner humiliated him before others, and he even punished him by various methods in order to maintain his authority over his slave.

But after slavery had been officially abolished for many years, the slave mentality still continued and was passed along for several generations. For instance, 20 years ago a negro in a southern town stole a pair of tires from the man he worked for on occasion. The man found out about the theft and, through a network of communication, found that this negro was the one who had stolen the tires. The plantation owner took a buggy whip and beat the negro until he confessed. He did more than make the confession. He promised to return the tires and assured the boss that he should have the thrashing. He was definitely intimidated.

We have dealt briefly with slavery and its aftermath. Slavery has been the curse of society from the time of early man down to our present generation, and it is the ultimate in intimidation.

The Youth Gang

Of recent years, we have been aware of youth gangs which have roamed through our cities. Many of the older people have been paralyzed by the gang activity. Also, these gangs have tested their strength against rival gangs. Their stock and trade is leadership in this area by the force of intimidation.

The Union Boss

Where trade unions are involved, workers on strike seek to intimidate non-union workers who wish to take their place of employment. The methods of intimidation vary, from massed demonstrations to acts of property destruction. These acts are not viewed by the Union Boss, or his Union leaders and members, as anything other than their "right to their jobs as a basic and undeniable condition of their welfare. On the other hand, the organs of public authority in objecting to intimidation of the strike breakers assume the abstract individual right of any worker to work whenever, wherever, and under whatever conditions he chooses. This was not the view of Charles W. Eliot when he declared the strike breaker 'a national hero.'"[2] The worker intimidator was pitted against the capitalist intimidator.

The Business Leader

Intimidation is practiced by big business on a wholesale basis. The business leaders may appear to be gentle and civilized, but these leaders know competition as a fiercely fought contest. They are the gladiators and they know the rules of the arena. Intimidation is a ready tool for the business leader. He is prepared to play the game with no holds barred. "Competitors resort to intimidation which may merge into violence. The oil industry of the earlier years presents many examples of the resort to violent intimidation. Lowering prices in order to force competitors out of business may be considered a form of intimidation. Price Associations and Cartels often resort to intimidation to force recalcitrants into line. Chain stores, by threatening to withdraw their orders, sometimes force onerous terms upon small manufacturers who have come to depend upon the Chain as their main market. Distributors of securities may be forced to handle certain objectionable issues by the investment banker's open or covert threat of ceasing further transactions. And financial groups out to secure control of particular corporations or to achieve other ends may make use of various forms of intimidation which flow from the possession of great power."[3]

Likewise, there is intimidation practiced by the radical minority leader or leaders. Intimidation is even utilized by the Church, the State, and social, economic, and educational persons and institutions.

Because of these far-reaching possibilities for leadership to practice the art of intimidation, it would seem to be the part of wisdom to illustrate how one individual became aware of the devastation of intimidation and set about to build a defense sufficient to enable him to protect his business and, at the same time, assume a style of leadership that gave him the initiative. First of all, he came to understand the theory of intimidation. He also discovered that the results a person obtains are inversely proportionate to the degree to which he is intimidated.

Mr. Ringer was a Real Estate Broker, and he states that it was in the deals in which he had been most intimidated that he had taken the worst beatings financially. Also, it was in situations in which he had been intimidated least that he had received the greater financial rewards. With these facts clearly in mind, it was evident that there must be a plan to keep from being intimidated. Thus, "the first step in organizing my philosophy into usable form was to lay out a specific plan to keep from being intimidated. I had to create a method for trading places with the principal; from now on I would have to be the intimidator and find a way to maneuver the principal into the role of the intimidatee."[4] How was this radical change to be accomplished? Mr. Ringer was a very able and talented person. His knowledge and ability were for the most part equal to or greater than those of principals with whom he dealt. His final conclusion was that his posture had been weak.

Posture Theory

"This theory states that it is not what you say or do that counts, but what your posture is when you say or do it. In real estate sales, for example, if your posture suggests that you are 'only a broker'—if the principals see you as nothing more than an unnecessary annoyance in their deal—then you are going to be intimidated no matter how great your knowledge and ability, and no matter what you say or do."[5]

Since a weak posture was seemingly the cause of intimidation, it was very evident that things must change until there was a strong posture. His image power must be upgraded. This was an abstract power. Moreover, he needed real power: In thinking it through, he came to the conclusion that he had to be backed up by "legal power"; he reasoned that if he had the proper legal tools on his side, he would then have the real power he needed. In addition to abstract or image power, there was to be real power and the necessary performance power. In the legal tool kit there were three legal tools which must be used in every sale. There must be a real estate license. There must be a written and signed commission agreement. There must be plentiful use of certified mail. These three legal tools gave real power. As salesman, the important steps for selling were these:

1. Obtain a product to sell.
2. Locate a market for the product.
3. Implement a marketing method.
4. Be able to close the sale.
5. Get paid. "The bottom line step."

In searching out a technique for establishing image power without having to justify who he was or what credentials he possessed, he solved the problem by having a special "calling card" designed. The calling card accomplished both objectives. It was a spectacular brochure which cost $5.00 per copy. It was also a clever piece of advertising, and anyone who used a spectacular $5.00 brochure as his calling card must be *somebody*. In short, the brochure was intimidating. After mailing the brochure to the potential seller, it was necessary to wait for a week or 10 days before calling him again. This was meant to give ample time for the "calling card" to arrive and make its impact.

"As a result, the casting of the roles was beginning to take shape. I was positioning myself to become the intimidator while giving the owner the opportunity, for the first time, to try out for the part of the intimidatee. I was developing abstract strength in the form of an impressive image."[6]

It is my sincere opinion that the leader must not allow himself to be placed or stay in the basement of intimidation. At the same time, because of the sacredness of human personality, the genuine leader shows respect and consideration for those with whom he labors. He should be able to build a strong defense and then lead from that point of strength.

The Pecking Order

There is yet another way to view the "Intimidation" theory of leadership. It is suggested by the Sociologist. The pecking order concept has to do with the barnyard ways of the chicken. It especially applies to the roosters. Let a new rooster from the neighborhood be placed in the chicken yard with 10 or 12 other roosters. His work is cut out for him. He immediately takes on one of the aggressive roosters, who is out to defend himself and his flock. The fight is long and it is bitter. He loses the fight with the first rooster and soon has to defend himself against another. This time he is more successful and the second rooster is running for his life. These battles continue for several days, or for a week or more, until each one knows whether to fight, peck, or run. In this way the pecking order is established. Each one knows his place in this order of things. In a more refined or civilized manner, each individual falls within a pattern of being equal, of less importance, or of more importance than friends, colleagues, or competitors in society. This theory certainly leaves many of us less than satisfied. It is the law of the jungle, for the most part, and it does not dress up very much for Sunday.

The "Intimidation Theory" of leadership is a ruthless philosophy for the most part. It is the procedure of being walked on because of one who wishes to dominate situations and people. Power, position, talents, or riches give the "intimidating leader" a handle to push others aside while he climbs toward his desired goal. The intimidator, many times, embarrasses on purpose. On other occasions the intimidator is a clever manipulator. He builds himself up and he puts others down. Sometimes he will make special deals and, through cooperation with other performers, take credit for successes which are really not his own. He passes out compliments or petty awards in order to build prestige for himself.

LEADERSHIP THROUGH INTIMIDATION
IS DESPICABLE

10.

The Lucky-Break Theory

EACH EVENT, SMALL OR GREAT, IS LINKED BY A
THOUSAND SUBTLE CHAINS TO ALL OTHER EVENTS. WE,
WHO CANNOT SEE THE LINKAGE, CRY CHANCE. THUS TO
THE FALLIBLE EYE OF MAN LUCK RATHER THAN DES-
TINY SEEMS AT MOMENTS TO OPERATE.

—*Leo Tolstoy*

There is a school of thought that believes in fate. "It has been a lucky break." "The wheel of fortune spins and where it stops nobody knows." A leader is born under a lucky star or he was born under an unlucky star. "The gods have determined it." "No matter what he does, a happenstance is responsible for the outcome.

Max Gunther has this to say concerning "The Luck Factor." "A hunch is a piece of mind stuff that feels something like knowledge but doesn't feel perfectly trustworthy. Some people trust their hunches more than others do and, of those hunches that are trusted, some turn out to be accurate while others do not. It is obvious that a capacity to generate accurate hunches, and then to trust them and act on them, would go a long way toward producing 'luck.' Lucky people as a breed do, indeed, have this capacity to a notable degree."[1]

It is interesting to note that Conrad Hilton, the hotel man, once said that much of his monumental success was due in part to a hunching skill so finely tuned that at times it seemed occult. He steadfastly denied that any paranormal forces were at work in him or around him, but he did sometimes admit to being baffled. "Most of the time I can reconstruct the circumstances of these hunches," he once said, "and I can figure out in general where it came from. I mean I can explain it—not completely—but enough to make it seem less strange. There have been times, though, when I could not come up with a good explanation."

However, Benjamin Franklin qualifies his position on the luck factor by stating that "Diligence is the mother of good luck." There is no question but that the accident of birth, riches, race, and intelligence is a very powerful factor in determining what we do, and how successful we are in that which we attempt. Nevertheless, we need not allow our leadership to be paralyzed by the thought that "Whatever will be—will be!"

It is possible for one to entrust his leadership to mere chance. Wait for fate to decide the matter, since "Whatever will be—will be"; there is no need to do anything about it. This theory is very weak at best; however, it is really dangerous because it freezes leadership at exactly the place where it has already arrived. "We will wait and see what the outcome will be." It is far better to believe that the human will, and the force of personality, can influence results and that there is always the possibility of human error or of feats performed miraculously. Perhaps we can best illustrate this by a study of both individual leadership and group leadership on the gridiron. Please note the influence of psychological and sociological factors.

It was on a New Year's Day. The "Rose Parade" and the "Rose Bowl Game" were keenly awaited. All of the Bowl Games promised an exciting day to usher in the New Year. The papers were filled with stories of these thrilling events. The television clips and comments inspired us to anticipate every hour of the day. The theme of the parade was: "On the Road to Happiness." What a thrilling theme! What exotic floats! What lavish beauty! Then came the series of Bowl Games. As the day wore on, the football games challenged us for the first two or three hours. Then we settled back in our easy chairs to watch the gridiron "Greats." The day was indeed a study in the psychological and sociological factors which made for success or led to losses. It was an interesting study in leadership. Does luck decide which team will win on the football field?

It is my contention that it does have a small part to do with the outcome of the game. But it is only a small part. It is my belief that Tolstoy is right when he ascribes little place to chance. In fact, he states that there is no such thing as chance. He reasons that each event, small or large, "is linked by a thousand subtle chains to all other events. We, who cannot see the linkage, cry chance. Thus to the fallible eye of man luck rather than destiny seems at moments to operate."[2]

In the Pasadena Rose Bowl, the awesome Michigan Wolverines were pitted against the Washington Huskies. The Huskies were the underdogs. The Wolverines were favored to win by at least 13 points. For the occasion, the Rose Bowl was filled to capacity with over 104,000 spectators. Finally, the hour came for the contest. There seemed to be unanimity on the part of all the "wise-ones" to believe that Michigan was superior in talent and experience. However, there was a psychological factor which favored Washington. *Washington was UP for the Game!*

Could it be that Michigan had prepared well for the game and had peaked early? Could it be that Washington had prepared well for the game and had peaked just at the right time? It was evident they were up for the game. It was a losing day for Coach Bo Schembeckler and his Michigan Wolverines. By the time the Rose Bowl game was over, the Huskies were the champions over a team that was expected to defeat them by two touchdowns. In fact, mighty Michigan was down at the last quarter by a score of 24 to 0. Then, the *momentum changed,* and with one minute and 21 seconds left to play, the score stood at 27 to 20. It was then a duel between two great coaches, two great quarterbacks, and two great teams, right down to the final second. Warren Moon, quarterback for Washington, was especially up for this game. The goal of the entire team was to win this most important game. They were "psyched up" for the occasion. It was also the supreme goal of the Quarterback. He had another high and worthy goal; this was to be selected as the "Best Player."

The game was won by the Washington Huskies, 27 to 20. Quarterback Moon was selected "Player of the Year" following this stunning defeat of the mighty Wolverines from Michigan. The headline

on our morning paper proclaimed: "MOON PROVES HE'S A WIN-
NER."[3]

It was excellent Coaching.
It was the desire to Win by All the members of the Team.
It was the Right Mental Set.
It was Peaking for the game at the Right Time.
It was being Up for the Game.

These were the important factors, rather than LUCK, determining
which Team would win.

Let us pursue the luck factor a little farther in the "Orange
Bowl" game, which was played in Miami, Florida, immediately following the "Rose Bowl" game. Was luck the deciding factor as Oklahoma challenged Arkansas? The football pundits put it negatively.
"The chances are dim for Arkansas." Even the Arkansas Coach, Lon
Holtz, agreed with them by saying: "After looking at Oklahoma and
then looking at us, I wouldn't give us much of a chance either." No
doubt the Coach was thinking about his three suspended players—
the leading rusher, the leading receiver, and a very good running
back. Also, Leotis Harris, an All American Guard, was out with an
injury. The entire University had been torn by the strong discipline
stand taken by Coach Holtz. Yes, the suspension of the three talented
players contributed to the belief that Arkansas was overmatched. Oklahoma was given the edge to win by 18 points.

Maintaining Momentum

But there was a positive side to this unfavorable assessment of
the situation; that was a statement given by Ron Calogni, the quarterback for Arkansas: "It has brought us closer together." The team
was a powerful and united force. In spite of the losses, Coach Holtz
put it this way: "Our defense and our kicking game got us here and
they are intact."

Oklahoma was the team favored to win by three touchdowns.
They made it no secret that they believed their Team was Number 1
in the nation, or at least would be if they won this one and if Texas
lost their game. Everyone knew that Oklahoma had a great blend of
size, speed, strength, and quickness. The underdog was Arkansas,
and everyone felt sorry for them in this widely declared uneven
struggle. In spite of all this, Coach Holtz declared: "We are ready to
play. We are UP for this game!"

Roland Sales ran through the staggering Sooners and set an Orange Bowl record with 205 yards in 23 carries. Sales scored Arkansas' first touchdown on a 1-yard plunge and raced 38 yards to set up the second as the Razorbacks jumped to a 14 to 0 lead in the first quarter. The amazing clincher, a churning 4-yard plunge by Sales, put Arkansas out in front by a 24 to 0 lead in the third quarter. It was a remarkable Arkansas defense that had only two Starters who weighed more than 215 pounds. It simply bewildered a Sooner offense that heretofore had banked on its blazing speed. Roland Sales rushed for an Orange Bowl record of 205 yards to ignite Arkansas to a stunning 31 to 6 victory over second-place Oklahoma.

The Razorback Coach put it this way: "We knew we were up against adversity, the press, and the nation. We just stuck it out ourselves." His analysis a little later was even more penetrative: 'I've never seen a team fight like the dickens like we did. A lot said we'd fall apart. But we're probably closer than ever. We were ready to play the game."

Yes, they were ready! Was it luck that caused the underdog, Arkansas, to win over a great Oklahoma team 31 to 6? In my opinion it was not luck but rather a supreme desire to win and several other factors.

The Coach said, "We Are Ready."
The Team said, "We Are Ready."
They were UP for the game.
They PEAKED at the Right Time.
There had been Thorough Preparation.
They Maintained their Momentum.

When it seemed as if the momentum would pass to Oklahoma, Arkansas sacked the Oklahoma quarterback. Thus, the Razorbacks kept the Sooners off balance and were able to maintain their momentum.

We believe that Benjamin Franklin was right in saying: "Diligence is the mother of Good Luck." Leader, don't rely on fate, chance, happenstance, a hunch, the wheel of fortune, a bit of luck, or the fact that you were born under a lucky star. Rather, it is far better to:

PLAN carefully,
PREPARE fully.

Get "up" for the important game, the assignment, the conference, the task. Maintain Momentum.

The Accidental or Lucky-Break Theory of Leadership accepts the idea that one may be born into a family of great wealth. He may be in line to receive political advantage or he may be favored with superior intelligence or educational privileges. These facts give to him what might be termed "a streak of luck," or "a lucky-break." Others may wait for luck to fall upon them, only to wait in vain.

President Gerald R. Ford did not sit idly waiting for luck to come his way.

He was a successful Congressman.
He was a hard worker.
He was highly respected as a leader.
    Then luck came his way.
He was appointed Vice-President of the United States of
    America.
    Was it because of his lucky star?
The President of the United State resigned.
This fact thrust Gerald R. Ford into the White House.

It was because of a series of happenstances. Could it have been the throw of the dice, or was it the working out of the plan of destiny? At any rate, Gerald R. Ford was in the right place at the right time to be thrust into our nation's highest post of leadership.

The Lucky-Break leader must have genuine abilities in order to capitalize on his new and heavy responsibilities. He must be able to work with others. Auren Uris states: "The leader's accomplishments are usually the sum total of the achievements of his group."[4]

The Lucky-Break leader must have a well organized and clearly defined program if he is to lead successfully. His task is:

To plan the work that is to be done.
To decide in what order the work should be accomplished.
To select people to do the work.
To tell them why it needs doing.
To tell them how to do it.
To tell them when to do it.
To listen to reasons why it cannot be done, or should be
    done in a different way, or at another time.

And then, to have the leadership ability to get a group to do what he wants them to do, when he wants it done, in a way that he wants it done, because they want to do it.

Moreover, the leader who has been catapulted into a high place of leadership must grow continually if he is to maintain his new place of leadership.

In spite of the Lucky-Break;
In spite of the favorable roll of the dice;
In spite of a lucky star;
In spite of an unlucky star;
In spite of a certain hunch;
In spite of the fortunate happenings;
IT IS TRUE—that eventually—EVERY MAN IS THE AR-
CHITECT OF HIS OWN FORTUNE.

DILIGENCE IS THE MOTHER OF GOOD LUCK

11.

The Conjuncture Theory

THE CONJUNCTURE, OR FALLING TOGETHER OF *PER-SONALITY TRAITS, SOCIAL SITUATION, AND EVENT*, DE-TERMINES LEADERSHIP FROM HOUR TO HOUR IN THE RELATIONS OF OBSCURE PERSONS, AND FROM TIME TO TIME IN THE AFFAIRS OF THE WORLD.

—Clarence Marsh Case

My study of the philosophy of leadership was set aflame by the late Clarence Marsh Case, Professor of Sociology at the University of Southern California. He was a great teacher by any standard. In his course on "Leadership," he propounded a theory which he called, "Leadership and Conjuncture—A Sociological Hypothesis." In my opinion it is perhaps the most important contribution to the study of leadership which has been made since the work produced by Thomas Carlyle on the "Great Man Theory." In studying the eight theories of leadership, I feel there is none which equals, or excels, Case's dynamic theory.

In the "Great Man Theory," there is posited one who is sent into the world. He is possessed of those abilities which make him the achiever. *Personality traits* are the dominant factors in his contribution to society. Other students of leadership emphasize the place of the *social situation* as a moving force in society.

In the thinking of Tolstoy there is interaction between the prominent leader—be he a military genius like Napoleon or some other great one—and the masses. Out from this interaction there emerges something new which was not intended by either the one or the other. Thus, there are the two elements at work in moving society. The one is the leader and the other is the followers. The one emphasizes the personality traits and the other emphasizes the social situation.

In Doctor Case's hypothesis, the conjuncture, or falling together, of *personality traits, social situation, and event* determines leadership from hour to hour in the relations of obscure persons, and from time to time in the affairs of the world. Now, with this definition of the *CONJUNCTURE THEORY OF LEADERSHIP*—A Sociological Hypothesis[1] before us, let us try to outline it in a more meaningful manner.

*Personality Traits**	*Social Situation***	*Event*
1. Physical Characteristics	1. Mood of the Day	1. Noteworthy Happening
2. Temperament	2. Climate of the Group	2. Unusual Occurrence
3. Character	3. Economic Situation	3. Momentous Milestone
4. Social Expression	4. Cultural Situation	4. Something of Historic Interest
5. Prestige	5. Historical Background	
6. Individual's Conception of His Role	6. Political Situation	5. Epochal Occasion
	7. Educational Theories of the Time	6. Some Form of Change
7. Perceptual Ability		7. An Intrusion into the Affairs of Men
8. Emotional Breadth	8. Attitude Toward Science	
9. Insight	9. Religious Mood	
10. Drive	10. Attitude Toward Present Day Institutions	
11. Charisma		

*Viewpoint of the Psychologist
**Viewpoint of the Sociologist

It seems advisable to attempt a definition of the word "Charisma," number 11 under *Personality Traits*. This is a word rich in meaning, but it is a bit ethereal when one attempts to give exact meaning to the term. "Charisma, a term first used in Sociology by Max Weber, means literally 'a gift of divine or spiritual origin.' It is among other things a product of total personal commitment. This quality endows an individual with the power of personal loyalty in his followers. The usual model of the charismatic leader is that of the hub of a wheel with the spokes as inner circle disciples and the rim as the larger circle of followers. Too many studies of movement dynamics have been hindered by the limitations of this model, which attributes the success of a movement to a single charismatic leader."[2]

What then is charisma in addition to commitment?
Is it uniqueness?
Is it simply talents?
Is it special charm?
Is it a gift of divine or spiritual origin?
Is it mere mysticism?
Is it special attractiveness?

There are some who definitely have it (charisma), and there are others who do not. It is possible for this inner power to be heightened through time, growth, and experience. It is possible for there to be elements of each of the above present in charisma.

In the opinion of Doctor Case, personality traits represent the more abiding aspects of leadership, although they themselves are conceived of as in the process of change and development. Among those characteristics which affect one's social status and efficiency are: (a) physical traits, (b) temperament, (c) character, (d) social expression, (e) prestige, and (f) the individual's conception of his role. The more permanent traits of personality are: (a) perceptual ability, (b) emotional breadth, (c) insight, and (d) drive.

The second factor in the CONJUNCTURE THEORY OF LEADERSHIP is the "Social Situation." This is a rather broad term which includes the ten elements listed earlier in this chapter. The social situation has been defined as involving three kinds of data: (1) The objective conditions under which the individual or society has to act, that is, the totality of values—economic, social, religious, intellectual, etc.—which at the given moment affect directly, or indirectly, the conscious status of the individual or the group; (2) the pre-existing attitudes of the individual or the group which at the given moment have an actual influence. upon his behavior; and (3) the definition of the situation, that is, the more or less clear conception of the conditions and consciousness of the attitudes.[3]

Thus, the person with his *traits*, facing a constellation of *social values* and attitudes in other persons, gives us two of our factors. The third factor which we shall now consider is *event*.

The "Event" is a noteworthy happening. It is an unusual occurrence. It is a momentous milestone. It is of historic interest. It is an epochal occasion. However, in this theory of leadership, *event* has a technical meaning, since it is used in connection with *personality traits* and *social situation*. "At this point we have to point out that these three factors are not mutually exclusive, since the definition of the situation by the person in itself constitutes part of the social situation, but is also included under the individual's conception of his role, which we have accepted above as a personality trait. The same overlapping appears when we consider the event, which seems at first glance to be an aspect of the social situation. This, to be sure, is but a special aspect. *An event is a form of change* just as a social situation is a process of many changes in itself. Moreover, the growth of personality is a process of mental integration and disintegration in large part. So it appears that all our factors are aspects or forms of change. Yet this need not disconcert us, since leadership, the very thing we are seeking to factor, is itself a form of change, a process of society, or interaction between the person and his associates, or with the group as a whole.

"An event is, as historians have always regarded it, a significant or outstanding change. It is part and parcel of the stuff that the world is made of, namely activity and change, but it receives, and deserves a special name."[4]

An "event" may also be identified as an "intrusion." To help clarify the term "intrusion," let us consider an illustration given by Fredrick J. Teggart, in his *Theory of History*.[5] He suggests that in order to come to an understanding of "how things work" in the course of time, we may envisage the facts of experience as arranged conceptually in a series of concentric circles. Outermost, we would have the stellar universe; within this, the physical earth; within this, the world of organic life; within this, again, the world of human activities; within this, the larger group, or nation; within this, the local community; and finally, within this, the individual. In such a series, it is obvious that change in any outer circle will affect all that lies within it. We may, then, define an "event" as an intrusion from any wider circle into any circle or condition which may be the object of present interest.

This interpretation of "intrusion" is our ground for regarding, in the present theory of leadership as conjuncture, any intrusive change, no matter how trivial or private, as an act if it disrupts the smooth flow of routine change, of some recurrent social process, within the field of interest or leadership under consideration at the moment. No sociologist need be told that leadership of an alley gang is just as valid a case as leadership of the allied nations, although not, of course, so important for human affairs.

Perhaps it will help to clarify this theory further if we were to consider a brief analysis of the leadership of the late E. Stanley Jones, one of the world's greatest Christian leaders. Again, we are dealing with the conjuncture, or flowing together, of three factors: *Personality Traits, Social Situation, and Event.*

E. STANLEY JONES: Minister—Missionary—Author— Evangelist—Bishop—Statesman— World Citizen

Personality Traits	*Social Situation*	*Event*
1. Good Character	1. Deeply Religious Family	1. Early Conversion
2. Religious Concern	2. Christian College Environment	2. Ministerial Call
3. Kindly Facial Expression	3. Leader of a Campus Prayer Group	3. First Sermon
4. Sensitive		4. Missionary Call to India
5. Friend to All	4. An Understanding Church	5. Illness in India
6. Perceptual Ability	5. Great Spiritual Hunger in India	6. Physical and Spiritual Renewal
7. Ill Health in India		7. "Round Table" Discussions with High Caste
8. Brilliant Mind	6. Caste System of India	
9. Prolific Writer	7. Illness Due to Climate	8. Ashrams for High and Low
10. Keen Insight	8. Need for Printed Gospel Material	9. Elected Bishop of M.E. Church
11. Superb Speaker	9. Need for a Spiritual Leader in India	10. Declined Election
12. Great Drive	10. Spiritual Hunger in the U.S.	11. World Evangelist
		12. Author of Scores of Books
		13. Preaching Missions World-Wide
		14. Ashrams at Home and Abroad

(You may find it helpful to select a leader of your own choosing and analyze his leadership in the light of the CONJUNCTURE THEORY.)

At this juncture, we now come to the very heart of this theory. We need a clearcut and definitive statement of the CONJUNCTURE THEORY OF LEADERSHIP. The definitions of "Personality Traits" have been given. The meaning of the "Social Situation" has been clarified. We have carefully defined the term "Event" and have given to it a special technical interpretation from the sociological point of view. The CONJUNCTURE THEORY, or PHILOSOPHY, of LEADERSHIP cuts through the maze of superficial thinking in current thought and literature on "Leadership," and gives to us a theory with penetrative insight into this vital subject. To define the term with depth, and yet with clarity, Doctor Clarence Marsh Case gives us this very lucid and definitive statement.

"The present hypothesis is that the conjuncture, or falling together, of personality traits, social situation, and event determines leadership from hour to hour in the relations of obscure persons, and from time to time in the affairs of the world."[6]

In concluding this chapter, I would like to suggest 10 ascending categories of leadership. There is a strong relationship between these "steps" and the "Conjuncture Theory of Leadership."

We have leadership from the beginning or BUDDING LEADER up to and including the WORLD LEADER. It is my fervent belief that any person who understands and puts into practice the "Conjuncture Theory of Leadership" can advance. To ascend will be more difficult without a clear understanding of this Theory. However, through a clear understanding of our own *Personality Traits*, the *Social Situation*, and the *Events* that occur, we can rise from a BUDDING LEADER to an EMERGING LEADER. Furthermore, as these "Factors" converge, or flow together, we may become a DYNAMIC LEADER or even a WORLD LEADER.

GOOD SUCCESS!
LET'S MOVE UP A STEP OR TWO, MY FRIENDS.

TEN CATEGORIES OF LEADERSHIP

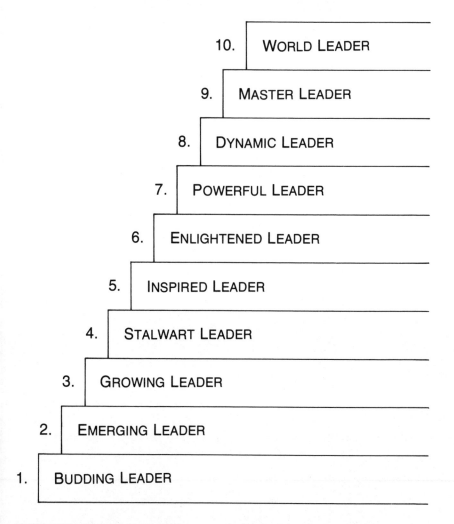

THE CONJUNCTURE THEORY OF LEADERSHIP GIVES DIRECTION TO
LEADERS IN EACH OF THESE 10 CATEGORIES.

12.

The Reed Theory

WHEN WE ATTEMPT TO SOLVE A PROBLEM, WE LOOK FOR
A CORRECT ANSWER. WHEN WE MAKE A DECISION, WE
LOOK FOR A CORRECT METHOD.

—James F. Fixx

IN MY VIEW, THE TIMING OF ACTION IS PERHAPS THE
MOST IMPORTANT SINGLE FACTOR IN LEADERSHIP. TIM-
ING CANNOT ALWAYS WAIT; BUT IT MUST EVER REMAIN
THE PRIME FACTOR IN LEADERSHIP.

—Harold W. Reed

In the preceding chapters we have given careful attention to a
definitive understanding of the word LEADERSHIP. Further, we
have attempted to consider the basics with which we have to deal in
setting parameters for this study. Moreover, as we have developed
these issues, we have been searching for the important theories, or
philosophies, set forth by the great minds of the past and present, or

they are being set forth by the general public until we are compelled to give them a place. These theories challenge our best thought. We have included in this study eight theories, or philosophies, which attempt to give the serious student of leadership some penetration into the very heart of the matter. These eight theories are:

The Great Man Theory
The Follower Theory
The Situationist Theory
The Creative Artist Theory
The Intimidation Theory
The Lucky-Break Theory
The Conjuncture Theory
The Reed Theory

The "Conjuncture Theory of Leadership," as set forth by the late Clarence Marsh Case, gave crystal clarity to three of the most important factors in leadership on any level. These three factors are *"Personality Traits," "Social Situation,"* and *"Event."* These three elements flow together, and they are present whenever, or wherever, leadership takes place. However, there is one problem which immediately appears, and that has to do with the term "event." There is no automatic time set for the tripping of the trigger. Therefore, it seems to me that there is need to deal with two additional factors, namely, *"Timing"* and *"Decision Making."* However, these factors build upon the CONJUNCTURE THEORY. In the words of Sir Isaac Newton, "If I have been able to see farther than others, it was because I stood on the shoulders of Giants." Thus, in the eighth theory, which we refer to as "The Reed Theory of Leadership," there are five powerful factors that emerge. Again, these factors, or elements, are:

PERSONALITY TRAITS
SOCIAL SITUATION
EVENT
DECISION MAKING
TIMING

Consequently, the Reed Theory of Leadership may be set forth as follows: The EVALUATION of *Personality Traits, Social Situation,* and *Event,* PLUS the elements of *DECISION MAKING* and *TIM-*

ING, DETERMINES LEADERSHIP and the EFFECTIVENESS of the LEADER.

This simply means that the leader MUST be a master of his craft. He must be able to interpret his personality traits. He must be able to understand and cipher the facts which have to do with the social situation. He must be able to see the event as a dynamic factor. Furthermore, he must utilize the two vital factors of *decision making* and *timing* in order to deal with *event* with precision.

Again, let me emphasize that the Reed Theory of Leadership assumes the coming together, or flowing together, of five clearly defined factors. These factors are the five powerful tools used by the skillful leader.

TOOL NUMBER ONE—An accurate appraisal of his personality traits.

TOOL NUMBER TWO—A keen understanding of the social situation.

TOOL NUMBER THREE—An awareness of the historic meaning of the event.

TOOL NUMBER FOUR—A correct method for coming to a decision—whether it be affirmative or negative.

TOOL NUMBER FIVE—A clear insight into the timing of action. The inner assurance that "now" is the time to act.

It is possible for one to understand quite clearly the personality traits involved. It is possible for one to give adequate attention to the social situation. It is possible for one to be fully aware of the event and, at the same time, to do absolutely nothing about it. There must be movement on the part of the leader if there is to be true leadership. This is implied, if not stated, in the Conjuncture Theory.

However, to the extent that the leader's personality traits are acceptable, to the extent that he understands and interprets the social situation, to the extent that he correctly understands and interprets the event, and to the extent that his actions are correct, that they are made decisively at the right time—then, and only then, will his leadership be positive and successful. Nevertheless, if the *timing is off*, his leadership will be ineffective and greatly inferior to what it could have been if the *timing were on target*. In my view, not only must the effective leader be a careful student of personality traits, social situation, and event, but he must be an astute student of DECISION MAKING and TIMING.

THE ELEMENT OF TIMING

It was the late Emory S. Bogardus, in his excellent book entitled *Leaders and Leadership*, who made this significant statement: "By anticipating situations one person may become a leader while other persons are running around in circles. Leadership involves both (1) analysis, and (2) controlling situations."[1] It has been of great interest to me, while conducting a large number of seminars on "The Dynamics of Leadership," to find that there are many Executives and Professional persons who are unaware of the important factor of timing in leadership. To many, this new concept comes alive and seems to be something that turns on the light and offers a new dimension of understanding.

TIMING is important when an investment is to be made.

TIMING is important when a politician throws his hat into the ring.

TIMING is important when an Administrator launches a 10-year development program.

TIMING is important when the Business Executive expands his growing enterprise.

TIMING is important when a Minister desires to launch an extensive building program.

TIMING is important in recognizing when a new Idea's "time has come."

Timing is very important when one makes the big decisions. Timing cannot always wait. However, it must ever remain one of the most important factors, if not the most important factor, in leadership.

DECISION MAKING

Timing scans the horizon for the most appropriate time to make an important move, while DECISION MAKING determines whether it is the Right time, or the Wrong time, to make such a move.

After attending a DECISION-MAKING Seminar, James E. Fixx, writer and editor, wrote an article entitled, "The Fine Art of Making

Up Your Mind." In this article he calls attention to Doctor Charles Steinmetz, a Manhattan physician, whose work as an Industrial Preventive-Medicine Specialist led him deeply into a study of the theory of decision making. He states that "Decision makers of today have available to them at least two new tools of unprecedented power. The first is the computer (which is not infallible), which by its versatility and precision has lately been shedding valuable new light on the entire decision-making process. The second is the practice of assigning exact numerical values to subjective, essentially nonmathematical entities such as personal feelings. A practiced decision-maker will ask, for example, 'How much more do I want to take a vacation in Europe than I want to save money for my retirement?' Only by putting a question that way, Steinmetz points out, can a simplistic, either-or answer be avoided.

"Such tools and techniques are currently ushering an entire new industry into existence. It is an industry dedicated to the proposition that decision-making can be made significantly more scientific and predictable than it has hitherto been."[2]

The one universal mark of an Executive is his ability and willingness to make decisions. This is also true, no matter in what capacity he serves; a leader must be *able* and *willing* to make decisions—to make decisions and to stand by them. This includes the hard decisions as well as the routine decisions of every-day living. The result of those decisions determines whether the leader is strong or weak. Thus, all leaders are greatly interested in the various theories of Decision Making and how they can use them most effectively in their own particular situation. Decision Making has been defined as follows: "Decision Making is the selecting of an alternative, from two or more alternatives, to determine an opinion or a course of action. Moreover, it is the psychic and creative event in which thought, feeling and knowledge are brought together for action."[3]

Decision making also includes setting up objectives. It means that one must see with clarity the goals one wishes to reach. For, "to achieve objectives, he must decide upon what specific actions are necessary, what new means can be introduced, and what to do in order to maintain a satisfactory work output. Decision making takes place in every part of an enterprise."[4]

Now, let us consider seven ways in which the leader can approach the task of decision making. The methodology has to go with the choice of the leader as to how he chooses to make his decisions.

He may be interested in Marginal Analysis. He may be more interested in the Psychological Approach. He may rely upon his Intuition, or hunch. He may feel relaxed and certain with Experience as his guide. He may logically and scientifically trust his decision after careful analysis.

Marginal Analysis

"This technique compares the extra cost and revenue resulting from the addition of one more unit. The profit maximizing point is that volume where, for the last unit added, the additional revenue equals the additional cost. At any lesser volume, the marginal revenue exceeds the marginal cost, and at any greater volume, the marginal cost exceeds the marginal revenue."[5]

Psychological Theory

There are many decisions one has to make that do not have much to do with economic advantage. Rather, these decisions may have to do with our own preferences. When one decides on building a home, he may prefer Colonial architecture, or he may prefer Spanish design. It is merely a matter of personal preference.

Intuition

For some, there is a feeling that now is the time to make a trip abroad, or now is the proper time to change jobs. It is a deep-down feeling that may turn out well, or it may lead to an unhappy ending. Usually, however, if this method follows long thought and careful study, it proves to be the wise move to make. Many times if decisions are based solely on an intuitive flash, it may not be a wise choice. Intuition is not a safe guide when one is down physically or emotionally.

Experience

Experience is a valuable tool in making an important decision.

When one has gone through the processes of major decision making, many times there are some things that one comes to understand quite fully. There are some ways that turn out well, and there are others that bring terrible defeat. However, there is a tendency for one to become too conservative in fearing that he will make the wrong move. As a result, he may not come to any decision at all, only that of trying not to decide.

Follow-the-Leader

This is the most conservative of all the possible patterns of decision making. This appears to be an easy solution. It merely follows the pattern that has already been established. It may turn out as wise, or it may turn out as disastrous, depending upon the wisdom, or lack of it, on the part of the leader that is being followed.

Experimentation

This is an important method used by large corporations in deciding upon launching a new product. It may also be used judicially in determining one's vocation or calling. It is also a valuable instrument in determining extension of group programs by the leader.

Analysis

It is my opinion that Analysis is the most important method which can be used in determining the solution of a problem. The various elements can be broken down and considered in detail. They can be seen in relationship to one another. This makes it possible for one to give careful consideration to the *parts* and to the *whole*. This approach narrows the facts, believed essential for the decision, to the most important specifics. The ability to conceptualize the problem is an important step in making a decision.

In the light of these seven methods of decision making, let us now consider an illustration which would call into play several of these methods. A decision was to be made concerning the possible purchase of an eighty-acre tract of land.

The Objective

The objective was to purchase fast-appreciating land in order to insure funds for retirement. This included a desire to speculate as far as possible, with the assurance that if things did not work out well, the loss on the venture would not impair other retirement funds. In other words, to be aggressive, but secure.

Discovery of an 80-Acre Tract of Land

This acreage was for sale at $2,000 per acre. It was situated only six blocks from a Liberal Arts College that had an enrollment of nearly 2,000 students. It had excellent frontage on a State Highway. This major decision meant that there should be careful analysis.

PROCESS OF DECISION MAKING

List of POSITIVE Factors:

1. Population is moving out past the College campus. Expansion seems to be moving northward up Highway 45. This acreage is directly on the highway.
2. Land is being improved on all four sides of this tract.
3. A multimillion-dollar Library and Learning Resource Center is under construction at the local College.
4. This land can go either residential or commercial, and that with profit.
5. Most land resources of any size are already taken on all sides of this tract.
6. All real estate is appreciating throughout the county.
7. Experience in purchasing land and residential property indicates that within five years this land should double in value.

List of NEGATIVE Factors:

1. There is no assurance of continued prosperity.
2. There are about 75 realtors in the community, and none

of them are buying this property, nor have they been successful in selling it to their clients. Why?

3. An attorney thinks that $2,000 per acre is a bit too high.
4. A banker cautions that developers could skip over this
   tract of land and secure land further out for a lesser figure.
5. It would be impossible to handle this indebtedness without a partner who could share in financing the project.
6. Other financial commitments are fairly heavy.

Conclusion

Now is the time to act! The timing is right!

Results

1. The right partner was found who could carry his share of
   the load.
2. The details of interest, down-payment, and annual payment were agreed upon, and these were satisfactory to
   both partners.
3. Money for the down-payment was secured.
4. Ten years later this tract of land was sold to a group of
   developers at a sizeable profit. The primary objective had
   been achieved.

THE TIMING WAS RIGHT.

THE DECISION TO MAKE THE MOVE IMMEDIATELY
WAS RIGHT.

What were the crucial methods which came into play?

There was *EXPERIENCE* in buying properties.
There was *INTUITION* or an *INNER FEELING* of assurance.
There was a careful *ANALYSIS* in which the pros and cons
were considered fully and in detail.

From this illustration, one perceives something of the dimension
of leadership. Ultimately, the chief executive's decision-making zone

is one in which he must transcend being a mere manager and must be a real leader. This is for him the creative challenge in the individual or institutional planning process, the meeting of which requires the exercise of:

VISION
IMAGINATION
JUDGMENT
PERSUASION—and sometimes really having the intestinal fortitude to go out front. This is the dimension that requires of the Executive CAREFUL DECISION MAKING and ASTUTE TIMING.

Part III

MOTIVATING FORCES IN LEADERSHIP

The mathematics of high achievement can be stated by a simple formula:

BEGIN with a DREAM—
DIVIDE the PROBLEMS and conquer them
*   One by One.*
MULTIPLY the exciting POSSIBILITIES in
*   your mind.*
SUBTRACT ALL NEGATIVE THOUGHTS to
*   get started.*
ADD ENTHUSIASM.
Your ANSWER will be the ATTAINMENT OF
*   YOUR GOAL!*

—Louise Hinkey

13.

The Transforming Force of Vision

LEADERSHIP IS THE TRANSFERENCE OF VISION.

—Hal Reed

One of the great motivating forces experienced by man is *VISION*. It is the ability to see clearly and to see at great distance. "All men who have moved the world have recognized the necessity of vision. Solomon, the wise man of the Old Testament, declared: 'Where there is no vision, the people perish.' Hannibal, cut off from Italy by the rugged mountains, exclaimed: 'Beyond the Alps lies Italy.' And it was the cold, calculating military genius from Corsica, Napoleon Bonaparte, who said: 'Imagination, or vision, governs the Universe.'"[1] Without vision, no creative work of significance has ever come to birth.

Imagination, or vision, is the fuel through which information is converted into creative energy. Through the power of vision, "We have the ability to create entirely new images, castles by the sea, phantasies, satires, social comments, new impressions of man, or a fresh interpretation of the commonplace subjects in our own environment. Our imagination enables us to recreate part or all of the present world, or entirely new worlds of our own."[2] It was the inspired poet, Tennyson, who exclaimed: "For I dipt into the future, far as human eye could see, Saw the vision of the world, and all the wonder that would be."

Imagination, or vision, rules the universe of great events. Moreover, imagination, or vision, rules the universe of small events. This is true whenever and wherever men are inspired to climb the heights. And those heights may be hillocks or they may be great and majestic mountains. Theodore Roosevelt, early in life, began scaling the hillocks, and with masterful courage continued throughout life to scale ever greater mountains.

Not only was Theodore Roosevelt a man of great determination and courage, he was a man of far-seeing vision. The rise of Roosevelt to power and to the Presidency of the United States of America is a saga of accomplishments in at least five fields. He was a writer of considerable understanding and talent. He was a naturalist of the first order. He was a big-game hunter. He was a fearless rough-riding soldier. But above all, he was a first-class statesman. All of these accomplishments merged at the age of 42 to make him the youngest President of the United States in history. While Roosevelt was a man of action, he was also a man of far-seeing vision. From his teen years, and on through early manhood and mature manhood, he believed that he would inevitably be President.

Let us note how he was able to attract men of real ability to his cause. One such powerful voice was that of William Allen White, editor of the *Emporia Gazette*. White said of Roosevelt: "I have never known such a man as he, and never shall again. He overcame me. . . . He poured into my heart such visions, such ideals, such hopes, such a new attitude toward life, toward patriotism and the meaning of things, as I never dreamed men had. . . . So strong was this young Roosevelt—hard-muscled, hard-voiced even when the voice cracked in falsetto, with hard, wriggling jaw muscles, and snapping teeth, even when he cackled in raucous glee, so completely did the personality of this man overcome me that I made no protest and accepted his dictum as my creed."[3]

Years later William Allen White attempted to analyze the charismatic effect which Roosevelt exerted over men. It was not social superiority; it was not political eminence; it was not erudition; it was youth afire with ideas of expansion and grandeur. It was a vision of a new order. "It was youth and the new order calling youth away from the old order. It was the inexorable coming of change into life, the passing of the old into the new."[4]

Roosevelt was possessed of a great vision of expansion for the United States of America. He was an ardent supporter of U.S. expansion of its Navy. As the Assistant Secretary of the Navy, he worked toward putting the Navy on a war basis for the coming war with Spain. After the outbreak of the Spanish-American war, he resigned from his Navy post in order that he might organize, with Leonard Wood, the Volunteer Regiment that came to be known as the "Rough Riders." The "Rough Riders" were famous because of their exploits in Cuba. Roosevelt returned to America as a very popular hero. At this time, he ran for the Governorship of New York State and was elected. Some have said of him that he was the most famous man in America at that time.

In 1900 Roosevelt was nominated as Vice-President of the United States, while William McKinley was nominated for the Presidency. His vision of the Presidency at some future time seemed to be a greater possibility now than ever before. The McKinley-Roosevelt ticket offered an opportunity for the realization of dream fulfillment. After all, is it possible that Roosevelt is to be "the man of destiny?" Here we see a man of vision and one who understood the importance of timing. When the Republican Convention was gaveled to order and the band struck up "The Star Spangled Banner," Teddy Roosevelt made one of his most famous delayed entrances. Here we see him as a master of timing. Marching down the aisle with slowness and purposefulness, he advanced toward the New York delegation. Some 15,000 pairs of eyes were upon him, and the Convention broke into applause and a thunderous chant of "We want Teddy." For two full minutes Roosevelt held his broad black hat, so irresistibly reminiscent of Cuba, over his heart while making his way to his delegation.

One of the forceful speeches which he made at the Convention is given to us in Edmund Morris's excellent biography of this exciting leader: "We stand on the threshhold of a new century, bit with the fate of mighty nations. It rests with us now to decide whether in the opening years of that century we shall march forward to fresh triumphs or whether at the outset we shall cripple ourselves for the contest. Is America a weakling, to shrink from the work of the great world-powers? NO. The young giant of the West stands on a continent and clasps the crest of an ocean in either hand. Our nation, glorious in youth and strength, looks into the future with eager eyes and rejoices as a strong man to run a race."[5]

McKinley and Roosevelt were nominated by votes of 926 and 925 respectively. The tasks of the nominees were assigned: McKinley would hold front-porch receptions for visiting deputations, and Roosevelt would do the traveling and make the speeches. By November 3, 1900, Roosevelt had made some 673 speeches in 567 towns and cities in 24 states. The Republican Party won by a landslide, and a large portion of that victory was due to the vision, courage, and hard word of Teddy Roosevelt. On March 4, 1901, the day of inauguration, William McKinley became President and Theodore Roosevelt became Vice-President. However, this situation was not to last for long. The following September, McKinley rode the "Presidential Special" north to the exposition in Buffalo, New York. While the President was in Buffalo's "Temple of Music," a young anarchist blasted two bullets into him, and a few days later the awesome responsibilities of the Presidency fell upon the shoulders of Theodore Roosevelt.

As a young lad he had climbed Mount Pilatus in Switzerland. As a big-game hunter he had climbed the Big Horns in Wyoming. In his early maturity he had climbed Capital Hill in Albany, New York. He had planted his shield in Cuba. Now, he had climbed Capitol Hill in Washington, D.C., thus reaching the highest peak of this long-sought ambition. Far-sighted vision, undaunted courage, and his will to victory gave to him the supreme power which he had craved. Through the transforming force of vision he was able to realize the leadership role that he had sought so long.

After this lengthy consideration of the brilliant rise of Theodore Roosevelt and the tremendous vision which possessed him, it may be well to take a clear look at the way in which vision can be a motivating force in the life of a very ordinary youth.

During my high school days I was privileged to attend a band concert in which the featured soloist was a cornetist. His tones were sharp and clear. The brilliance of his muiscal runs was thrilling. Immediately, I aspired to play the cornet. I envisioned myself as a Master Cornetist heralding forth beautiful clear notes and playing dazzling musical runs. It was a beautiful thought, but it did not occur to me that there was the need for talent and the necessity of spending long hours in practice as well. My immediate concern was to secure an instrument that could make this dream become a reality.

One evening I noticed that there was a beautiful cornet displayed in the window of the Allen Music Store in Colorado Springs, Colorado. It was a silver trumpet with a gleaming golden bell. This was just the musical instrument that I needed. The next week I made it a point to visit the Allen Music Store in order to try out its silvery tones. The price of the instrument was a mere $60, and it could be secured by paying $2 per week. My custodial position in those depression days, which paid me $3 a week, made it possible for me to buy the trumpet under those conditions. Usually it was easy to make the regular payment, but occasionally an expenditure on a high school date would make it impossible to bring in the full amount. When this would happen, there was only one thing to do—go and see Mr. Allen and promise to make up the deficit the following week. This plan was carefully followed, and through it an excellent credit rating was obtained.

A few years later, while attending Colorado College in the same city, during the depths of the "Great Depression," my finances were so stringent that there was a strong temptation to drop out of college. However, it was my Junior year and my studies were going well. There must be a way to raise sufficient finance to continue my college career for one more year. Realistically, the situation looked impossible. There were literally hundreds of men on the streets of the city without work. These were indeed desperate years.

One afternoon, while walking to the College, for there was no money for streetcar fare, I stopped in front of another music store. The large window was filled with pianos and there was an announcement which stated that the store was in receivership and that these instruments were for sale at a greatly reduced price. My friend, Mr. Allen, of the Allen Music Company, had purchased this entire inventory. He now had scores of pianos and other instruments for sale at bargain prices. These facts set my mind to turning, and the more I thought about it, the faster my mind turned. The transforming force of vision was beginning to take effect. Perhaps a low down payment could be made on one or two of these pianos and then they could be taken out into a rural area and sold at a profit. But—there were two big problems.

THERE WAS NO PROSPECT OF ANY MONEY FOR THE
    DOWN PAYMENT.
THERE WAS NO TRANSPORTATION AVAILABLE FOR
    THE PROJECT.

But as the afternoon passed and evening came, there was born a vision. YES, these problems could be worked out, and I could remain in college and complete my Baccalaureate degree.

Then came this sobering thought: "If something could be worked out, why was it not being done by one of the hundreds of men on the streets who were in such dire need?" Could it be that all of these men lacked the vision which was mine? Does vision make the difference? Whatever the truth of this situation might be, I determined that there must be a way through for me. I made up my mind to visit my good friend of high school days, Mr. Allen. He seemed delighted to see me, and I told him of my dream, or vision. The plan envisioned the purchase of two or three pianos on credit, and then to transport them to some rural area and sell them to people who desired pianos for their families.

After a few moments of thought, Mr. Allen made this observation: "You established credit with me when you were in high school. I will give you an excellent price on the pianos. You can take them out on credit and sell them at a profit and pay me after you have sold them." Hurdle number one had been cleared, and now it was necessary to find a way to secure transportation. One of my friends had a little Ford car which he had made into a makeshift truck. Nonetheless, it was large enough to transport two pianos. After I had worked out an agreement with him to pay $5 per day, furnish gasoline and oil, plus lodging and meals, we were ready to load two pianos and to begin our journey. The destination was to be Southeastern Colorado. The vision that I had gave clarity to the project; but as the little truck, heavily laden with pianos, pulled out onto the highway, there was some apprehension. Ten dollars stood between us and our first piano sale. However, we were very fortunate to be able to spend the night with friends in LaJunta, Colorado, and this included a free breakfast. Early the next morning we drove out into the country to begin our "sales pitch." Late in the afternoon we came upon a very prosperous-looking farm. The farmer and his young daughter were unloading a hayrack of feed. No doubt this young girl needed a piano! With this inspired thought, I grabbed a hayfork and helped the farmer unload his feed. After it was all unloaded, I requested 10 minutes to talk to him about my beautiful "Story & Clark" piano. He gave me the time and showed some interest. He listened to my sales pitch, as did his daughter. She was especially interested, and we soon had her trying out the piano. She was delighted, and the farmer looked on with admiration and pride. Shortly, the piano was sold for

$200. We were in BIG business! A College Junior was now both trucker and salesman. The second piano was sold the following day, and a triumphant homecoming was assured. All bills were paid, and there was some money in reserve.

Now, a larger truck was hired, three pianos were contracted, and we were on the road again. Once again the pianos were sold at a good profit, and our vision was becoming enlarged. We would initiate some new plans. The thrill of selling was exhilarating. A 3-ton Chevrolet truck was purchased, and a plan was launched to go out and sell pianos every weekend. Ambition, initiative, and hard work were expanding our horizons so that we envisioned doing greater things. A contact with a music teacher, Miss Rockhill, gave me access to scores of families who had children that needed pianos. For a $10-dollar bonus on each piano, Miss Rockhill gladly went with me to demonstrate the pianos for prospective students and their parents.

Soon I owned a small automobile; I had already purchased a good 3-ton Chevrolet truck; and I was in business with all college bills paid to date and was assured of completing my Senior year of college. I had experienced on a small scale, in very difficult times, the *TRANSFORMING FORCE OF VISION* in leadership.

Let us consider yet another illustration of the motivating force of vision. Often on a Sunday morning I will turn to the thrilling television program of the Reverend Robert Schuller, which is known as "The Hour of Power." It is always inspiring and uplifting. It is built on the solid premise that where there is a vision, ways will be found to accomplish great things. The story of Dr. Schuller's ministerial beginnings in Garden Grove, California, is most unique. He received his education at Hope College in Holland, Michigan, and at Western Theological Seminary. At one time in his Seminary career, he was very fortunate to decide on writing a thesis on the life of Dr. George Truett, the great Baptist preacher of Dallas, Texas. George Truett promised, as a young minister, to make his little struggling church into the greatest church in America. He had envisioned a program whereby this could be possible over his 40-year ministry in Dallas. At the close of that period, his vision had unfolded, and he was able to leave the largest, and perhaps the greatest, Baptist Church in America. This study fired the soul of young Schuller and, sparked by the experience of Dr. Truett, he was imbued with the thought that "The greatest churches have yet to be organized."[6] My, what a vision! He believed that his task was to build that Church. He was a man with great vision, but he was not visionary.

As a young clergyman, just out of the Seminary, he was assigned the formidable task of securing a place of worship, securing a congregation, and building a church in Garden Grove, California. This tremendous task was begun with very little subsidy. There seemed to be no place available for him to begin conducting church services. He attempted to rent from the Seventh Day Adventists, but they were already renting to another denomination. He attempted to rent an auditorium from the School Board, but it, too, was already being rented. He attempted to rent a Chapel from one of the Mortuaries, but another denomination was renting there. Finally, he was able to rent the "Orange Drive-In Theater." Something new and exciting was about to happen. At the first service there were over one hundred people present, and the press read: "Southern California's first 'Drive-In' Church got off the ground yesterday with an attendance of over half a hundred cars." After the service, the young pastor counted $83.75 in the offering. This was a small beginning, but his vision continued to grow. Soon more people were coming to the "Drive-In" Church and more money was being received in the offerings. There was a spirit of great expectancy, and an assurance that they were in the beginning days of great things.

A few years later a "Walk-In"—"Drive-In" church was built. This was a beautiful facility, and the congregation increased rapidly. Some stayed in their automobiles and listened to the inspiring messages, while others filled the large sanctuary to its capacity. BUT THE VISION CONTINUED TO GROW! Soon three services were needed each Sunday morning, and the church was not large enough to meet the needs of the great congregation which overflowed its sanctuary. They came by the thousands. Other thousands, or perhaps millions, were listening and viewing the inspiring services by radio and over television. What should be done?

A new and greater vision gripped Dr. Schuller, and soon the congregation caught the vision as well. They would build a "Crystal Cathedral," at a cost of some $14,000,000. This Cathedral would seat some 4,000 persons at each service. The "Drive-In" church concept would continue, since the Cathedral would be almost entirely constructed of crystal. To envision a great cathedral is one thing; to envision the method of financing such a project is yet another.

His vision for financing the construction of the cathedral, which was to be the largest cathedral in the United States, included the idea of 10,000 persons giving $500 each to purchase one of the crystal windows as a Memorial. Suddenly the project moved from "unbelievability" to "achievability"; all 10,000 windows had been reserved. With this impetus, actual construction was begun. A little later, on a special Sunday morning, the "Garden Grove Community Church" gave, in cash and pledges, over $1,000,000. In addition to this, several wealthy individuals personally gave $1,000,000. Momentum was up and going strong. The *TRANSFORMING FORCE OF VISION* was making the "Crystal Cathedral" a reality.

In a letter to his constituents, Dr. Schuller urged: "Now, we must make this All-Glass, Star-Shaped, Crystal Cathedral come alive with light and sound! To do this we shall need interior furnishings; an altar; a pulpit; an organ; the lights and television equipment." The money for these furnishings had to be secured. Then came another vision in the form of a beautiful idea: "The Crystal Cathedral of Memorial Stars." Suspended from the ceiling above the altar would be 10,000 sparkling stars reflecting thousands of twinkling starlights throughout the length and breadth of the mirrored Cathedral. The Cathedral itself was to be 414 feet in length. The name of the individual designated would be inscribed on each of these "Stars." A gift of $500 would make this possible. The names of my two lovely young granddaughters are inscribed on two of those "Stars" that sparkle from the vaulted ceiling of the "Crystal Cathedral." This great vision moved me to action, as well as the many thousands of other persons who had a part in this thrilling creation. Robert Schuller is a man of vision, but he is not visionary. The "Crystal Cathedral" is now a magnificent reality.

> THE TRANSFORMING FORCE OF VISION enabled Teddy Roosevelt to ascend to the highest place of leadership in our land, the President of the United States of America.
>
> THE TRANSFORMING FORCE OF VISION enabled a young man to find ways and means of completing his college education during the days of the "Great Depression."
>
> THE TRANSFORMING FORCE OF VISION enabled a young minister to accept creatively that which seemed impossible and to erect one of the great Cathedrals of our world.

THE TRANSFORMING FORCE OF VISION IN LEADERSHIP IS A POWER-PACKED, MOTIVATING DYNAMO.

14.

The Creative Force
of Ideas

IDEAS, AND CONNECTIONS WITH IDEAS, POURED FORTH
IN A CONTINUOUS AND ONLY PARTLY PREMEDITATED
FLOOD, LIGHTED FROM ABOVE BY LIGHTNING FLASHES
OF INTUITION. WHEN THIS HAPPENS, ALL THOUGHTS OF
TIME ARE FORGOTTEN AND WE REALIZE ALL OVER
AGAIN THAT AN IDEA IS THE MOST EXCITING AND POW-
ERFUL THING THERE IS.

—*New York Times*

There are certain untimed and apparently uncontrolled flashes
of insight which certain persons experience. These might be termed
flashes of genius. This experience is one which is shared by many
and is sometimes referred to as a "hunch." It often occurs after seemingly very difficult problems have been faced. Then suddenly the
solution or solutions seem to burst upon the mind with creative insight.

While serving as President of an Institution of Higher Learning,

I found it not uncommon to be faced with the hard realities of a major building program or an all-out financial drive to meet the needs of an expanding campus. With these tremendous pressures upon me, it was not unusual for the difficult problems to lay dormant in my thinking process for a time; then would come the incubation of an idea, followed by flashes of insight which suggested what could be done. One's insights become stronger as new and better ideas rush into the mind, until it is astir and the whole person is awakened to great possibilities. New insights, or lightning flashes of understanding, give outline to the steps which can be taken to accomplish the task, even to the planning, financing, and constructing of an important building. However, there is one thing very important to remember—that is, the necessity of writing out fully the steps which are to be taken. On occasion these flashes of insight have been experienced, only to fade away because they were not written out fully with precision. Especially can this situation be true when in the night one is awakened as flashes of understanding come and continue to unfold until one is aflame with inspiration for the task. How tragic to wait until the following day to write out the plans and procedures, only to find that the creative inspiration has slackened and the flood of ideas is gone.

The stages in the creative-thinking process are described by Graham Wallas as: *"PREPARATION, INCUBATION, ILLUMINATION and VERIFICATION."* Though derived from his own introspection and scattered observations rather than systematic empirical observation, the stages in the process of creative thinking that he set forth have been widely accepted by theorists and investigators of creativity. A questionnaire was sent out by the American Chemical Society regarding the frequency of insight in scientific problems. Of the 232 Directors of Research Laboratories, American Men of Science, chemists, mathematicians, physicists, biologists, and men of high standing generally, 83 per cent admitted to assistance from this experience. We know that these insights are not infrequent among those who are creative thinkers. In fact, they are a motivating force that can and should be used by the creative leader.

As we consider the creative urge, we are aware that we can find illuminating or inspired instances which relate to the solution of problems in which the degree of difficulty and frustration is great, and the drive toward accomplishment persistently strong. Many of these illustrations relative to flashes of insight can be utilized by the leader who recognizes the possibility of this creative urge in others and also in his own pattern of thought and thinking. The solution to the problem situation through insight or inspiration seems to be a brilliant shortcut toward a determined goal.

Bertrand Russell writes concerning an example of insight: "In all the creative work that I have done, what has come first is a problem, a puzzle involving discomfort. Then comes concentrated voluntary application entailing great effort. After this, a period without conscious thought, and finally a solution bringing with it the complete plan of a book. This last stage is usually sudden and seems to be the important moment for subsequent achievement."[1] The birth of a great idea, the unfolding of a plan for a superb Medical Center, the establishment of a significant Institute for the study of leadership all involve the creative urge. The creative urge is a mysterious thing. It surrounds and inspires the will and is a catalyst which gives a thrust to leadership.

The story is told of Leo Tolstoy that upon his marriage to Sophia Behrs, he decided to place a two-year suspension on his literary endeavor. However, before the two years had passed, he began to yearn to continue his literary activities. At first there seemed to be little or no success. But, as time went on, the creative urge seemed to possess him, and he could find no contentment or peace of mind until his pen was active once again.

As he attempted to start a literary project, the urge to create became strong within him, so strong that it overwhelmed him and "touched off a fuse which led to a creative explosion. It was the theme of the world's greatest novel, *War and Peace*, which now possessed him."[2] There was an unusual urge to write. The theme which he had conceived some seven years earlier for a short story was again forcing itself upon his mind. As the theme grew in his thinking, it developed into a full-orbed novel of great scope; it expressed quite fully his philosophy of history. Within his mind there was implanted the idea that he was doing a great work, and one that would be world-wide in significance. His basic thought was to write a psychological novel about Alexander and Napoleon, and about all the baseness, passion, madness, all the contradictions of these men and the people surrounding them. Yet, while there is a thrill to the creative flashes and the birth of powerful ideas, there is an accompanying cost which must be paid by the leader. It is the pain and "letdown" which follow. Tolstoy worked so hard on his task that his health became threatened. He could not cease from his fierce labor, and gradually he developed dizzy spells and feverishness. Finally, after two grueling years of thinking and writing, the masterpeice was completed. He was of the opinion that any work destined to live through the centuries should "come singing from the author's soul."[3] What a relief after his constant enslavement to this momentous task! What a Work of Art! "The cosmic heights to which Tolstoy aspired to lift his novel had been achieved. 'War and Peace' marks an enormous advance over all his previous works. It achieved great contemporary success and put him in the front ranks of the world's novelists."[4]

For the leader who is attempting to deal with the creative idea, it should be noted that Tolstoy did not then write significantly for a period of seven years. This was a time in which his mind lay fallow in preparation for another great literary thrust, the writing of his well-known *Anna Karenina*. It is Stanwood Cobb who calls attention to these creative cycles in this way: "First a fallow period; then a vague urge to be creating; next an urge which becomes so constant and so strong as to lead to the choice of a theme and the beginning of actual work on the creative task selected. A new phase now begins, one of demonic obsession in which the creator has no rest night or day until the creative vision has assumed full form."[5]

The creative vision was experienced by George Handel as he wrote the transcendental musical composition, "The Messiah." It is said of him that "so great was Handel's inspiration, so intense his creative urge, that he completed this great oratorio in twenty-two days, during a period of intense struggle with debt, with public detractors, and enemies. The greater this external pressure upon him, the greater became his reliance upon his spiritual power. As he worked upon this majestic composition, the very gates of Heaven seemed open to him and he was lifted up in ecstatic vision to both see and hear the celestial chorusing of angels. 'I did think I did see all Heaven before me and the great God Himself.' As he feverishly worked upon this creation, tears of joy and gratitude flowed from him. And because he felt assured of the supernal heights from which this music was derived, he never considered it his own personal achievement, nor would he accept any financial remuneration for it."[6]

While we have been considering the leadership of men of great genius, such as Tolstoy and Handel, it is well for us to recall the four phases of the creative process, the giving birth to ideas. These four stages are: preparation, incubation, illumination, and verification.

This cycle is present for all creative leaders, whether they are in the category of the genius or of lesser abilities. This creative process is true for all of those in the professions, in science, and in business, as well as those in the arts. It has been said that "when the creative urge is strong enough, it generates a power that seems to become self-operative and self-guiding. It is on this cosmic plane that genius operates, through a force that is characterized by immediacy and perfection."[7] He who would create, he who would experience the creative force of ideas must learn to operate on this plane.

My contention is that the great achievers in our world are men and women who are willing to thrust out creatively for the new, the untried, the unexplored, and the progressive. They are not daunted by obstacles, nor are they afraid of the fact that it has not been done before, or that it has never been done in that fashion. There is a freshness about their approach toward tasks that is exhilarating indeed. The truly creative person, with creative ideas, plows ahead through all conditions and circumstances. He eternally continues the process of expansion and extension of his powers. In the words of Disraeli: "Imagination governs the world."

We have pointed out with clarity that insight and ideas which are creative develop best in problem situations which involve a pattern of behavior that consists of four creative cycles: the stage of preparation, the period of incubation, the flash of illumination, and the time of verification. There seems to be little doubt that creativeness is innate, but the very important question is: "Can it be developed or stimulated?" According to Albert Einstein: "Imagination, or ideas, is more important than knowledge." Since the creative force of ideas is of such paramount value to all who aspire to leadership, its encouragement and cultivation is of exceeding importance. The qualities which are essential factors in the process of creativeness include imagination, sensitivity, and intuition. These factors are to be desired and must be nurtured and cultivated.

"MEN ARE MORTAL,
BUT IDEAS ARE IMMORTAL."

15.

The Driving Force of Goal Setting

NOT HAVING GOALS BEYOND YOUR GOALS IS MORE CRIP-
PLING THAN NOT REACHING YOUR GOALS. THE "IS"MUST
NEVER CATCH UP WITH THE "OUGHT."

—*Victor Frankl*

One of the most powerful tools for the leader is the motivational
force of GOAL SETTING. Whether the goals are derived from the
thinking and planning of the group or whether they are derived from
the master thinking and planning of the leader, they are able to significantly increase the level of production. Since this force is of so
great importance in leadership, it behooves the leader to understand
it as far as possible and to capitalize on ways and means of utilizing it
to the full.

The problem of how to motivate the individuals or groups has
caused leaders to be frustrated for generations. Perhaps the reason is
to be found in the fact that motivation at the very root ultimately lies
within the person and, therefore, cannot be observed directly. How-

ever, the leader, while unable to change the personality structure of the members in his group, is in a position to use incentives to encourage and inspire the individuals or the group to use their energies in reaching worthwhile goals.

What are some of these incentives? One of the most important is that of money. This is a primary incentive for almost everyone. One has a position; he gets up early; he drives across the city; he gives a full day's work; then he returns home in the evening a bit tired and worn. Why? His major incentive is that he needs and wants money. Nevertheless, money is not the only incentive that we have to use. There are incentives such as participation in decision making, job enrichment, behavior modification, and organizational development. These have all been tried with varying degrees of success. However, a large number of research studies have shown that one very straightforward technique, that of goal setting, not only is probably more effective but is the driving force by which these other incentives affect motivation.

Perhaps I can best illustrate the driving force of goal setting from my own experience, first as a pastor and later as a college president. As a pastor, it was my responsibility to preside at the Annual Meeting of the congregation. At this time goals for the new year were presented, studied, and adopted. Prior to this meeting, as their leader, I would give careful thought to outlining challenging goals for every department. It was necessary for the pastor to think, and to think *BIG*. These goals always included at least a 10 per cent increase in church membership, a large increase in financial giving, an increase of 100 per Sunday in Church School attendance, and an outreach program that would challenge both pastor and people. It was my responsibility to inspire and encourage my congregation to use their energies in reaching these important goals. In the words of Stan Wanczyk:

> *We may not always reach our goals,*
> *But there is recompense in trying;*
> *Horizons broaden so much more,*
> *The higher we are flying.*

Later, as the President of a Liberal Arts College, it was my responsibility to use this powerful tool of GOAL SETTING in the process of lifting and building this Institution into one of the great Christian Colleges of America. There was the continuing challenge of setting greater and higher goals each year. But, there was also a conscious effort, while lifting the goals higher each year, to not lift them so high that it would be impossible to reach them.

At the beginning of the college year, the motivational force of goal setting was very evident. Challenging goals were presented to each of the several groups that comprise an Institution of Higher Learning. These were: Administrators, Faculty, Student Leaders, and Staff, and the Alumni and Board of Trustees, who held their annual meetings a little later in the year.

The first challenge was to the Administrative Officers and the Faculty. There had been an initial input by them into the goals for the new year through special studies during the preceding year and throughout the summer months. These goals were highlighted during this first Faculty meeting. This seemed to engender an optimistic spirit as the faculty caught something of the spark of adventure surrounding them when the "College Ship of State" was launched into the new year. Following the early morning faculty meeting, on the first day, was the President's "Annual Dinner" in the evening. This was an occasion of great significance as three hundred administrators, faculty members, staff personnel, and their spouses came together for a banquet in beautiful "Ludwig Center." This was an event to which they had all looked forward. Included on the program for the evening was the recognition of those who had completed further graduate studies and those who had published learned articles, books, or music. For those who had published some work there was a monetary reward. Also, trophies were awarded, by vote of the Faculty, to the "Faculty Member of the Year," and by vote of the Staff, to the "Staff Member of the Year." In this way, outstanding leadership was recognized.

Again, the incentive of recognition came into play as "Service Pins" were awarded to both faculty and staff members on the basis of length of service. The climax of the evening was a challenging address by the College President, in which I set forth the goals for the new year, as seen by the Administration.

It was a challenge to make the new year a year of great achievement.

It was a challenge to continue to lift the level of the academic program.

It was a challenge to the Faculty to strive for excellence, so as to better serve our growing Student Body.

It was a challenge to the Staff to strive for excellence in their area of service. A beautiful and an immaculate campus is an important goal.

It was a challenge to ALL to accept new, yet reasonable, far-reaching goals that would require each one to THINK BIG, and to reach toward ever higher heights.

The following morning in a Chapel-Assembly, once again the Administrators, the Faculty, the Students, and the Staff were challenged as a "Family," or "Community," as I forcefully set forth the *Goals for the New Year*. A new academic year was being launched, and the aims and goals for the College year were indelibly stamped on the minds of everyone. Thus, from within the college community, these aims and goals had been delineated in a way that they were fully understood by all.

Following the opening convocation, we met with the student leaders in their "Student Council Workshop." This was a time for planning as well as goal setting in areas related to student life. I was to host a dinner meeting for this group, at which time we could share with them our goals, especially those that primarily related to the students. This was an attempt to secure the full cooperation of the student body and to challenge these student leaders to think, and to THINK BIG. The first sessions of the "Workshop" were held on campus, and then it was moved to a campsite for a more informal setting. Here, as we talked together and played together, a strong admixture of administrative and student goals made possible a strong and happy thrust into the college year.

Two other groups who are involved in the goal-setting process of an Institution of Higher Learning are the Alumni and the Board of Trustees. However, the sector that is in reality the "deciding group" relative to the future plans of a college or university is the Board of Trustees, or the Board of Regents. This group of eminent leaders met twice each year as a full Board. This Board was legally responsible for the following four responsibilities:

1. To select and to elect the President of the College.
2. To submit contracts to the Administrators and to the Faculty members.
3. To decide on the major policies of the Institution.
4. To be fully responsible for all of its finances.

Consequently, the aims and objectives of the Institution are scrutinized by the Board, and the allocation of finance is determined by it also.

Obviously, the record of finance raised, being successful in operating on a balanced budget, and the wisdom exhibited in administering the entire scope of the University program gives the President prestige with his Board. It also helps if he is a person of far-sighted vision and has keen insight into all areas of the Institution's operation. On the other hand, if there have been glaring failures and obvious weakness in the areas of finance and administration, the Board will move very slowly in accepting his goals or adopting large projects. Nevertheless, the future of the Institution is in the hands of an Administration and Governing Board, and goal setting must be considered, whether "for better or for worse," and objectives must be accepted. It is not difficult to predict success for the Institution where the Administration, the Faculty, the Board of Governors, the Student Body, the Alumni, and Staff all unite in accepting challenging goals, both short-term and long-range objectives.

Again, the leader is the one who finally has to come forth with goals. As the leader formulates these goals, he must be able to think "BIG." It is imperative that the President of a University, the Chief Executive of a Corporation, the Owner of a Business Enterprise, the Minister of a Church, and Leaders at every level dare to aim high for their enterprise. They should heed the advice given by Emerson: "Assume in your imagination it is already yours, the goal you aspire to have; enter into the part enthusiastically, live the character just as does the great actor absorb the character he plays."

Goals and plans that challenge the very best in each leader are the magic keys that open for him the doors of success. Someone has said that "only 3 per cent of all people have goals and plans and write them down. Ten per cent more have goals and plans, but keep them in their head. The rest—87 per cent—drift through life without definite goals or plans." If one should analyze these assertions, it would be revealed that "the 3 per cent who have goals and plans that are written down accomplish from fifty to one hundred times more during their life than the 10 per cent who have goals and plans and merely keep them in their heads."[1] Clearly, delineating our goals is extremely important.

We have emphasized the fact that goal setting is a tremendous motivational force in leadership. But goal setting is not enough; plans must be set in motion to enable us to achieve our goals. In addition, it is of prime importance to set up a time frame in which these goals are to be realized.

One of the most forceful illustrations of the necessity for setting up target dates for the completion of projects is that of the "Space Program" and the "Lunar Landing." In 1960, President John F. Kennedy addressed the nation and set forth a "10-year" program designed to put a man on the moon. This effort, that became a gigantic success, began with a towering objective. No nation, or people, had ever succeeded in such a fantastic endeavor, but America became fully committed to this goal of PUTTING A MAN ON THE MOON. Even more daring was the fact that the announcement was made to all the world that this goal would be achieved in 10 years. The second step was to set up a basic plan of action. Thus, there was a GOAL—a PLAN—and a TARGET DATE.

It was a mind-boggling goal, one which men and women worked toward with great excitement and with great expectation. Many who are reading about this miraculous event today remember the enthusiasm and the unbelievable thrill which possessed us all as we witnessed Neil Armstrong set foot upon the moon. For the first time in the history of mankind, on July 20, 1969, there were men standing on the moon. Neil Armstrong recalls that he had given thought as to what he would say as he stepped upon the lunar surface. But he had not fully decided until after the moon landing was successful. "At 9:56 p.m., Houston time, Neil Armstrong stepped out of the dish-shaped landing pad and onto the surface of the moon: 'THAT'S ONE SMALL STEP FOR A MAN, ONE GIANT LEAP FOR MANKIND.'"[2] We are still inspired and thrilled as we remember this shout of triumph.

While there were many unknowns to face in this gigantic project, there was strong faith that the goals could and would be attained. The difficulties were overcome and the goal was achieved. The task was accomplished, and America was intensely proud of her Astronauts. A miracle had been performed, and it remains a high-water mark in our sophisticated world today. This unbelievable achievement, PUTTING A MAN ON THE MOON, should cause us to never doubt the power and the wisdom of planning and the driving force of goal setting.

The "Space Program" applied every principle for successful goal setting; there were NO alternatives for failure. The Goal: A Man on *the Moon within 10 Years*! The moral to this gigantic effort may be stated in four action-packed words: DARE TO THINK BIG!

In the "moon launch" we detect at least seven important steps:

1. A goal was set.
2. A plan was made.
3. A firm target date was established.
4. Group thinking was utilized to the full.
5. Everyone kept the goal in mind and did his part.
6. Action was employed.
7. The word IMPOSSIBLE was ruled out.

They were keenly aware of the importance of reaching their goal within the time-frame reference. They gave their all. Goal setting was the driving motivational force that thrust them onward and upward.

The greatest benefit of a dynamic goal is that you yourself measure up to the fullest possibility of the total capacity of all of your talents, mind power, and potential. In the words of Daniel Burnham:

Make no little plans. They have no power to stir men's blood and probably in themselves will not be realized. Make BIG PLANS in the hope that they will live through the ages and become a thing of living, burning intensity.

GOAL SETTING IS A DRIVING MOTIVATIONAL FORCE WHICH WORKS. LET IT WORK FOR YOU!

16.

The Miracle Force of Enthusiasm

ENTHUSIASM IS A CATALYST
WHEN UNITED WITH EXPERIENCE AND WISDOM—
IT PRODUCES MIRACLES.

One of the most powerful forces that a leader has at his disposal is the *miracle force of enthusiasm*. It is nothing more than faith in action. You are full of it. Turn it loose! It is more powerful than money or influence. The world pays the highest price for this prodigious power. It pushes aside slander, hate, and egotism. If you give the world all your enthusiasm, you can sweep aside all opposition that would hinder you. Enthusiasm is the greatest miracle force within your body.

The mere possession of a sound purpose is not enough. It is necessary to be charged, and surcharged, with a mighty emotion.

THERE MUST BE A WILL TO WIN

There must be an abounding sense of joy, and a strong supporting drive. It must be self-assertive and self-sustaining. It must be, above all else, contagious. When this is the stituation, it is evident to all that this kind of enthusiasm is genuine.

If the leader is possessed on the physical side with great vigor, and on the mental side with definiteness of purpose, than the normal result will be enthusiasm. This does not mean that enthusiasm is mechanical, but it does mean that the essential ingredients for its achievement are present, and that they can be and should be increased. On the other hand, "it means that its creation is a derived fact and that out from the springs of great energy and of deep intellectual conviction will pour that emotional exhilaration which is essential for arousing others."[1]

Throughout this book you will observe that enthusiasm has played a vital role in the lives of the great leaders which we have considered. These men and women have felt deeply and have thought carefully in order to reach their high goals. In a sense, they were driven to accomplish their objectives. Great leaders feel deeply; they are emotionally primed and have the power to summon and elevate the desire of others which wholly transcends the rational level. Good leaders are enthusiasts. They feel themselves commanded by a power and strength which they in turn command.

It is of interest to note that the word "Enthusiasm" is derived from two Greek words which mean, "Possessed, or Inspired, by Divinity." As a leader, are you so fully inspired and caught up in your task that it drives you forward? Are you so fully charged with a sense of the importance of a purpose to be realized that you are conscious of being carried forward and dominated by some power working through you and out from you? Are you so confident, so determined, so mobilized in your whole personality, that your leadership effort has its own way, and in action and human contact gives off light and heat that draws others to it?

In examining and strengthening the sources of our energies, and the vitality of our purposes, we are able to increase our enthusiasm and power. "The good leader is not ashamed of the fact that he is an enthusiast. He knows intuitively that he has to be one. His zeal is in large part the measure of his influence. Ultimately, such impelling enthusiasm is related also to the basic life faith or outlook which one holds. The pessimist, the cynic or the nihilist is no enthusiast."[2] Henry Thoreau once said: "None is so old as the person who has outlived enthusiasm." A person of 80 or a person of 20, if he is devoid of enthusiasm, is old.

Let me state our formula for MIRACLES in the form of an equation. ENTHUSIASM + EXPERIENCE + WISDOM = MIRACLES.

1. *ENTHUSIASM* breathes life into that which is commonplace or mundane.
2. *ENTHUSIASM* lifts life to a new and higher level.
3. *ENTHUSIASM* creates confidence in the tasks we undertake.
4. *ENTHUSIASM which is sustained* assures victories and miracles.

ENTHUSIASM is one of the greatest words in the English language. "It is not a pollyannaish, sweetness-and-light, moonlight-and-roses kind of word. It is a word that is built deeply into the victorious spirit of man himself."[3] Charles Schwab, of the great Steel Empire, considered that his most precious personal asset was his capacity to arouse enthusiasm among his men. He exclaimed: "Take away my plants, take away my inventory, but leave me these men, and I will build another steel empire."[4] Inspired men have accomplished the impossible, and the spirit that inspires them is the *genuine enthusiasm* of their leader. Enthusiasm never wells up from the bottom; it always filters down from the top. It is this spirit of inspiration that sets the machinery of human enterprise in motion.

ENTHUSIASM BREATHES LIFE INTO THAT WHICH IS COMMONPLACE AND MUNDANE

It happened in my early ministry, but I have remembered it across the years. The District Convocation was over, and we were preparing to leave for a new pastorate. The prospect before us was not the most auspicious, and it included the building of a new church. As we said, "Good-bye," to the Presiding Superintendent, he placed his hands upon our shoulders and said, "Young people, you can Smile your way through all of the difficulties that you will face during the coming year." It was an inspiring "blessing." It gave encouragement to a young minister and his wife who were facing a most difficult task, one in which there was little glamor. It was another way of saying, "You will need to exude enthusiasm at all times. You will have to maintain your enthusiasm when everyone else has little or none." But the Bishop had stated it so beautifully: "SMILE YOUR WAY THROUGH." Keep your enthusiasm going for you. I have thought of this inspirational statement many times. In fact, it has become an admonition to be followed daily.

As a young College President, in my late twenties, I determined to never meet my faculty, staff, or students without a smile. It was not always easy. Sometimes the long hours, the tremendous pressures, and the difficult decisions would cause me to pass a professor or a student in the halls or upon the campus without noticing him. As soon as this situation was perceived, I made it a rule to slip away from my office for a few days of rest until I could get my perspective, be genuinely enthusiastic about my task, and meet everyone with a smile.

Enthusiasm breathes new life into that which is commonplace and mundane. Enthusiasm makes life exciting and creative. Enthusiasm enables us to accomplish the seemingly impossible. This is true in every area of leadership. The proverbial "Butcher, Baker, and Candlestick Maker" can breathe new life into that which is commonplace or mundane, through genuine enthusiasm. No one will be more excited about the task than is the leader. The leader dare not expect enthusiasm to come up through the ranks, but must ever remember that it always filters down from the top. This, too, was a lesson learned early in my ministry. I shall never forget a member of my official Board whose level of enthusiasm for an exciting new plan, or a challenging new project, was usually expressed in these words: "I can't find anything wrong with it." He was a very able professional person and possessed many find qualities, but it was a definite challenge to my leadership to be able to infuse enthusiasm into this member of my Board as well as all the other members. Miracles are possible for the leader who can do this.

ENTHUSIASM LIFTS LIFE TO A NEW AND HIGHER LEVEL

Let us consider another equation before returning to our original premise. ENTHUSIASM + ENERGY + INTELLIGENT AGGRESSIVENESS = PROGRESS. The rate of progress being made is of concern to every leader. Again, from this equation, we find that ENTHUSIASM is a vital component. However, if we are striving to accomplish the seemingly impossible, let us remember that ENTHUSIASM IS A CATALYST; WHEN UNITED WITH EXPERIENCE AND WISDOM, IT CAN PRODUCE MIRACLES.

One of my most challenging and rewarding experiences as a College President was the establishing of a collegiate-level Department of Nursing. The need for professionally trained nurses was without question. It was a project for which I had great enthusiasm and one to which I had given careful consideration. There were many who recognized this need, but a thorough evaluation of the project assured me that it would take a miracle to accomplish it. All of those affiliated with such a School of Nursing warned me of the very high costs involved, this being partially due to the very low ratio permitted between students and faculty. The securing of qualified faculty members could be one of the gravest problems. However, the need for more professional nurses was acute in both of the local hospitals. In fact, the need was so urgent as to cause one hospital to offer a substantial subsidy, on an annual basis, for the program.

After numerous studies were completed and a Director secured, the Nursing Program was launched with a small, but highly trained, faculty. A concerned and enthusiastic Pharmacist and his wife were responsible for providing the necessary funds to build a splendid facility for our new Department of Nursing—a most adequate building, which bears their name. As soon as the announcement was made that the Department of Nursing Education was opening, students began seeking admittance. They came in ever increasing numbers and, as a consequence, the faculty and staff were overloaded. As a result, unhappiness and tension developed, both within the faculty and among the students. After being away from the campus for several weeks, I returned to find that there was confusion and conflict in the Nursing Education Department. I learned that it was largely over the fact that there were not sufficient faculty members to meet the needs of the every growing Division. Some of the upper-division students were threatening to leave. Some of the professors were threatening to resign. The entire cause was in jeopardy. Enthusiasm was gone. A request came to my office for a meeting with all of those involved in the Nursing Department. When, along with other administrative leaders, we arrived at the beautiful auditorium in the Nursing building, it was filled to capacity, with many having to stand. The atmosphere was highly charged. What should a College President do under those circumstances? Should I speak or should I run for cover? The answer: I would speak and believe for the best.

I began by stating: ENTHUSIASM IS A CATALYST THAT UNITES WITH EXPERIENCE AND WISDOM TO PRODUCE MIRACLES! I repeated it again and then asked them to repeat it with me. YES! We had already witnessed some miracles in the Nursing Division. We recalled how the Nursing Education Department was begun because of the great need for professional nurses in our

Community, in our State, in our Nation, and within our World. Yes, we were filling a very real need. I called attention to the fact that the Riverside Medical Center was helping to subsidize this Department of the College because of its need for qualified personnel.

IT WAS A MIRACLE that in such a short period of time we had reached the place in the field of Nursing Education that we now held.

IT WAS A MIRACLE that we had secured such a well qualified faculty in such a new program.

IT WAS A MIRACLE that we had a multi-million-dollar "Wisner Nursing Education Building," equipped with the most modern equipment available—in fact, a facility equal to the very best in the State of Illinois.

IT WAS A MIRACLE that we had "Reed Hall of Science," equipped with the very best in both classrooms and laboratories. Another MIRACLE was that most of the professors in the Natural Science Division were young and held earned Doctorates from prestigious Universities. Moreover, these outstanding professors were anxious to give adequate support in the field of Science to the Nursing students.

IT WAS A MIRACLE that some of our graduates were writing to us, from places where they were serving throughout the world, praising the College for the excellent training and preparation they had received as undergraduates.

Yes, we had witnessed MIRACLES! ENTHUSIASM had been the catalyst that had made these miracles possible. Our only problem was the fact that we had too many well qualified students and that we needed many more qualified professors. Furthermore, our greatest need at the moment was for ENTHUSIASM, since enthusiasm united with experience and wisdom still produces MIRACLES.

The entire atmosphere changed. An infusion of enthusiasm was lifting the motivation of this Division to new and higher levels. I challenged the Senior students to enthusiastically prepare for their final exams and to be ready for their State Board Examinations. I offered to give several weeks to full-time recruiting of faculty members for this exciting program. This I did, and peace fell beautifully over the entire campus. Enthusiasm had been restored to the Nursing Division.

ENTHUSIASM CREATES CONFIDENCE IN
THE TASKS WE UNDERTAKE

Enthusiasm is a powerful motivational force. It makes things happen. "Get full of *enthusiasm*, the kind that keeps you excited about your job and about people."[5] There is never a time when the leader can allow himself to be overcome with lethargy. The enthusiastic leader is wholehearted, ardent, and eager. He is spirited, exuberant, and unstinting. If the task is not exciting, the leader must enthuse it and keep it continually exciting. "Develop the powerful motivation that comes from *deep inner enthusiasm* that never runs down."[6]

For me, my little church with 200 members was a great church. New members were congratulated upon becoming a part of a great church. It was indeed exciting.

For me, Bresee College, with its 150 students, was a great college. The students were congratulated upon being a part of a great college. It was exciting to be a part of a growing institution.

For me, a larger church with 500 members was a great church with exciting possibilities. New members were made to feel that they were an integral part of a great and growing church.

For me, a Liberal Arts College with 2,000 students and over 100 highly trained faculty members, was a great college. New faculty members and incoming students were constantly made aware of the fact that the College was a great Institution. They were made aware that they were highly honored to be a part of this rapidly growing and prestigious College. The building program was phenomenal, with a major building being erected at an average of every two years, and all of this on a sound financial basis. New academic achievements were duly reported and these genuine accomplishments were attributed to the faculty and to the students. Consequently, there was a sharing of these thrilling developments. The College Community was able to sense in the Administration real enthusiasm and genuine commitment to the task of building a great University. As a result, there was confidence in believing that the tasks attempted could, and would, be accomplished. Each time that there was a breakthrough seen in reaching our goals, there was greater assurance that there would be other successes as well. There was ardent enthusiasm and fervid excitement, as difficulties were met and overcome.

Enthusiasm always creates confidence in the tasks we un-

dertake. So keep full of wholehearted enthusiasm that will make you excited about your task.

ENTHUSIASM WHICH IS SUSTAINED ASSURES VICTORIES AND MIRACLES

It is one thing to experience a burst of enthusiasm and yet quite another to sustain it. Have you ever noticed the "cooling off" of enthusiasm until an entire project slows down or comes to a complete halt? The genuine leader is aware of the natural lessening of inspiration and drive with the passing of time and, therefore, the continual demand to sustain enthusiasm.

Some years ago, while attending a conference, I heard three great men speak on the subject of "Leadership." The first speaker urged upon the convention the necessity for a leader to be a great and growing person. He emphasized that the leader must grow as the institution, or organization, which he serves enlarges and expands. Thus, to him, the most important task of the leader was to be a vitally alive and growing person.

The second speaker urged that organization was the most important tool for leadership. He made an excellent case for the usage of the organizational force in leadership. Without the powerful force of organization, the leader could not hope to reach his goals.

The first two speakers had presented a challenging case for their views on leadership. However, I was anxious to hear the third speaker's presentation. As he addressed the conference, it seemed as if he were inspired. He concurred with those who had preceded him; a leader must continually grow and develop, and if his leadership is to be successful, he must be able to use the powerful tool of organization. But, in addition to this, the great leader must be *filled with enthusiasm*. To illustrate this fact, he related a story from his early career. He told of how he and a friend were traveling in the Dakotas during the days of the old Model T Ford. It was late at night, and they were following a highway that paralleled the "Great Northern" railroad. It was bitter cold. The snow was falling rapidly, and it was being driven by a howling wind. The little Model T had its side curtains buttoned tightly, and the tiny heater struggled to warm the little car. The road turned so as to cross the railroad tracks. As they approached the turn, far in the distance a "Great Northern" passenger train threw its powerful light down the track, piercing the darkness. The driver brought his little car to an abrupt halt, and the two men sat motionless, facing the railroad tracks. While they waited, shivering in the cold, the mighty train roared into the face of the wild storm at a rate of over 60 miles per hour. The speaker recounted his vivid recollection of watching the great engine as it passed before them. The fireman had the fire-box open and was shoveling in more coal. It seemed as if they were looking into the very heart of that locomotive. It seemed as if the entire engine were on fire.

Said the speaker, the leader must be like the fireman stoking the fire. To face the storms, to overcome the difficulties, the heart of the thing must be on fire. The "Great Northern" was able to speed into the face of a mighty blizzard that swept across the Dakota prairies because its heart was on fire. The fireman did not allow the heat to die down nor the fire to burn out. The true leader must be able to ignite the flame of enthusiasm in those whom he seeks to lead. The leader's heart must be aflame with real enthusiasm that burns continually.

Yes, enthusiasm which is sustained assures victories and miracles. The successful business executive who takes a small, struggling business enterprise and builds it into a solid, growing corporation has learned not only that enthusiasm creates confidence, but that enthusiasm which is sustained can bring victory out of defeat and success out of failure. Likewise, the college or university president who lifts the academic standing of his institution to new and higher levels, and who builds one major building after another, has learned that enthusiasm, which is sustained, is necessary if these miracles are to take place. A leader must continually breathe enthusiasm into every sector of his constituency.

However, this can only be done as the leader is able to discover the OPPORTUNITIES in every DIFFICULTY—rather than the *difficulties in every opportunity.* It can only be done as the soul is re-fired and the mind is stimulated and inspired by a deep and abiding enthusiasm. It can only continue to be done as the leader goes forth with definite plans worked out in the crucible of experience and wisdom.

ENTHUSIASM breathes life into that which is commonplace or mundane.
ENTHUSIASM lifts life to a new and higher level.
ENTHUSIASM creates confidence in the tasks we undertake.

ENTHUSIASM which is sustained assures victories and miracles.

ENTHUSIASM IS A CATALYST—WHEN UNITED WITH EXPERIENCE AND WISDOM IT PRODUCES MIRACLES!

17.

The Stimulating Force of Optimism

THE OPTIMIST BELIEVES, ATTEMPTS, ACHIEVES. EVERY
OPTIMIST MOVES ALONG WITH PROGRESS AND HASTENS
IT, WHILE EVERY PESSIMIST WOULD KEEP THE WORLD
AT A STANDSTILL. OPTIMISM IS THE FAITH THAT LEADS
TO ACHIEVEMENT; NOTHING CAN BE DONE WITHOUT
HOPE. OPTIMISM, THEN, IS A FACT WITHIN MY OWN
HEART.

—*Helen Keller*

Roger W. Babson, the famous economist, was not naturally an optimist. However, he developed a technique which could transform his depressions into optimistic views of life and of the future. He put it this way: "I can turn myself into a shouting optimist within an hour."[1] He suggests that his method is to read history and then attempt to get perspective. In the light of the centuries, his troubles and anxieties become small and trivial. The pages of history point to the fact that tragic wars, famine, disease, and man's inhumanity to man have been the lot of man through the ages. Thus, when Babson became depressed, he used this technique to become a "shouting optimist." The genuine optimist rises above the historic present. He rises above human limitations, and he faces the new day with its new opportunities, with real optimism for its new plans and new programs.

It is possible for one to have this spirit of optimism within himself. Helen Keller states that "optimism is a fact within my own heart." It lives with us all, but it needs to be cultivated and developed. If this spirit is permitted and encouraged to grow within you, the stimulating force of OPTIMISM will greatly enhance your leadership.

Helen Keller's is a familiar story of one who faced life with what appeared to be insurmountable obstacles in her path. In fact, there are few life stories that begin with such difficulties and reach to such heights as did hers. You will recall that before she was two years old she experienced a serious illness that was diagnosed as brain fever. This devastating illness destroyed both her sight and her hearing. Consequently, she was cut off entirely from the world about her. It appeared as if she must live all of her life as a deaf-mute. However, she had the good fortune of having for a teacher, Anne Sullivan.

Anne was able to make contact with her through the sense of touch. Through the brilliance of her teacher and her own fertile mind, Helen was able, within three years, to learn the alphabet and to read and write in Braille. Up and until the age of ten, she was able to talk only in the sign language of the deaf-mute. Nevertheless, there was within Helen Keller a burning desire to learn and to accomplish worthy educational goals. She decided to learn the art of speaking, and by the time she was 16, she had made sufficient progress that she was permitted to enter a preparatory school. Later she was graduated from Radcliffe College with honors. She had experienced the stimulating force of optimism. She had made the discovery that: NOTHING SUCCEEDS LIKE SUCCESS. She became a noted lecturer and writer. During her lifetime, "she lectured in more than twenty-five countries on the five major continents. Her books are best sellers and have been translated into more than fifty languages."[2]

Helen Keller was a unique person, with tremendous potential. She believed that outward circumstances do not determine one's destiny. She believed that the stimulating force of optimism could enable her to conquer all the obstacles which surrounded her life.

She refused to allow her childhood circumstances to keep her from developing and unfolding her full potential as a person. She was firmly committed to the fact that nothing succeeds like success.

Another illustration of the dynamic force of optimism is revealed in the life of Charles Schwab. This young stable boy, with the cheerful spirit and the warm smile, caught the attention and interest of the rich and powerful Andrew Carnegie. He proposed to the youth that he should come and work for him for a good salary. Mr. Carnegie believed that this young man, with his optimistic spirit, would be a great asset to his business. As a result, he was launched into a career in the steel industry where he could utilize and capitalize upon the stimulating force of optimism. Since this spirit was within his own heart, he was able to climb the ladder of success with rapidity. As a vibrant business leader soon in his own right, he was able "to sell the elder J. P. Morgan the idea of combining small steel companies to form a giant one. Older men had been unable to sell this idea to the financier, but smiling, optimistic Charlie Schwab did it."[3] And all the while, smiling, optimistic Charlie Schwab was earning a million-dollar-a-year salary.

Recently, while traveling through New Mexico, I found a very clever story in an advertising journal that had been placed in our motel room. *Optimism* versus *Pessimism* is a thought that we would all do well to consider. This little story graphically deals with this thought.

> There was a man who lived by the side of the road and sold hot dogs.
> He was hard of hearing, so he had no radio.
> He had trouble with his eyes, so he read no newspapers.
> But he sold good hot dogs.
> He put up signs on the highway telling how good they were.
> He stood on the side of the road and cried: "Buy a hot dog, Mister?"
> And people bought.
> He increased his meat and bun orders.
> He bought a bigger stove to take care of his trade.
> He finally got his son home from college to help him out.
> But then something happened.
> His son said, "Father, haven't you been listening to the radio?

"Haven't you been reading the newspapers?

"There's a big depression.

"The European situation is terrible.

"The domestic situation is worse."

Whereupon the father thought, "Well, my son's been to college; he reads the papers and he listens to the radio, and he ought to know."

So the father cut down on his meat and bun orders, took down his advertising signs, and no longer bothered to stand out on the highway to sell his hot dogs.

And his hot dog sales fell almost overnight.

"You're right, Son," the father said to the boy. "We certainly are in the middle of a great depression."[4]

The moral of this story is plain for all to see and to understand. Pessimism leads inevitably to failure. Optimism leads inevitably to success.

THE STIMULATING FORCE OF OPTIMISM

It was my intent as the President of a Liberal Arts College to always meet the students, faculty, and administrators with a smile, a smile of friendship, assurance, and confidence. It was an expression of my commitment to the stimulating force of optimism. It was meant to give encouragement and inspiration to all of those on the campus. It was an expression of a philosophy of positive thinking. Again, this philosophy can be stated succinctly in seven words: THERE IS NOTHING WHICH SUCCEEDS LIKE SUCCESS.

The opposite of an optimistic spirit is that of a negative spirit. One should beware of those who live in a negative world where CAN'T is the most frequently used word in their vocabulary. Suppose Thomas Edison, as well as other scientists and explorers, had listened to the so-called experts. Listen to what they had to say:

1840—"Anyone traveling at the speed of thirty miles per hour would surely suffocate."

1878—"Electric lights are unworthy of serious attention."

1901—"No possible combination can be united into a practical machine by which men shall fly."

1926—(From a scientist) "This foolish idea of shooting at the moon is impossible."

1930—(Another scientist) "To harness the energy locked up in matter is impossible."

Yes, the pessimistic experts can be wrong. This kind of a negative spirit throws a wet blanket over every plan or enterprise. There is no possibility of success for the leader who sees only the reasons why it cannot and should not be done. A negative person forfeits the possibility of successful leadership. The optimistic leader recognizes the difficulties and is not blind to the hardship which may be encountered. On the contrary, he accepts these hard facts of life, but he is challenged by a hundred ways through and over the difficulties. "The optimist believes, attempts, achieves."[5]

In my own career I have found that one of the most important ingredients in accomplishment is that of optimism. This is true whether it be in a large corporation or in a small retail shop, whether in the halls of government or the halls of learning, whether in the laboratories of scientific research or in the confines of office or home, whether in old age or in youth. "Optimism is the faith that leads to achievement; nothing can be done without hope."[6]

As a young man of 26, I was asked to meet with the governing Board of a small Christian College. At the appointed time, I met with the Trustees, and they talked to me about assuming the Presidency of this Liberal Arts College that was in dire financial circumstances. However, there were some of the Trustees who believed that I was far too young and inexperienced to undertake the salvaging of a church school during the days of the "Great Depression." Consequently, the Board turned their attention to someone older and wiser and elected a professor of History from a sister institutuion. The Professor came and looked over the College, with its deficits and its lack of financial support, and then took the first train back to his home in California.

Again, the Trustees requested that I come to Hutchinson, Kansas, and meet with them. They informed me that one-third of the faculty had resigned in order to take positions where their salaries would be more certain. This was quite understandable, since they had not been paid for several months during the past year. They informed me that there was over $5,000 due in current obligations in the city; in fact, it was past due. There was more bad news; the central heating plant was broken, and there was no money in the current funds. Their report was most discouraging, but there were those of the faculty and administration who believed in the cause of Christian Education. Also, the Board of Trustees was anxious that the College should continue.

That night when I went to my room to make my decision, there was little or no sleep for me. As I turned and tossed on my pillow, there was a verse of scripture that came very vividly to my heart and mind. It seemed to stand out in large, bold letters in my thinking: "I can do all things through Christ which strengtheneth me."[7] It was a challenging verse. It was a verse freighted with optimism, the kind of optimism that could cause one to "believe, attempt, achieve." Early the next morning, as the sun appeared on the eastern horizon, there was a calmness and an assurance within. "I can, with Divine assistance, do that which seems impossible." I was willing to accept the challenge to rescue a Liberal Arts Church College from bankruptcy, even in the midst of a great despression.

Now was the time to harness the motivational forces available to ALL leaders: VISION—IDEAS—GOAL SETTING—ENTHUSIASM—OPTIMISM—ORGANIZATION. I had been schooled in the powerful force of organization at my previous assignment, which I shall relate in the following chapter. These dynamic forces could enable me to succeed.

1. VISION—Maintain a strong Liberal Arts College in the Heartland of America, where young people could receive the best in education in a Christian environment.

2. IDEAS—Establish an "education budget," to be paid on a per-capita basis by the sponsoring church. (This was a "first" in the denomination at that time.) Initiate a script system whereby the faculty would receive sixty per cent of their salaries in cash and 40 per cent in script (goods and services). This would help the students as well as the faculty.

3. GOAL SETTING—Inaugurate a city campaign to raise $10,000 to pay our current obligations. (Successful.) Purchase a large apartment house in the city and have it moved onto the campus to serve as an additional dormitory. This would comfortably house 40 girls. (Enrollment was increasing.)

4. ENTHUSIASM—Capitalize on the services of an out-standing male quartet. Take these enthusiastic young people out into the community and into all of the churches in our Educational Zone. This helped us to secure payment of the budgets promised and to secure many personal gifts of cash and produce.

5. OPTIMISM—"Optimism is the faith that leads to achievement."[8] Money was raised to fix the furnace. Money was raised to purchase coal by the carload. Friends supplied food from their farms. Groceries could be purchased wholesale. Excitement was running high.

A young leader, and those associated with him, were seeing the motivational forces of leadership at work. While this was on a rather small operation, it proved to be excellent training for a future assignment on a vastly larger scale. Nevertheless, the same dynamics of leadership proved valid.

One day when a staff member suggested to me that I enlist support by telling our constituents that "we were too poor to buy toothpaste," my reply was swift and forthright—"NEVER! Our people are fully aware of our financial needs. We shall tell them of the thrilling progress that is being made. NO ONE WANTS TO INVEST IN A SINKING SHIP."

One of the most optimistic persons that I have had the privilege of knowing is Robert H. Schuller of Garden Grove, California. We enjoyed having him lecture on our campus, and we have attended his church on several occasions. He is one of the most widely known churchmen in America today. When asked, during a television interview, whether he felt that his supersuccess was in danger of becoming a numbers game, Dr. Schuller's answer was given immediately. "I take my cue from the unfinished tasks."[9] He pointed out that the wise business executive would not look at what accomplishments were already made or at the size of his competitor. Rather, he would look at the untapped and undeveloped markets all around him.

While he was a Seminary student in Dallas, Texas, a study of the life and work of the late Reverend George Truett set his heart aflame. This caused him to pray: "Lead me, Lord, into a community where there will be so many spiritually hungry and hurting people that I can spend my whole life in one place and make it great. You only know, Lord, how big a job I can handle."[10] Garden Grove, California, has proven to be that place. The story of the Garden Grove Community Church is well known. Dr. Schuller always greets his congregation with this familiar salutation, "This is the day that the Lord has made. We will rejoice and be glad in it."[11] He exudes optimism from the beginning until the final benediction.

Without optimism, Pastor Schuller could never have led his little congregation, worshipping in a "Drive-in" theater, with such a humble beginning, into the magnificent "Crystal Cathedral" where thousands now worship. Robert Schuller has been utilizing, to the full, the motivational forces that are available to every leader. The stimulating force of optimism is very evident.

Almost everyone can recall a thrilling story from childhood about a "Little Engine" that was faced with an overwhelming task. One will recall that the tiny "Engine" was asked to take a train of freight cars over a high mountain. This appeared to be an impossible assignment, but the "Little Engine" became optimistic and said, "I THINK I CAN." With this stimulating force at work, the little wheels began to turn and the little train began to move. The climb was steep and difficult, but the "Little Engine" kept saying, "I think I can. I THINK I CAN!" As the little train moved up the mountain, the "Little Engine" never lost its optimism, for optimism is the faith that leads to achievement. It believed that, "INCH BY INCH—ANYTHING'S A CINCH."[12] Finally, the summit was reached and, with great enthusiasm, the "Little Engine" raced down the other side of the mountain exclaiming, "I THOUGHT I COULD! I THOUGHT I COULD!"

While this is just a child's story that has inspired many a child to attempt a difficult task, the moral is very evident. *ONLY THOSE WHO HAVE FAITH TO DARE—ACHIEVE.* Whether you are an Executive in a giant corporation or a Mayor of a large city, whether you are President of an Insurance Company or the Director of a private firm, whether you are Pastor of a Church or President of a College: EVERY LEADER must utilize *THE STIMULATING FORCE OF OPTIMISM* if his leadership is to be successful.

ALWAYS REMEMBER: NOTHING SUCCEEDS LIKE SUCCESS.

18.

The Powerful Force of Organization

THE SMART LEADER IS NOT THE LEADER WHO CAN DO THE WORK OF TEN MEN—THE SMART LEADER IS THE LEADER WHO CAN ORGANIZE TEN MEN TO DO THE WORK OF TEN MEN.

THE SMART LEADER IS NOT THE LEADER WHO TRIES TO DO THE WORK OF ONE HUNDRED PEOPLE—THE SMART LEADER IS THE LEADER WHO CAN ORGANIZE ONE HUNDRED PEOPLE TO DO THE WORK OF ONE HUNDRED PEOPLE.

THE SMART LEADER IS NOT THE LEADER WHO AT-TEMPTS TO DO THE WORK OF A THOUSAND PEOPLE— THE SMART LEADER IS THE LEADER WHO CAN ORGANIZE A THOUSAND PEOPLE TO DO THE WORK OF A THOUSAND PEOPLE.

Organization is the powerful force that activates the machinery of leadership. The leader who has not mastered the technique of this dynamic force is ill-prepared to lead. "Organizational effectiveness is generally defined as the extent to which an organization achieves its goals or objectives."[1] Leadership's primary task is to cause organizations to operate effectively, while also having the ability to organize unstructured situations and to see the implementation of their organ ization. A critical role in the formulation of objectives and goals of the formal organization is played by the chief executive or administrative head. It is assumed that he has the wisdom to design its structure and to provide the mechanisms for its successful performance.

In a study of "Organizational Dynamics," it is important to understand that the executive, whether in a small enterprise or in a large organization, becomes a statesman of that organization as he makes the transition from Administrative Management to Institutional Leadership. In fact, "outstanding leaders convey their knowledge, skills, and personality to their organization, thereby stimulating growth and movement toward worthwhile goals. And often organizations bring out hidden talents in those who are chosen to lead them."[2]

Once the organizational pattern is established and is operating effectively, woe to the leader who is forever "tinkering" with the machinery. Our nation was shocked, during the Carter Administration, to hear that the entire membership of the Cabinet, which had existed for only two years, was requested to resign. This action by the President verified what many had feared: the leadership of the United States was weak. Theodore Roosevelt once said: "The best executive is the one who has sense enough to pick good men to do what he wants done and self-restraint enough to keep from meddling with them while they do it." This is not to say that there are not times when change is necessary and desirable, but quality of leadership is called into question by the leader who is continuously tampering with his organizational pattern or chart. The driving force of organization is seriously dissipated in such a process.

THE SMART LEADER IS NOT THE LEADER WHO CAN DO THE WORK OF TEN PEOPLE—BUT—THE SMART LEADER IS THE LEADER WHO CAN ORGANIZE TEN PEOPLE TO DO THE WORK OF TEN PEOPLE.

This statement by the late J. B. Chapman was indelibly impressed on my mind in the very early days of my ministry. I had been assigned to a new pastorate, in a small city in Central Kansas. The congregation numbered very few, and the need for a new church building was very evident. The present facility was a store-front building with an adjoining apartment which was to serve as our manse. A congregation in the nearby city of Salina had declined my appointment there because of my youth and inexperience, for they, too, wanted a minister who could build a church for them.

In order to understand the immensity of this assignment, we must recall the economic situation that prevailed in the early thirties. This will be difficult to comprehend for those who have grown up during an era of prosperity and by those who are now experiencing the era of inflation. The "Great Depression" was so devastating, it is hard now to believe that our nation could have survived such an ordeal. Butter was selling for 10¢ a pound at the corner grocery, and gasoline was abundantly available at the pump for 25¢ a gallon. Farmers were receiving 25¢ a bushel for their wheat, and hundreds of men stood on the streets hoping and praying for work. The oft-repeated statement, "Brother, can you spare a dime?" was a painful reality. Our salary was $7.50 a week. The church furnished a tiny three-room apartment. The tiny icebox in the little apartment was adequate to care for the amount of food that we could afford on a $3-a-week food budget. The "poverty line" that we hear about today would have been the "luxury line" during the days of the "Great Depression."

In the midst of this, a young minister was busy pastoring his flock and seeking for ways and means to build a church. First, he must motivate this small group of people to attempt something that would challenge their best efforts, always remembering that: "there are an infinite number of degrees of motivation, from the slightest, almost imperceptible urge, to the deepest and most overpowering drive, which consumes all our available energy and dominates our thinking until the goal is achieved. People of tremendous potential may fail to achieve what they should because they are not sufficiently motivated. On the other hand, people of mediocre endowments can go far beyond their apparent potential under the pressure of a consuming motivation."[3]

As a youthful leader, I was faced with the task of utilizing the force of motivation that was becoming apparent in the little group, enabling them to accomplish the impossible: BUILD A CHURCH DURING THE DARK DAYS OF THE GREAT DEPRESSION. I had to capitalize on the *powerful force of organization.* "It is conceivable that the youthful vigor of a newly organized group bears a close relation to the vigor of its leader. A leader who is old in spirit tends to create around him an organization from which the fires of enthusiasm are gradually burning out."[4] The fires of enthusiasm were beginning to burn brightly in spite of the darkness of the times. At this time, I vividly recalled the statement: *THE SMART MAN IS NOT THE MAN WHO CAN DO TEN MEN'S WORK. RATHER, THE SMART MAN IS THE MAN WHO CAN ORGANIZE TEN MEN TO DO THE WORK OF TEN MEN.*

The task appeared gigantic. Envisioned was a church with a sanctuary that would seat 350 people. We had faith to believe that it could be done. It was Emerson who declared: "They conquer who believe they can. Do the thing you fear and the death of fear is certain."[5] We began to take stock of our assets, believing that "There are infinite possibilities if God is in them."[6]

1. Our congregation consisted of 50 beautiful people who were very dedicated and highly respected in the community.
2. A large lot, in a nice residential area, had been given to the Church.
3. One member, Manager of a local store, was unusually gifted in the area of creative ideas.
4. Another member was a skilled carpenter and builder.
5. Another source of strength was our elderly, retired German farmer.
6. Yet another was a quiet man employed by the Railroad; father of seven children, committed to the task of helping to provide a suitable church facility for his family.

It was time to organize and to utilize *ALL* of our resources. We must act while the momentum was rising.

Harry Lytle, Manager of the Duckwall Store, was a great sales leader and a very successful organizer. He suggested a project that would accomplish a threefold purpose: (1) Distribute little paperbank churches throughout the community, thus acquainting the city with the fact that we were planning to build a new church. (2) Secure the Boy Scouts to distribute and to collect the banks. This would further advertise our project and would enlist the participation of these energetic young men. (3) Ask the families who accepted the "Little Churches" to deposit an offering each week, for six weeks, in the paper banks. Although we knew that the funds received through this project would not be large, we felt that the participation and goodwill of the community would be of inestimable value. When the little banks were collected and the Building Committee met to open them, it took some time to count all the small change. Perhaps there never had been such a large penny offering. The total amount of money received was slightly over $34, but this was a BEGIN-NING—we were MOVING. The community was talking about the project, the congregation was building momentum, and the pastor remembered a slogan from his college days: *NOTHING SUCCEEDS LIKE SUCCESS!* The Board of Trustees and the entire membership were asking: "Where do we go from here?"

The next step was to establish a building fund, and to decide on the size of the building and on the type of structure it would be. It was my responsibility to help the congregation to *THINK BIG*, and to *BELIEVE* that their goal could be realized. It was an enthusiastic group that met on the building site for a simple "Ground-Breaking" ceremony. Another of our resources was a lady who was a talented musician; as she accompanied the songs on her piano accordion, the beautiful music inspired the hearts of all who were present. Now, we would need manpower to excavate a 40 by 60 basement. Should the pastor volunteer to man a shovel, or should he go into the city and hire 10 men to come and work while he returned to places of business and homes of friends and members, securing the money with which to pay them at the close of the day? Again, the deep and cruel depression was upon us; there were scores and scores of men on the streets unemployed. Remembering my theory of leadership and organization, I would secure 10 men to work on the church while I secured the funds with which to pay them. Our proposition to these men was to pay them $2 a day, $1 in cash and $1 credited as a donation on the new church. In addition, they would receive a hot meal at noon, furnished and served by the ladies of the church. It was an easy matter to secure the men. They were thrilled with an opportunity to be meaningfully employed in the building of a church and to have something with which to feed their families. Securing the needed funds each day was not so easy, but the men were never disappointed. Momentum continued to increase as more and more people participated in the project. WE WERE BUILDING A CHURCH.

As the work progressed, interest in the project grew. A stonemason, a master craftsman, volunteered his services on the same basis as the other men. The quarry donated the stone for the basement walls, and the stonemason supervised the laying of it. In addition, he chiseled a beautiful cornerstone to be imbedded in the foundation. Another friend, with a little Model T truck, volunteered to haul the stone from the quarry if the church would pay for the gas and oil. The funds brought in by the Boy Scouts was designated for this purpose. The day came for the laying of the cornerstone. Scores of members and friends lifted their voices in praise with the accompaniment of Vina's accordion. Prayers of thanksgiving were offered. The tide of enthusiasm was rising.

It was now time for the Building Committee to come to grips with a major decision: how to proceed further and how to obtain the necessary funds? The weekly building fund offering was increasing. There were new families becoming involved in the church. Several Army Personnel, from nearby Fort Riley, were adding their interest and support to the project. Our own carpenter and builder offered his services at a very minimal wage to supervise construction. However, the Lumber Company had declined to extend credit for the dimensional lumber, and the banks had taken the position that a church project was a poor credit risk. This was a time when all of the motivational forces in leadership were needed.

In early spring, a mobile sawmill moved into the area and set up its operation along the Republican River. The creative force of ideas was at work. Why not discuss with the owners of the sawmill the possibility of securing our dimensional lumber from the cottonwood trees along the river? The contact was made and, after a time of calculating their costs, they offered to furnish all of the dimensional material needed for the sum of $325 cash. The man with the Model T truck would transport the lumber to our building site, and the men and youth from the church would be organized to stake down and cure the green lumber lest it curl up and return to the river. While the summer sun was curing the lumber, the stimulating force of optimism was at work. I was responsible for securing the funds necessary to pay for the lumber. In these days of extreme inflation and runaway prices, the sum of $325 seems almost insignificant, but not so in 1935. Mr. Schmutz, our retired farmer, offered to pay $100 if we were successful in securing the entire amount. Mr. Peterson, the father of a large family, offered to borrow $100 on his home in order to help insure the erection of the church. Others gave lesser amounts, and a joyful congregation saw this obligation paid in full.

Our goal of completing the project within the year kept driving us forward. By this time, the Manager of the City Lumber Company realized that a church was going to be built without his help or without any profit to his business. The banks could see that there was an organizational force at work in the project that assured its success. The materials necessary for completing the building were offered by the Lumber Company on credit. The funds necessary for a furnace and other fixtures were made possible through a loan by one of the banks. Genuine enthusiasm, plus wisdom and experience, was producing a *MIRACLE*. The powerful force of organization was assuring Victory! Literally, scores and even hundreds had given of their *time, talents, labor,* and *money,* in order to see this beautiful church completed.

We had achieved our goal. The day of Dedication was announced. Invitations were sent to all who had participated in the project. The District Superintendent was invited to give the dedicatory message. This would indeed be a time of celebration. As the day drew near, the temperature in Central Kansas plummeted. With a forecast for sub-zero weather, the District Superintendent suggested that it would be wise to postpone the service, since few would brave such bitter weather to attend. We felt that this would be a colossal mistake, since hundreds of personal invitations had been sent out.

The "Day of Dedication" dawned crisp and clear. The thermometer stood at 14 degrees below zero. The hour of service had been set at 3 o'clock in the afternoon. The local florists had sent lovely floral arrangements to add to the beauty of the sanctuary. The District Superintendent was utterly amazed as we entered the church to find it filled to capacity with over 500 people present. This fact alone gave evidence of the powerful force of organization in leadership. The service was simple, dignified, and beautiful. A dedicatory offering of $500 was received, which enabled the congregation to dedicate their church very nearly debt-free.

The organizational force that was set in motion as the Boy Scouts distributed the little paper banks throughout the city continued to direct and motivate throughout the entire project. The proposition that *the smart leader is not the leader who can do the work of ten persons, but the leader who can organize ten persons to do the work of ten persons,* had proven valid. ORGANIZATION is a powerful tool that every leader must use with the skill of a master craftsman. This is true in business and industry, as well as in corporations and institutions.

We have illustrated this principle as it worked on a rather small scale and at an extremely difficult economic period. Now, let us enlarge our proposition from that of 10 persons to 100 persons, or even 1,000 persons. Again, from personal experience, I have proven this to be true. The setting is a Liberal Arts College in Illinois. I assumed the Presidency in 1949. It was a church college, and the sponsoring denomination had been generous in its support. Full accreditation had been achieved in 1956, and the enrollment was increasing rapidly. As we entered the decade of the "sixties," the dire need of a College Center building and a Science Facility was pressing in upon us. During the "fifties" we had erected a Library and three large Dormitories. We recognized the need, but we had established a policy to fully fund all nonrevenue-producing buildings before construction could begin. We were now thinking in terms of millions rather than dimes and dollars.

The Board of Trustees had authorized the construction of both buildings. The College Center could be largely financed through government funds. It would need to be a facility that could serve the needs of a student body of 2,500. We wanted it to be functional and yet a thing of beauty. We believed that our architects could design such a building. However, I determined to make priority "Number One" the Science Complex.

Much time was devoted to a study of the needs of the Natural Science Division. The science facilities of many colleges and universities were visited. Notes were taken on the superior features and equipment of these facilities. The findings were shared with the Building Committee and with the Architects. The first drawings were unacceptable, for they did not embody many of the innovative ideas and features that had been reported. The President, the Natural Science Division, the Faculty, and the Board of Trustees were all deeply involved in this project. After further study, which included a first-hand observation by the Architects of several facilities that had been visited, plans were submitted that would care for the needs of over 2,000 students. The preliminary drawings were exciting and included a Planetarium. Once the architect's plans had been approved, the price tag for these plans weighed heavily upon the Board of Trustees and their President. In 1964, $2,250,000 loomed quite as large as $2,250 in 1934. It should be noted that this Church College had never raised $1,000,000 in any of its previous drives for capital funds.

The President and the Board of Trustees began to consider ways, means, and plans to meet this challenge. It meant that, if successful,

1,000 college students would attend classes and utilize the laboratories in this facility every day that the College was in session. This would mean that a constant stream of doctors, nurses, scientists, and teachers would flow from this facility. This gave inspiration to our task. The plan adopted was as follows:

The Educational Zone would raise $1,250,000.
The President's Club would raise $300,000.
The city of Kankakee would raise $200,000.
A Federal Grant of $500,000 would be secured for the
    Planetarium.

It was a great plan, but it had to be organized, stimulated, and set into motion. The powerful force of organization must be utilized. The lessons of past years were most helpful. Now was the time to organize 100 people, or more, to do the work necessary to achieve our goal. The ball was in my court, and the next move was up to me. *DECISION MAKING* and *TIMING* were of prime importance. To gain perspective for this Herculean task, it seemed wise to spend 10 days in tropical Florida, resting and getting the organizational machinery ready for action.

As we neared the close of our vacation, my thoughts were continually upon this overwhelming project. One night I awakened with this thought burning in my mind and heart. It caused me to roll and toss. We must succeed, but it would not be easy to raise the necessary funds for building and equipment. Science equipment is very costly. Finally, my thoughts began to zero-in on my special task to raise $300,000 through the "President's Club." In previous projects we had personally given $1,000. This would not be sufficient for this much larger project. It was evident to me that night that my friends would plan their giving quite in relationship to mine. This caused me to roll and toss all the more, for we must reach our goal if we were to expect the others groups to reach theirs. After a troubled night, my decision was made; I would personally, at great sacrifice, pledge $10,000. This would enable me to seek out 29 more to join me in the "President's Club."

Immediately upon our return to the campus, an organizational pattern was put into action. First, I would invite five prosperous and dedicated Alumni to be my guests for a steak dinner at the local hotel. All kindly responded. After an enjoyable meal, we retired to a private room where we could discuss the "Science Building" project. Some had been science majors and were painfully aware of our great need for an adequate science facility. They were all young and were doing well financially. For two hours I poured out my heart to these successful young Executives, one of whom was a Physician. We talked and we prayed. They called their wives and, as we parted, they gave me five pledge cards which totaled $50,000. This was the breakthrough needed to assure success. At early breakfasts, late luncheons, and delightful dinners, this story was retold and assisted in the securing of additional pledges for $10,000 to $50,000. Soon this segment of the total amount was underwritten. The stimulating force of optimism was propelling the project forward. The good news of success was being told in the Churches, at Zone Conventions, in District Assemblies, to Chambers of Commerce and Business Groups, and it was being shared with Alumni Chapters worldwide.

While this was in process, the organization of 800 pastors and 200 laymen, along with 42 enthusiastic Trustees, was being superbly directed by Vice-President Gibson and his able assistant, Ruth Anderson. The principle of the organizational force was utilized to the full. Hundreds, even thousands, had become involved in this exciting project. Every segment of the master financial plan was succeeding. Our goal of $2,250,000 was in sight.

Contracts were let for both of these major buildings in May of 1964. The timing was right. We were able to get excellent bids. Both were to be completed in 1966. Beautiful "Ludwig Center" was dedicated in the spring of that year. Magnificent "Reed Hall of Science," including a Planetarium, was dedicated, debt-free, in September of 1966.

The dynamic principle of the *POWERFUL FORCE OF ORGAN-IZATION* had again been utilized in leadership. The successful leader must be able not only to organize but to carry that organization through to the achieving of his goals. Very few are ever given the privilege of captaining an organization of All-Stars, but the skillful leader is the one who can organize what he has, wherever he is, to do what needs to be done. It should always be remembered that the leader who can organize 10 people demonstrates greater leadership than the one who attempts to do the work of 10. In fact, the leader who tries to do the work of 10 may be a menace to the enterprise, since the involvement of others is vital to almost every endeavor.

THE SMART LEADER IS NOT THE LEADER WHO
TRIES TO DO THE WORK OF ONE HUNDRED

PEOPLE—BUT—THE SMART LEADER IS THE
LEADER WHO CAN ORGANIZE ONE HUNDRED
PEOPLE TO DO THE WORK OF ONE HUNDRED
PEOPLE.

Part IV

THE HEART OF
THE MATTER

Hold fast to dreams, for if dreams die, life is a broken winged bird that cannot fly.

—Langston Hughes

A DREAMER LIVES FOR ETERNITY.

19.

The Basics of Leadership

IF THE ESSENCE OF LEADERSHIP IS THE ABILITY TO
LEAD—AND
IF THE WORLD STANDS ASIDE TO LET PASS THE LEADER
WHO KNOWS WHITHER HE IS GOING—
A CLEAR UNDERSTANDING OF THE DYNAMICS OF LEAD-
ERSHIP IS IMPERATIVE.

Almost every study of the secret of the successful leader has agreed that the possession of a generous and unusual endowment of physical and nervous energy is essential to leadership ascendency. Those who rise in any marked way above the mass of aspiring leaders have conspicuously more drive, more sheer endurance, and greater vigor of body and mind than the average person. "The leader is entitled, if not required, to invest his cause with some excitement and glamor. The energy displayed in espousing it is a big factor in this glamor."[1] To keep one's organism at "concert pitch" requires an adequate understanding of the health factor. An excellent definition of "health" is set forth by Ernst van Aaken:

199

> *Health is a constantly changing, multi-faceted sensation with feelings of freshness, endurance, comfort, strength and performance capacity . . . with optimistic, reliable vigor, mental and emotional strength, and a strong life of the soul.*
>
> *Health consists of a rhythmic rise and fall, a kind of dance of life. It is not static but full of movement, and it has to be re-won, maintained and heightened daily, through the years and decades, up to highest old age. Health is not an average but a heightened norm, an individual's highest achievement. It is the will become visible, the strength of will expressed as durability.*[2]

As I see it, there are three great things which have much to do with supplying us with energy for our task. We can energize ourselves through a great cause, a great inspiration, or a great confidence.

LEADERSHIP:
    THE ABILITY TO LEAD.
    THE ABILITY TO CREATE AND PERSUADE.
    CONCILIATION—EDUCATION—PATIENCE.

According to the late Dwight D. Eisenhower, "It is long, slow, hard work." Some believe that leadership has to be persuasive rather than authoritarian, inspirational rather than arbitrary, based on proclamation rather than on defense. But what are some of the fundamental components of the Leader who demonstrates the ability to lead?

First, I would list *COMPETENCE.* This includes intelligence—native intelligence but more "effective intelligence." It also includes knowledge—multi-dimensional knowledge of what one does (the business one is in), and more broadly, an awareness of the environment, in the economy, in the society, and at a point in history. By competence, we mean forward thinking, imaginative ideas, and creative approaches to problems—a creative competence.

Second, *AN ARTICULATE SET OF VALUES.* This refers to the underpinning of life supports, such as inner drives, faith, and deep commitments. It includes honesty, dependability, and responsibility, and a sense of high ideals. This commitment is basic to a belief in the sacredness of human personality, both on the part of the leader himself and on behalf of those whom he leads. It includes, above all, having humane interests, signifying not fragility and weakness, but a commitment to human ends and a serenity that comes from having made peace between the heart and the mind, a depth of sensitivity that brings idealism and action into harmony.

Third, *DIRECTION.* Is there a clear concept as to where the leader wants to go? A story is told regarding a race sponsored by the Knights of Columbus. "The Annual Ten-Mile Race, at Quincy, Massachusetts, got off to an excellent start. The leading runners had already reached the first turn. 'Hey, that's the wrong way!' shouted two boys standing at the corner. Uncertain as to where they were going, the hard-pressed runners grasped at the youngsters' directions. But, what appeared to be the 'right way' found the entire field of forty athletes piled up in a dead-end street. Exasperated officials decided to call the race off until the following week."[3] Direction is a combination of understanding where the goal is located, and the strategy for reaching the goal. In other words, it is a combination of being goal-centered and strategy-minded.

The fourth essential is *SPIRIT.* H. W. Johnson defines spirit as "a combination of personal curiosity, enthusiasm and physical energy that welcomes challenge and accepts risk-taking ventures with a cheerful attitude."[4] It is an inner drive—deep and strong. It is the result of abundant health of body, mind, and spirit. LET SPIRIT COME ALIVE! Spirit provides an element of mystery and yet has a remarkable assurance and certainty.

These four fundamental components—COMPETENCE, ARTICULATE SET OF VALUES, DIRECTION, and SPIRIT—can make possible leadership possessed of the signs of the extraordinary.

In the techniques of creative thinking we use both science and art. It is true that every art develops techniques in order to give it acceptable effects. This is certainly true, to a great extent, in the exercise of leadership. There is a sense in which leadership is both a science and an art. As a science its very essence is what is usually called scientific management. It is vastly important to understand the various building blocks which are utilized in building the basics of leadership. Moreover, it is of tremendous import that the leader be able to take these basics of leadership and mold them into a work of art. For a master of the craft of leadership there is a variety of methods which may be used in the exertion of that leadership. Furthermore, the master craftsman must be able to consciously use the tools of his craft in order to blend the FOUR BASICS OF LEADER-

SHIP, which we shall now consider, into the personality of the master leader.

I. A PHILOSOPHY OF LIFE

You may think that a philosophy of life is irrelevant to the best in leadership, but I would strongly disagree. Again, let me say, your philosophy of life colors the type of leadership which you embrace. If your philosophy of life is to win at all costs, your leadership will be tainted by dishonesty. It will be of an inferior quality. Adolph Hitler accepted a philosophy of "Rule or Ruin." Millions were killed under his ruthless dictatorship. His philosophy of life was responsible for the direction of his leadership.

On the other hand, Abraham Lincoln had a philosophy of life which embraced the position that "Honesty is the best policy." This was extended to all of his activities and gave guidance to his philosophy of leadership. The late golf immortal, Walter Hagen, stated his philosophy very simply, "You're only here on a short visit—make sure you smell the flowers." And as he ambled merrily through a productive and fun-filled life of over 70 years, Hagen managed to smell a lot of flowers. He was the winner of two U.S. Opens, four British Opens, and five PGA Championships.

Yes, the quality of your leadership is largely determined by your philosophy of life. Your philosophy of life gives color and depth of shade as well as direction to your leadership. Perhaps, sharing with you my personal experience in reaching a philosophy of life will help to make this *basic of leadership* more meaningful.

It was in my senior year at Colorado College, Colorado Springs, Colorado. We were nearing the time of graduation. The President of the College, the late Doctor Mierow, called me into his office. He had a graduate scholarship for me. However, it had been requested that I formulate my philosophy of life and submit it to him in writing. Up until that time I had thought of a philosophy of life as something that would give ballast and direction to life, something that would be reliable for the long-distance run. Now, I must write out a statement which would incorporate these elements into my life. It must be a solid philosophy which would stand life's strain and stress. Yes, it must be able to stand the severe tests of life.

Several days later it came clear to me—just as if it had been written for me and for no other person. It was a familiar verse of scripture. It was *my* verse. From this time forth, Romans 8:28 would be *my guiding light.*

And we know that all things work together for good to them that love God, to them who are called according to his purpose.[5]

This verse assured me of Providential Guidance! It suggested a Divine Partnership which would not fail! It was an exciting philosophy of life!

However, immediately came the question: Will it work? Will it work when life gets hard? Will it work when you are confronted with life's real tests and stresses? Will it work when sickness strikes you down? By faith, I would believe and stand fast on this solid rock for a lifetime. It has worked! It is still my philosophy of life!

For several years the Senior class at the College where I served as President requested that I meet with them as a group and share with them my philosophy of life. Over a period of years it was my privilege to speak to successive classes on this basic fundamental of leadership. I emphasized to them that my philosophy had enabled me many times to wrench victory from what seemed to be utter defeat. I told them of how my philosophy had been tested over a period of years:

the test of a closed door—
the test of serious illness—cancer—
the test of multiple open doors—
the test of dreaded polio—
the test of moving an Institution—
the test of a high-level post in Higher Education.

Through it all, my philosophy of life had held me steady; it had given me ballast.

It had given me direction.
It had given me assurance and courage.
It had given me poise and confidence to believe that *"All things work together for good."*

Yes, my philosophy of life was sane. It was meaningful. It was a "Gibralter" upon which to build my philosophy of leadership. Let me repeat it again: *The quality of one's leadership is largely determined by one's philosophy of life.*

What is your philosophy of life? Is it strong as Gibralter? It must be if it is to stand the crucial tests of time and the storms of life.

II. A PHILOSOPHY OF LEADERSHIP

The second essential in the basics of leadership is a well defined philosophy of leadership. A superficial attempt to substitute "the tricks of the trade" for a thorough study of leadership will not do. The greatest need in our world today is for great and good leaders. The greatest need in these United States is for leadership, men and women of integrity. The greatest need in Government, at every level, is for tall leaders who are truly statesmen, leaders who give their best interests and highest priority to their nation.

The greatest need of business and industry is for keen and honest leaders who can lift the economic level of their countries. The greatest need of the Church World today is for a steady stream of dedicated and growing leaders, with a world vision, equipped for a powerful ministry. The greatest need in the several professions is for truly committed leaders who sincerely serve their fellow men. These leaders are not "born leaders," THEY ARE MADE. *Yes, they are made—not born.* Some are endowed with five talents, some with two talents, while others have only one. Thus, they have potential in varying degrees. However, through a thorough understanding of the basics of leadership, that potential can be increased.

Charles Arthur Nelson, in his book entitled *Developing Responsible Public Leaders,* tells of corresponding with 52 leading Americans and asking the question: "Is there a leadership crisis?" Their answers were an emphatic "YES." There were none who thought in terms of "business as usual." Courses in "Leadership" should be priority No. 1 in our great centers of learning. By this, I am not referring to such specialized courses as "Business or Educational Leadership," nor to such courses as "Church Management," nor to the many courses that are offered on "Management." These are helpful, but they do not go deep enough.

To have an adequate philosophy of leadership, one must have a thorough understanding of the various theories of leadership. Thus, our second basic of leadership is a study, at some depth, of at least eight of these theories. We have dealt with these at length in Part II. However, we wish to state them again, briefly and succinctly, so that the aspiring leader may bring together, in a logical manner, these important theories of leadership.

1. THE GREAT MAN THEORY. This theory of leadership was propounded by Thomas Carlyle and was the first such theory to be presented in a systematic manner. It was the first to be fully formulated and quite fully understood by the educated populace. This view accepted the position that leadership was a great gift to the chosen few. In this theory, the focus is upon the personality of the leader.

2. THE FOLLOWER THEORY. This theory suggests that *faithful followership* is responsible for leadership. The alert and consistent follower eventually becomes the leader. In reality he earns a place of leadership. Thus, the thesis of this position assumes that the only road to leadership is through the gateway of followership. This theory, also, accepts the view that followership is focused upon the personality of the leader.

3. THE SITUATIONIST THEORY. This view is an environmental approach. There are certain environmental factors which work to the leader's advantage, while in other instances the environmental factors greatly restrict what he is able to accomplish. This is true for the leader as he is faced by society. He is often restricted by both people and environment. On the other hand, these factors may give to the leader special opportunities for development. This view passes over personality traits and seems to mostly feel the grip of environmental forces.

4. THE CREATIVE ARTIST THEORY. This view considers the artist as a leader and the leader as an artist. "Creative leadership emerges when a personality becomes the propulsive force for a value or complex of values, or in certain circumstances for a systematic program, rallying about himself a group of men which on a small or a vast scale creates a stronger pressure than can emanate from any individual."[6] The path breakers of the early Italian Renaissance discovered the paramount importance, in architecture, sculpture, and painting, of an eye-satisfying proportion between the various components of a work of art. The German reformers developed the doctrine of "Justification by Faith," which liberated the layman from the priest and gave him immediate access to a personal God. Externally the strength of the creative leader is embodied in the followers who gather about them. Their distinctive mark, in contrast to other leaders, is the creativeness of their work.

Not only does the creative artist affect the period of his own time, or his own century, but in many cases his leadership influences the continuing centuries.

5. THE INTIMIDATION THEORY. This view emphasizes the personality traits of this type of leader. He achieves his desired goal through influence, fear, power, threats, agitation, warnings, persuasion, sweet talk, gifts, and sometimes by raw force. Intimidation is a powerful force which is for the most part totally incompatible with true leadership. It is a type of leadership that we all have witnessed and a type which we all should deplore.

6. THE LUCKY-BREAK THEORY. This philosophy of leadership believes in fate. It posits the view that either the leader is born under a lucky star or the stars are against him. Leo Tolstoy believed, as many of us do, that there is no such thing as chance. He reasoned that each event, small or large, "is linked by a thousand subtle chains to all other events. We, who cannot see the linkage, cry chance. Thus, to the fallible eye of man luck rather than destiny seems at moments to operate."[7]

7. THE CONJUNCTURE THEORY. This scholarly theory is thought by many, including this writer, to be the most complete philosophy of leadership which has been formulated. Consequently, every leader should be informed of it. It is because of this fact that The Reed Institute for the Advanced Study of Leadership was established in 1976. The "Conjuncture Theory" brings together three very important elements, which become tools for the interpretive play in leadership situations. This philosophy fully recognizes that *personality traits* are an important element in leadership. It further recognizes that the *physical and social environment* is an important factor every time and in every place that leadership is exhibited. The third powerful factor is that of *event.* An event is thought of as a noteworthy happening. As these three mighty forces unite, or converge, there ensues or flows out from them, leadership. The effective leader is the one who masters an understanding of these three elements, or factors, which flow together, and in so doing produces leadership, or the act of leading.

The leader who is able to keenly interpret his own *personality traits,* understand fully the *physical and social environment,* and to interpret them correctly in the light of the *event* or *events* which occur, is in a position to exercise leadership in a superb manner. I am persuaded that this theory of leadership can give both understanding and depth of insight into the problems faced by every leader. It is my reasoned judgment that by taking advantage of these principles, every leader has the possibility of increasing the effectiveness of his leadership by a wide margin.

8. THE REED THEORY. It was Sir Isaac Newton who once said: "If I seem to see farther than others, it is because I stand on the shoulders of Giants." If this eighth theory has merit, it is because of my association with the late Doctor Clarence Marsh Case and the impact that his "Conjuncture Theory of Leadership" has had upon my own life and leadership. However, I believe that there are two additional factors which play vital roles in the art of leadership. The prime importance of *Decision Making* and *Timing* cannot be over-emphasized. These elements, or tools, are basic in leadership. They are of utmost use for the leader who knows what he wants, what he must have, and what he must do, if he is to utilize the science of leadership.

Moreover, as the leader masters the elements of decision making and timing, he becomes more adept in understanding what he can do at a particular time and what the result will be under the present, past, or future conditions. There is a time to seize an opportunity, and there is a time when it might even be catastrophic to act. In the words of Marcus Brutus, in *Julius Caesar:*

> *There is a tide in the affairs of men,*
> *Which, taken at the flood, leads on to fortune;*
> *Omitted, all the voyage of their life*
> *Is bound in shallows and in miseries.*
> *On such a full sea are we now afloat;*
> *And we must take the current when it serves,*
> *Or lose our ventures.* [8]

Great intelligence cannot be effective without timing. Timing scans the horizon for the most apropos time to make the important move, and decision making determines that now is the best time, or that it is the wrong time, to make that move.

My philosophy of leadership fully embraces the "Conjuncture Theory." However, it is the extension of this theory to include the elements of *decision making* and *timing*, that gives to me a philosophy of leadership which I feel is totally adequate.

III. THE MOTIVATIONAL FORCES

Comprehending and utilizing the motivational forces that are at the disposal of every leader is basic to leadership. Only those persons with *Vision*, with *Ideas*, with *Goals*, with *Enthusiasm*, with *Optimism*, and with the art of *Organization* can hope to be effective leaders.

VISION sees what needs to be done.
IDEAS reinforce that vision.
GOALS extend the horizon of our dreams.
ENTHUSIASM sets afire our desire to achieve.
OPTIMISM says: "IT CAN BE DONE!"
ORGANIZATION devises ways and means of getting it done.

It is not enough for a leader to have defined his philosophy of life and to have embraced an adequate philosophy of leadership— these are basic to the best in leadership—but he *must fully understand, and utilize*, the dynamic forces that motivate.

IV. A SENSE OF MISSION

It is of vital importance that the leader possess *a sense of mission*. This is a powerful ingredient in the life of every truly great leader. It leads one ever onward and upward; moreover, it drives one to reach his goals. It is a full commitment of all of one's talents and energies, and a definite focus upon his objective or objectives. It is the thrust of dedicated personality.

A sense of mission demands the declaration: "I must." It was present in the life of Jesus Christ. "I must needs go through Samaria," and again, "I must work while it is day." It is the strong sense of oughtness. *Basic to the best in leadership is a strong sense of mission.*

This sense of mission was very evident in the life of Peter the Great, Emperor of Russia (1772-1825). He passionately believed in leadership training. The secret of his extraordinary success lay in the fact that he organized an informal, but highly effective, training system for preparing young men who would serve his revolutionary purposes. He was determined that at whatever cost, hardship, or inconvenience, Russia should be ruled by Russians. Before his death, every important place in the Empire was in the hands of capable Russians of his own training. Peter the Great was possessed of that sense of mission which would not accept a lesser goal for his people or for his Empire.

Florence Nightingale, the Lady of the Lamp, at the age of 31, had tired of her life of travel, wealth, and friends. She cried out, "My God! What is to become of me? Let me do something! Give me some mission in life."[9] Her prayer was answered, and she lit a lamp which will blaze for all time. As a ministering Angel, her long and honored service to the sick and to the dying was both vertical and horizontal—"Duty toward God" and "Compassion for Man"—with the vertical inspiring and sustaining the horizontal. It is doubtful that the leadership of Florence Nightingale, in the ministry of healing, would have ever reached such heights if she had not possessed this sense of mission.

Many of those who have felt this deep sense of "mission," this driving sense of "oughtness," have also sensed their own human inadequacy to fulfill that mission. It has been said that Saint Augustine was "the man the Roman Empire had come to regard as the most brilliant of his era, the aristocrat of theologians, the prince of philosophers, the most compassionate of pastors, the most human of preachers, in his generation the noblest Roman of them all."[10] Yet this dynamic leader often prayed for wisdom, strength, and guidance.

Another who felt his own inadequacy, as his sense of mission thrust him into a place of grave responsibility, was General George Washington. The touching and inspiring painting of General Washington kneeling in the snow at Valley Forge, as he prayed for Divine assistance, portrays to us a source of help and strength for leaders whose mission at times seems to overwhelm them.

My friend, have you ever watched a great leader who was totally given over to his task? A leader whose whole life was submerged in reaching high and purposeful goals? One who was being driven from within by a passionate sense of mission? And now, let me ask, are you possessed by a strong sense of mission? Is there a sense of "oughtness" as you see your task, your assignment, your goals? Would that every leader, whether in business or industry, in government or the professions, in education or religion, in community, state, and nation, were possessed with *a sense of mission*.

"It is not the critic who counts. The credit belongs to the man who is actually in the arena, whose face is marred by dust and sweat and blood, who strives valiantly, who errs and comes short again and again, because there is not effort without error and shortcoming, but who does actually strive to do the deeds, who knows the great enthusiasms, the great devotions, who spends himself in a worthy cause, who at the best knows in the end the triumphs of high achievement and who at the worst, if he fails, at least fails while daring greatly, so that his place shall never be with those cold and timid souls who know neither victory nor defeat."[11] It has been said concerning the late William Randolph Hearst that he lacked a consuming purpose in life, a dedication to a great cause. "The tragedy of Hearst was that he had all the equipment for first-rank eminence except the most vital ingredient of all. He was a Rembrandt struck color-blind, a Stradivarius out of tune."[12]

Would that every leader were so possessed with this basic of leadership, *this sense of mission*, that it would never be said: "Mission Scrubbed," or "Mission Impossible," but rather—"MISSION ACCOMPLISHED!"

What then are some of the basic qualities of an effective leader?

INTELLIGENCE
INITIATIVE
INTEREST
INTEGRITY
IMAGINATION
LOYALTY
ENERGY
ENTHUSIASM — (The Mainspring of the Soul)

What are the fundamental components necessary for leadership?

COMPETENCE
ARTICULATE SET OF VALUES
DIRECTION
SPIRIT — (Let Spirit Come Alive!)

What are the four *Basics of Leadership?*

A PHILOSOPHY OF LIFE
A PHILOSOPHY OF LEADERSHIP
UNDERSTANDING AND UTILIZING THE MOTIVATIONAL FORCES
A SENSE OF MISSION

An old Chinese proverb says: "A journey of a thousand miles begins with a single step." Likewise, the quest for the art of leadership begins with the basic factors which we have just considered. LEADERSHIP IS THE KEY TO SUCCESS—LET IT OPEN THE DOOR FOR YOU.

20.

Impossible Dreams That Live!

SOME MEN DREAM ONLY OF THE PAST.
 SOME SEE ONLY THE PRESENT AND SAY, "WHY?"
  OTHERS DREAM OF THINGS THAT NEVER WERE,
  AND SAY, "WHY NOT?"

          —Martin Luther King, Jr.

"Hold fast to dreams, for if dreams die, life is a broken winged bird that cannot fly."[1] What if Thomas Edison had listened to those who cried, *"Impossible,"* when he dreamed of an *"incandescent bulb"* that could illumine the world? Today, darkness has been turned into light; night has been turned into day: An IMPOSSIBLE DREAM THAT LIVES!

In his book, *A Time for Truth,* William E. Simon states that, "we have too many efficient technocrats and too few far-sighted visionaries."[2] Without these far-sighted visionaries, MAN WOULD NEVER HAVE WALKED ON THE MOON; THE SPACE SHUTTLE WOULD NEVER HAVE LEAPED INTO THE HEAVENS, with a thunderous roar, on April 12, 1981. IMPOSSIBLE DREAMS THAT LIVE!

Early in my career, the Chairman of the Board of Trustees presented to me a framed copy of a poem which has hung on the wall of my office across the years. Edgar A. Guest, in his homespun style, tells of his response to the cry: *IMPOSSIBLE!*

> *Somebody said that it couldn't be done, but he with a chuckle replied that 'maybe it couldn't,' but he would be one who wouldn't say so till he'd tried. So he buckled right in with the trace of a grin.... If he worried, he hid it. He started to sing as he tackled the thing that couldn't be done, and he did it.*

> *Somebody scoffed: 'Oh, you'll never do that; at least no one ever has done it.' ... There are thousands to prophesy failure; there are thousands to point out to you one by one, the dangers that wait to assail you. But just buckle in with a bit of a grin, take off your coat and go to it; just start in to sing as you tackle the thing that 'CANNOT BE DONE' and YOU'LL DO IT.*[3]

These words bring hope and courage to the *Dreamer of Impossible Dreams.*

While I was a young man in High School, a statement from Ralph Waldo Emerson was forcefully impressed upon my mind: "HITCH YOUR WAGON TO A STAR."[4] Coupled with this star studded vision were the more sobering words of Abraham Lincoln: "I will study and prepare myself and when my time comes I will be ready."[5] These thoughts stirred in my brain as I worked in the field to earn money toward a college education. The cultivator stirred the soil but great thoughts were stirring my heart and mind:

DREAMS of Higher Education.
DREAMS of World Travel.
DREAMS of Dedicated Service to God and Youth.
IMPOSSIBLE DREAMS for one who had no financial backing and no social advantage.

During my college days, at Colorado College, the late President Mierow challenged me to complete my college work; to press on and secure a Master's degree, and then to continue on until I had earned the Ph.D. degree. IMPOSSIBLE! How was I to finance these years at the University? But Lincoln had said: "Prepare yourself," and

Emerson had said: "Hitch your wagon to a Star." Dare to attempt the impossible. As my College President encouraged me, secretly I dared to dream of the day when I, too, would be highly educated and the President of a prestigious College.

The years passed swiftly. Many things which "Couldn't Be Done," had become reality. Now, it was nearing the time that I had elected to retire from the Presidency of Olivet Nazarene College, fully recognized as a Mature Institution on the Master's level.

We were in Miami Beach, Florida.

The year was 1972.

It was the beautiful month of June.

Political and Religious Conventions flooded the City along with an abundance of wind and rain.

Our Church was in its International Quadrennial Assembly.

The eight Institutions of Higher Learning, supported by the Church, were having their Alumni Reunions. Olivet Nazarene College was one of the largest, and strongest, of these Institutions. Our Reunion was held in the Grand Ballroom of one of the beautiful hotels. The room was filled to capacity. An abundance of good food and delightful fellowship was in evidence at every table. Our talented and highly trained "Orpheus Choir" sang and thrilled every Alumnus.

It was my privilege to address this meeting of our illustrious Alumni. This was to be my last quadrennial message to the Alumni as their College President. It was a thrilling moment, and yet a little twinge of sadness was felt deeply in my heart. As I arose to speak, the joy and thrill of accomplishment over a period of 25 years flooded my mind and soul. My subject for the occasion: "DREAMS THAT LIVE." For 25 years I had dreamed, worked, and dreamed. A great part of that time it had seemed to be "The Impossible Dream." And then, slowly but surely, the dreams had become reality. The campus area had been increased to 150 acres. One by one, buildings arose, averaging better than one every two years.

1. Williams Hall—A residential hall for women.
2. Memorial Library—The academic center of the campus.
3. Nesbitt Hall—A dormitory for women.
4. Hills Hall—A residential hall for men.
5. Chalfant Hall—A large auditorium, seating over 2,000, to be used for convocations, chapel services, and concerts.

6. McClain Hall—Another dormitory for women.
7. President's Home—A spacious, older home situated on the Kankakee River.
8. Ludwig Center—A beautiful and functional College center.
9. Reed Hall of Science—A great Science complex including a Planetarium.
10. Howe Hall—A motel to serve as a housing unit.
11. Gibson Hall—An apartment-type housing unit.
12. Brodien Power Plant—A large heating facility to serve the entire campus.
13. Parrott Hall—Another residential hall for women.
14. Miller Hall—A former dining facility, totally renovated and made into the college business center.
15. Milby Memorial Clock Tower—A beautiful memorial to Tom Milby, whose father served with distinction as a Vice-President.
16. Wisner Nursing Education Building—One of the best, fully equipped, Nursing Education facilities in the State.
17. Benner Library and Learning Resources Center—A magnificent Learning and Computer Center, including Television Studios.

There was a student body numbering nearly 2,000. There was a Faculty of over 100, with approximately 50 holding earned Doctorates from prestigious Universities. Our financial structure was sound and our indebtedness small. Full accreditation by North Central Accrediting Association, on the Master's level, had just been granted for another 10-year period. Yes, it was a great day to speak on the subject: "DREAMS THAT LIVE."

Twenty-five years had flown by swiftly. They were good years. They were exciting years. They were challenging years, years of daring. They were years of dreaming and hard work. Satisfying years of achievement. Many seemingly insurmountable difficulties had become golden opportunities. Many "Impossible Dreams" had become realities. And yet, there were many other dreams which had not been fulfilled—future goals which had not yet been achieved, visions far beyond our present dreams:

1. The dream of a beautiful Fine Arts-Chapel Building that would have an auditorium to accommodate 3,500.
2. The dream of a great Field House with an arena that could accommodate 10,000.

3. The dream of an enlarged Endowment Fund to assure adequate salaries for the Faculty.
4. The dream of Olivet Nazarene University with a "School of Education," a "School of Theology," a "School of Business Education," and a "School of Medicine."

These dreams were living, pulsating, thrilling, and challenging. However, when the Trustees asked me to continue for another five-year term, my response was to accept the Presidency for only one more year. I felt then, as I do now, that I should conclude my Administration at the close of my twenty-sixth year. Having previously served as the President of Bresee College, Hutchinson, Kansas, for 4 years, I would have a total of 30 years in College Administration. Friends, meaning to be complimentary, would remark: "You have earned retirement. Now you can rest and take it easy." But, frankly, the thought of not being involved in dreaming, and causing those dreams to live, was not a pleasant thought.

Then, while on an intensive speaking tour in Brazil, South Africa, Zimbabwi, Kenya, and Swaziland, in the Spring of 1976, I began to dream once more. I had the dream of establishing an International Institute for the Advanced Study of Leadership. Again, this seemed to be an "Impossible Dream."

There were no buildings.
There was no Board of Directors.
There were no Academic Regents.
There was no definite source of finance.
There was no academic accreditation.
There was no pattern to give guidance, for this was an entirely new concept.

It was simply a dream and nothing more. But dreams that will fulfill a great need have a tendency to find a way, or ways, of realization.

Now, this dream is beginning to live. Within a three-year period:

A Home Office was established in the city of Kankakee, Illinois.
A splendid Board of Directors was organized.
A group of distinguished Academic Regents was selected.
The Institute was fully incorporated as a not-for-profit Institution in the State of Illinois.
Full recognition was granted by the Illinois State Department of Education. This means that up to nine hours of

upper-division or graduate credit may be granted through directed study.

With "Directors" and "Academic Regents" in Brazil, Kenya, and Japan, as well as in the United States, my dream that the Institute would be an International Institute, with a world outreach, is fast becoming a reality. One of the tentative "Ten-Year Goals," adopted by the Board of Directors, is to have International Satellite Offices.

The copyright for the document "Eight Theories of Leadership" has been secured. This is used in connection with Seminars and Directed Study.

Yes, we are still dreaming, for we are keenly aware of the *driving force of dreams* in leadership. Some of these dreams are:

THE DREAM OF CONTINUING EDUCATION ON A GRAND SCALE

According to the National Advisory Council on Education in its Professional Development's Report to the Congress: "The entire population of the United States should be seen as a national resource, a society in which continuous and meaningful learning becomes a way of life, and within a variety of circumstances and formats." The report claims that: "Approximately 101 million Americans are now part of a learning society. Comprising the learning society are citizens and youth who are pursuing some form of structured educational experience or who are directly connected with the educational process as teachers, administrators and professional staff, or as trustees and Board members of schools and colleges. This would include approximately 66 million students enrolled full or part-time in American schools and colleges, and an additional 32 million adults pursuing informal educational programs of all kinds."[6]

The report continues with a recommendation that a national goal be established to encourage all educable American adults to continue their education. The goal also is to promote ways to involve the approximately 98 million American adults now excluded from the new learning society as full participants. We certainly agree with these conclusions and also agree that it is necessary for there to be access to many options, both formal and informal.

The dream of continuing education on a grand scale is a tremendous challenge to every alert and committed educator. The opportunities to train for leadership are staggering in the light of the great need for leadership in every field of endeavor. The possibilities of research, seminars, symposiums, workshops, lectures, and directed study simply boggle the mind.

THE DREAM OF UNDERSTANDING AND TEACHING
THE FUNDAMENTALS OF LEADERSHIP
AT A DEEPER LEVEL

It was Victor Hugo who said: "Nothing in the world is so powerful as an idea whose time is come."[7] I believe that the idea of an Institute which deals with the fundamentals of leadership, at a deeper level, is *an idea whose time is come*. There are many who are talking about leadership, and some organizations seem to have a hazy idea of leadership; but for the most part, there is no clear-cut understanding, or definition, of the term. In a thorough check of several college and university libraries, I was unable to find 100 serious books on the subject of "Leadership." Most books on the general subject were meant to inspire or stimulate the individual by way of motivation.

Also, from my experience, college and university courses are usually limited to the teaching of leadership from the narrow perspective of a specific discipline. For the most part, they offer such courses as "Business Education," "Religious Education," or "Educational Administration." Obviously these courses have meaning for those who plan to enter these fields, but they are little more than learning "the tricks of the trade." That which deeply concerns me is the learning of those fundamentals which apply to every field of leadership. It was a great surprise to me to find that there were so few clearly stated "Philosophies of Leadership." We have endeavored to outline, with clarity and logic, eight theories, or philosophies, of leadership.

The greatest need in our world today is that of able leadership.

Leadership in Government.
Leadership in International Diplomacy.
Leadership in Education.
Leadership in the Professions.
Leadership in the Arts.
Leadership in Human Services.
Leadership in Business and Industry.

Leadership in Science and Technology.
Trained and Dedicated Leaders!
Stalwart and Sensitive Leaders!
Able and Growing Leaders!

Leaders are made—not born. Yes, LEADERS ARE MADE—
LEADERSHIP CAN BE TAUGHT. The Reed Institute for the Advanced Study of Leadership is dedicated to this task.

Still dreaming? Yes! Impossible dreams? No! He who fails to
dream will never realize high moments of achievement. While most
of the dreams which we have recounted have been personal, I wish
to call attention now to an "Impossible Dream That Lives" in the
great country of Brazil.

BRASILIA, A DREAM COME TRUE

As our Pan American Clipper made its descent through the
dazzling sunlight into the airport of Brasilia, we caught our first
glimpse of the new Capital of Brazil. It had been impressive from the
air; but later, as we drove down its broad boulevards, it was
breathtaking. The architectural scheme was as modern as tomorrow.
*How had this scintillating city come into existence in so short a
time?* In spite of a heavy speaking schedule, I determined to spend
as much time as possible in finding the answer to this question. I was
intrigued by the leadership that had made this dream a reality.

On a national and international level there are leaders who have
revolutionized their respective countries. Their great thrusts have
pushed their nations out of the ruts of the past and have launched
them out into a place of world influence. These leaders have been
possessed with impossible dreams, and they were made to live. Such
a dreamer was Juscelino Kubitschek, President of Brazil from 1956
until 1961.

Kubitschek was elected President of Brazil on a platform of rapid
economic development. He vowed to transfer the nation's Capital
from Rio de Janeiro on the coast to the site of Brasilia in the interior
of the country. He set forth a list of some 30 specific objectives which
he determined would be accomplished in his five-year term as President. These objectives were chiefly production goals which were to
be met by 1960. They were goals in the fields of transportation,
power, food, and basic industries. In fact, "Kubitschek insisted the
Republic must have daring, imaginative leadership with confidence

in the future, willing to spend heavily to develop domestic sources of energy, determined to create a vast network of roads and highways to unite the distant regions of the country, and prepared to supply the credits, tariff protection, and other incentives necessary to speed the growth of private industry. He promised that his program would give Brazil 'Fifty Years of Progress in Five.' "[8]

It seemed to be this slogan, "FIFTY YEARS OF PROGRESS IN FIVE," that aroused the nation and caught its imagination. Kubitschek believed that only in this way would Brazil become a world power and be able to achieve its great destiny. Time was of the essence. A presidential term was for five years only. Hence, "FIFTY YEARS IN FIVE!" The majority of the President's highly publicized production goals, both in the public and private sectors, were achieved or surpassed. These great accomplishments stagger the imagination. In five years the Brazilian people surpassed the *impossible goals* which their leader had established.

However, constructing the city of Brasilia, and making it the Nation's Capital in 1960, seemed most certainly to be "The Impossible Dream." Opposition to this move was fierce, especially from the population of Rio de Janeiro, which was then the Capital City. Nevertheless, for three and one-half years construction was pushed at a frantic pace, with men and equipment being flown to the site until access roads were opened. Speed was required if Kubitschek was to finish his term in office at Brasilia as he had planned.

While pursuing our study of this great leader, we found a partial answer to our quest inscribed on a wall of the humble building that was used as the headquarters of the President while Brasilia was being built.

Here in this room, President Juscelino Kubitschek remained overnight for the first time on November 10, 1956, and it served him during several months when it was the only light to indicate the presence of man in the solitude in which a SHINING IDEAL and an UNCONQUERABLE WILL gave birth to Brasilia.

From this humble room, he sent out the first acts destined for the construction of Brasilia, with a rhythm of intensity which amazed the world and filled the Brazilians with a justified pride which has never broken.[9]

After decades of talking and planning, the physical work now commenced in a sudden burst. There were some 30,000 men at work on a three-shift basis. As Kubitschek stood on the site where soon Brasilia would rise, he said: "From this solitude of the Central Plateau, shortly to be transformed into a center where vital national decisions will be made, I look toward tomorrow and foresee the dawn of my country's great destiny with unshakable faith and unlimited confidence."[10]

Oscar Niemeyer, the brilliant architect, not only was able to capture the "SHINING IDEAL" of this powerful leader, but was able to design a city that represented modern city planning on an immense and colossal scale. It was Kubitschek who was able to take a city off of the drafting board and bring it to life. This indeed took an "UNCONQUERABLE WILL." "The heart of the city is a great triangle, a form which symbolizes equilibrium. The symbolism is not an accident; it represents the system of checks and balances on which the government was founded. The plaza of the three towers, as the triangle is called, is bordered by the headquarters of each of the three branches of the Government: the Congressional Palace, the Palace of Justice, and the Executive Palace. These gleaming, ultramodern towers of Brasilia, rising from the red-brown soil of the Central Plateau, signal Brazil's determination to open the great interior of the country to development."[11]

While the construction of the new Capital moved forward with a rhythm of intensity that amazed the world, "there were 20,000 at work on the Belem-Brasilia highway. And yet another 14,000 at work on the Fortaleza-Brasilia highway which was a 1,060 mile project. Also, the 400 mile highway between Belo Horizonte and Brasilia was paved in time for Brasilia's inauguration on April 12, 1960."[12] Brasilia was becoming the hub of a network of great highways connecting the Northern and Western sections of the nation with Rio de Janeiro. It also connected the new Capital with the great industrial city of Sao Paulo in the South. Over these roads multiple thousands of people were funneled into the new Capital city.

Kubitschek promised his fellow countrymen that he would give to them "FIFTY YEARS OF PROGRESS IN FIVE." His "Impossible Dream" was beginning to live. As he looked toward the East, and the South, the dawn of a great new day was already lighting cities and farms. "In the Northeast, fingers of light were spreading slowly over the countryside. Across the endless horizons of the Central Plateau and in the gloom of the Amazonian forest, a faint tinge of its illuminating rays was reflected in the night sky. Throughout this giant nation the people were stirring, preparing to deal confidently with a future that was already upon them."[13]

Industry boomed under this giant leader. To supply the desperately needed power for industrialization, the President authorized the construction of the gigantic Furnas Hydroelectric project and the impressive Tres Marias Dam on the Sao Francisco River. The principal heavy industry, steel, continued to expand. An automobile industry was also created. By May of 1967 a million and a half cars had rolled off the assembly lines of the ten automobile producers."[14] Tractors and trucks also went into production. Soon the companies not only manufactured enough automobiles to meet their own country's need, but began to export cars, tractors, and trucks to neighboring countries.

The Leader's promise: "FIFTY YEARS OF PROGRESS IN FIVE" had been fulfilled. Brasilia, a daring futuristic city with magnificent architecture, had captured the imagination and the admiration of the world. While the nation as a whole acclaimed this seemingly impossible feat, there were some who disagreed. One of the leading bankers in Sao Paulo told me in 1976 that he still regarded the moving of the Capital a dire mistake. Due to a conflict of schedules, I was not privileged to meet Juscelino Kubitschek and, because of the language barrier, my quest to learn more about the leadership of this dynamic man was not possible. However, his DREAMS and DARING call to mind the haunting melody and challenging words of the song "The Impossible Dream," from the musical *Man of La Mancha*. Truly, Juscelino Kubitschek reached the "Unreachable Stars"!

TO DREAM *"THE IMPOSSIBLE DREAM"* IS A BEGINNING.

TO MASTER THE BASICS OF LEADERSHIP AND CAUSE THAT DREAM TO *"LIVE"* IS: *THE HEART OF THE MATTER.*

REFERENCES
and
SELECTED BIBLIOGRAPHY

On the plains of hesitation
Bleach the bones of countless millions
Who, at the dawn of victory,
Sat down to rest, and resting, died.

—Fernando Edwardo Lee
São Paulo, Brazil

REFERENCES

PART I. FUNDAMENTALS OF LEADERSHIP

Chapter 1. *An Overview*

1. Thomas Carlyle, *Sartor Resartus & On Heroes and Hero Worship* (New York: Dutton, 1908), p. 1.

2. Ordway Tead, *The Art of Leadership* (New York: McGraw-Hill, 1935), p. 94.

Chapter 2. *A Definitive Meaning of Leadership*

1. John Kenneth Galbraith, *The Age of Uncertainty* (Boston: Houghton Mifflin, 1977), p. 330.

2. Ibid., p. 237.

227

3. Julius Gould and W. L. Kolf, eds., *The Dictionary of the Social Sciences* (New York: Free Press, 1964), p. 380.

4. Ibid.

5. David L. Sills, ed., *International Encyclopedia of the Social Sciences*, vol. 9 (New York: Macmillan, 1968), p. 91.

6. Ibid., p. 92.

7. George A. Theodorson and Achilles G. Theodorson, *A Modern Dictionary of Sociology* (New York: Crowell, 1969), p. 227.

8. Ibid.

9. Bernard M. Bass, *Leadership, Psychological and Organizational Behavior* (New York: Harper & Brothers, 1949), p. 89.

10. Ibid.

11. Roger M. Bellows, *Creative Leadership* (Englewood Cliffs, N.J.: Prentice-Hall, 1956), p. 9.

12. Kimball Young, *An Introductory Sociology* (New York: American Book Co., 1934), p. 403.

13. Sills, op. cit., p. 92.

14. Fred E. Fiedler, *A Theory of Leadership Effectiveness* (New York: McGraw-Hill, 1967), p. 7.

15. Sills, op. cit., pp. 91-93.

16. Fiedler, op. cit., p. 8.

17. Ibid.

18. Jerome Davis, *Contemporary Social Movements* (New York: Century Co., 1930), p. 13.

19. Young, op. cit., p. 410.

20. Fiedler, loc. cit.

21. Young, op. cit., p. 411.

22. Niccolo Machiavelli, *The Prince*, trans. James B. Atkinson (Indianapolis: Bobbs-Merrill, 1976).

23. Peter F. Drucker, *The Effective Executive* (New York: Harper & Row, 1966), p. 1.

24. Ted W. Engstrom, *The Making of a Christian Leader* (Grand Rapids: Zondervan, 1976), p. 23.

Chapter 3. *A Philosophy of Life*

1. Robert Payne, *The Life and Death of Adolph Hitler* (New York: Praeger, 1973), p. x.

2. J. G. McDonald, *Rhodes—A Life* (Bulawayo: Books of Rhodesia, 1971), p. 387.

Chapter 4. *Seven World Changers*

GOLDA MEIR

1. Terry Morris, *Shalom, Golda* (New York: Hawthorn, 1971), p. 14.

2. Ibid., p. 15.

3. Ibid., p. 33.

4. Peggy Mann, *Golda: The Life of Israel's Prime Minister* (New York: Coward, McCann & Geoghegan, 1971), p. 137.

5. Julie Nixon Eisenhower, *Special People* (New York: Simon & Schuster, 1977), p. 13.

6. Mann, op. cit., p. 176.

7. Ibid., p. 179.

8. Eisenhower, op. cit., p. 20.

THOMAS ALVA EDISON

9. Robert Conot, *A Streak of Luck* (New York: Seaview, 1979), p. 58.

10. Emory S. Bogardus, *Leaders and Leadership* (New York: Appleton-Century, 1934), p. 235.

11. *The National Cyclopedia of American Biography*, vol. XXV (New York: James T. White, 1936), pp. 2-3.

12. Zig Zigler, *See You at the Top* (Gretna, La.: Pelican, 1976), p. 6.

13. George S. Bryan, *Edison: The Man and His Work* (New York: Garden City, 1926), p. 271.

14. Ibid., p. 281.

MAO TSE-TUNG

15. Edgar Snow, *Red Star over China* (New York: Garden City, 1939), p. 121.

16. Hugh Purcell, *Mao Tse-tung* (New York: St. Martin's Press, 1977), pp. 18-19.

17. Ibid., p. 28.

18. Jerome Ch'en, *Mao and the Chinese Revolution* (London: Oxford University Press, 1965), p. 185.

19. Purcell, op. cit., p. 47.

20. Ibid., p. 50.

21. Ibid., p. 1.

22. Ibid., p. 62.

ALBERT SCHWEITZER

23. Norman Cousins, *Dr. Schweitzer of Lambarene* (New York: Harper & Brothers, 1960), p. 17.

24. Albert Schweitzer, *Memories of Childhood and Youth* (New York: Macmillan, 1963), p. 52.

25. Ibid., p. 70.

26. Ibid., p. 117.

27. Herman Hagedorn, *Prophet in the Wilderness* (New York: Macmillan, 1954).

28. Magnus C. Patter, *Albert Schweitzer: Life and Message* (Boston: Beacon Press, 1950), p. 190.

J. PAUL GETTY

29. J. Paul Getty, *How to Be a Successful Executive* (Chicago: HMH, 1971), p. 13.

30. Ibid., p. 12.

31. J. Paul Getty, *How to Be Rich* (Chicago: HMH, 1961), pp. 43-45.

32. J. Paul Getty, *As I See It: Autobiography of J. Paul Getty* (Englewood Cliffs, N.J.: Prentice-Hall, 1976), p. 269.

MICHELANGELO

33. Charles De Tolnay, *The Art and Thought of Michelangelo* (New York: Pantheon, 1964), p. 34.

34. Robert J. Clements, *Michelangelo: A Self-Portrait* (New York: New York University Press, 1968), p. 10.

35. Rolf Schott, *Michelangelo* (London: Thames & Hudson, 1963), p. 29.

36. De Tolnay, op. cit., pp. 7-8.

37. Irving Stone, *The Agony and the Ecstasy* (Garden City, N.Y.: Doubleday, 1961), p. 89.

38. *Lives of Seventy of the Most Eminent Painters, Sculptors, and Architects*, vol. 4 (New York: Traw Directory, 1896), p. 74.

39. Kenneth Clark, *Civilization: A Personal View* (New York: Harper & Row, 1970), p. 128.

40. Stone, op. cit., pp. 454-455.

41. Dino Formagio, *Michelangelo* (Milan: Uffici Press, 1955), p. 8.

42. Harold W. Reed, "The Thrust of Dedicated Personality," *Committed to Christ* (Grand Rapids: Baker Book, 1960), p. 15.

43. Stone, op. cit., p. 61.

DOUGLAS MacARTHUR

44. William Manchester, *American Caesar: Douglas MacArthur 1880-1964* (Boston: Little, Brown, 1978), p. 140.

45. Major E. Whon, Jr., *A Soldier Speaks* (New York: Frederick A. Praeger, 1965), p. 28.

46. Manchester, op. cit., p. 314.

47. Whon, op. cit., p. 122.

48. Ibid., pp. 132-133.

49. Ibid., p. 150.

50. Ibid., p. 241.

51. Ibid., p. 353.

PART II. EIGHT THEORIES OF LEADERSHIP

Chapter 5. *The Great Man Theory*

1. Leo Tolstoy, *War and Peace,* The Inner Sanctum Ed., trans. Louise & Aylmer Maude (New York: Simon & Schuster, 1954), p. 1335.

2. Thomas Carlyle, *Sartor Resartus & On Heroes and Hero Worship* (New York: Dutton, 1908), pp. 239-467.

3. Ibid., p. 248.

4. Ibid., pp. 250-251.

5. Ibid., p. 278.

6. Ibid., p. 280.

7. Ibid., pp. 290-291.

8. Ibid., p. 311.

9. Ibid., p. 239.

10. Ibid., p. 316.

11. Ibid., p. 333.

12. Ibid., p. 346.

13. Ibid., p. 357.

14. Ibid., p. 385.

15. Ibid., p. 405.
16. Ibid., p. 384.
17. Ibid., p. 430.
18. Ibid., p. 428.
19. Ibid., p. 440.
20. Ibid., p. 464.
21. Ibid., p. 467.

Chapter 6. *The Follower Theory*

1. *Guides to Good Supervision* (New York: American Management Assn., 1957), p. 38.
2. Ibid., p. 39.

Chapter 7. *The Situationist Theory*

1. John W. Gardner, *The Anti-Leadership Vaccine* (New York: Carnegie Corporation, 1965), p. 5.
2. Hubert Bonner, *Group Dynamics: Principles and Application* (New York: Ronald Press, 1959), p. 167.
3. Howard M. Carlisle, *Situational Management: A Contingency Approach to Leadership* (New York: American Management Assn., 1973), p. 130.
4. Ibid., pp. 102-103.
5. Ibid., p. 133.

Chapter 8. *The Creative Artist Theory*

1. Hal Reed, "The Artist as a Leader," address given to a leadership symposium at Kankakee, Ill., November 1979.
2. John Hersey, *The Writer's Craft* (New York: Knopf, 1974), p. 142.
3. Ibid., p. 14.
4. Arthur Koestler, *The Act of Creation* (New York: Macmillan, 1964), p. 649.
5. Ibid., p. 19.
6. Henry Hass, "Stimulating Creative Minds," *The Chemist*, vol. 32, no. 12, June 1955.
7. Koestler, op. cit., p. 27.

8. Richard Wolff, *Man at the Top: Creative Leadership* (Wheaton, Ill.: Tyndale House, 1969), p. 53.

9. Ordway Tead, *The Art of Leadership* (London: Whittlesey House, 1935), p. 33.

10. Robert H. Schuller, *Reach Out for New Life* (New York: Hawthorn, 1977), p. 71.

11. Reed, op. cit., p. 3.

Chapter 9. *The Intimidation Theory*

1. Edwin R. A. Selligman, Ed.-in-Chief, *Encyclopedia of the Social Sciences*, vol. 9 (New York: Macmillan, 1933), p. 239.

2. Ibid., p. 240.

3. Ibid., p. 241.

4. Robert J. Ringer, *Winning Through Intimidation* (Beverly Hills, Calif.: Los Angeles Book Publishing, 1973), p. 89.

5. Ibid., p. 90.

6. Ibid., pp. 96, 110.

Chapter 10. *The Lucky-Break Theory*

1. Max Gunther, *The Luck Factor* (New York: Macmillan, 1977), p. 121.

2. Leo Tolstoy, *War and Peace,* The Inner Sanctum Ed., trans. Louise & Aylmer Maude (New York: Simon & Schuster, 1954), p. xxxv.

3. *Valley News*, Northridge, California, January 3, 1978.

4. Auren Uris, *How to Be a Successful Leader* (New York: McGraw-Hill, 1953), p. 172.

Chapter 11. *The Conjuncture Theory*

1. Clarence Marsh Case, "Leadership and Conjuncture—A Sociological Hypothesis," *Sociology and Social Research Journal,* 17:510-18, July-August 1933.

2. L. P. Gerlach and V. H. Hine, *People, Power, Change: Movements of Social Transformation* (Indianapolis: Bobbs-Merrill, 1970), pp. 38-39.

3. Case, op. cit., p. 512.

4. Ibid., p. 516.

5. Fredrick J. Teggart, *Theory of History* (New Haven: Yale University Press, 1925), pp. 148-149.

6. Case, op. cit., p. 518.

Chapter 12. *The Reed Theory*

1. Emory S. Bogardus, *Leaders and Leadership* (New York: Appleton-Century, 1934), p. 269.

2. James E. Fixx, "The Fine Art of Making Up Your Mind," *Sky Magazine*, September 1977, p. 47.

3. George R. Terry and Roger H. Hermanson, *Principles of Management* (Homewood, Ill.: Learning Systems, 1968), p. 15.

4. Ibid.

5. Ibid., p. 17.

PART III. MOTIVATING FORCES IN LEADERSHIP

Chapter 13. *The Transforming Force of Vision*

1. Harold W. Reed, *Committed to Christ* (Grand Rapids: Baker Books, 1960), p. 49.

2. Carl W. Linderman, *Invitations to Vision* (Dubuque, Ia.: W. C. Brown, 1967), p. 11.

3. Edmund Morris, *The Rise of Theodore Roosevelt* (New York: Coward, McCann & Geoghegan, 1979), p. 583.

4. Ibid., p. 729.

5. Ibid.

6. Robert H. Schuller, *Move Ahead with Possibility Thinking* (Garden City, N.Y.: Doubleday, 1967), p. 7.

Chapter 14. *The Creative Force of Ideas*

1. Eliot D. Hutchinson, *How to Think Creatively* (New York: Abingdon Press, 1949), pp. 19-20.

2. Stanwood Cobb, *The Importance of Creativity* (Metuchen, N.J.: Scarecrow Press, 1967), p. 119.

3. Ibid., p. 97.

4. Ibid., p. 119.

5. Ibid., p. 120.

6. Ibid., p. 130.

7. Ibid., p. 132.

Chapter 15. *The Driving Force of Goal Setting*

1. Glenn Bland, *Success: The Glenn Bland Method* (Wheaton, Ill.: Tyndale House, 1972), p. 44.

2. Gene Farmer and Dora J. Hamblin, *First on the Moon: A Voyage with Neil Armstrong, Michael Collins, Edwin E. Aldrin* (Boston: Little, Brown, 1970), p. 268.

Chapter 16. *The Miracle Force of Enthusiasm*

1. Ordway Tead, *The Art of Leadership* (New York: McGraw-Hill, 1935), p. 98.

2. Ibid., p. 100.

3. Norman Vincent Peale, *Creative Help for Daily Living* (New York: Foundation for Christian Living, 1970), p. 3.

4. Charles Schwab, *Leadership on the Job* (New York: Holt, Rinehart & Winston, 1957), p. 17.

5. Norman Vincent Peale, *Enthusiasm Makes the Difference* (Englewood Cliffs, N.J.: Prentice-Hall, 1967), p. 38.

6. Ibid.

Chapter 17. *The Stimulating Force of Optimism*

1. Dale Carnegie, *How to Stop Worrying and Start Living* (New York: Simon & Schuster, 1948), p. 242.

2. Glenn Bland, *Success: The Glenn Bland Method* (Wheaton, Ill.: Tyndale House, 1972), p. 110.

3. Donald A. Laird, *The Technique of Building Personal Leadership* (New York: McGraw-Hill, 1944), p. 77.

4. *Clovis-Portales: Happy Home Finder* (Clovis-Portales, N. Mex., 1979), p. 14.

5. Helen Keller, *My Key of Life: Optimism* (New York: Crowell, 1926), p. 48.

6. Ibid., p. 54.

7. The Bible, King James Version, Phil. 4:13.

8. Helen Keller, op. cit., p. 56.

9. Robert H. Schuller, *Reach Out for New Life* (New York: Hawthorn, 1977), p. 135.

10. Ibid., p. 136.

11. The Bible, King James Version, Psalms 118:24.

12. Robert H. Schuller: quotation.

Chapter 18. *The Powerful Force of Organization*

1. Arnold S. Tannenbaum, *Control in Organization* (New York: McGraw-Hill, 1968), p. 76.

2. Ernest C. Miller, Ed.-in-Chief, *Organizational Dynamics Quarterly*, Winter 1980, p. 42.

3. Elton T. Reeves, *The Dynamics of Group Behavior* (New York: American Management Assn., 1970), pp. 26-27.

4. Ordway Tead, *The Art of Leadership* (New York: McGraw-Hill, 1935), p. 92.

5. Norman Vincent Peale, *The Power of Positive Thinking* (Englewood Cliffs, N.J.: Prentice-Hall, 1956), p. 15.

6. Robert H. Schuller: quotation.

PART IV. THE HEART OF THE MATTER

Chapter 19. *The Basics of Leadership*

1. Ordway Tead, *The Art of Leadership* (London: Whittlesey House, 1935), p. 90.

2. Ernst van Aaken, *Van Aaken Method* (Mountain View, Calif.: World, 1976), p. 12.

3. Auren Uris, *How to Be a Successful Leader* (New York: McGraw-Hill, 1953), p. 207.

4. Howard W. Johnson, "Education for Leadership." Address given to the symposium "Requirements for Leadership in the 1980's," University of North Carolina, Chapel Hill, 1967.

5. The Bible, King James Version, Rom. 8:28.

6. Edwin R. Selligman, Ed.-in-Chief, *Encyclopedia of the Social Sciences*, vol. 9 (New York: Macmillan, 1933), p. 283.

7. Leo Tolstoy, *War and Peace*, The Inner Sanctum Ed., trans. Louise & Aylmer Maude (New York: Simon & Schuster, 1954), p. 1335.

8. William Shakespeare, *Julius Caesar* (Cambridge, Mass.: Harvard University Press, 1955), p. 77.

9. Herbert Lockyer, *The Man Who Changed the World* (Grand Rapids: Zondervan, 1966), p. 247.

10. Henry W. Coray, *Son of Tears: Saint Augustine* (New York: Putnam's, 1957), p. 12.

11. Theodore Roosevelt, The Sarbonne, Paris, France, April 23, 1910.

12. W. A. Swanberg, *Citizen Hearst* (New York: Scribner's, 1961), p. 525.

Chapter 20. *Impossible Dreams That Live!*

1. Langston Hughes: quotation.

2. William E. Simon, *A Time for Truth* (New York: McGraw-Hill, 1978).

3. Edgar A. Guest, "It Couldn't Be Done," *The Path to Home* (Chicago: Reilly & Lee, 1919), p. 37.

4. Ralph Waldo Emerson: quotation.

5. Abraham Lincoln: quotation.

6. Richard E. Pesqueira, *Equal Opportunity in Higher Education: Choice as Well as Access*, Pamphlet 97 (College Board of Review, 1975).

7. Victor Hugo: quotation.

8. Bello, José M., *A History of Modern Brazil, 1889-1964*, trans. James L. Taylor (Stanford, Calif: Stanford University Press, 1966), p. 335.

9. Quotation trans. Charles W. Gates (Brasilia: 1976).

10. Richard P. Momsen, Jr., *Brazil: A Giant Stirs* (Princeton, N.J.: Van Nostrand, 1968), p. 124.

11. E. W. Egan, *Brazil in Pictures* (New York: Sterling, 1967), p. 49.

12. Ibid., p. 35.

13. Richard P. Momsen, loc. cit.

14. E. Bradford Burns, *Nationalism in Brazil: A Historical Survey* (New York: Frederick A. Praeger, 1968), pp. 92-93.

SELECTED BIBLIOGRAPHY

Adair, John. *Leadership, Training for Leadership.* London: MacDonald, 1934.

Allison, Graham T. *Essence of Decision.* Boston: Little, Brown, 1971.

Armerding, Hudson T. *Leadership.* Wheaton, Ill.: Tyndale House, 1978.

Baklanoff, Eric N., ed. *New Perspectives of Brazil.* Nashville: Vanderbilt University Press, 1966.

Baldridge, J. Victor. *Power and Conflict in the·University.* New York: Wiley, 1971.

Basil, Douglas C. *Leadership Skills for Executive Action.* New York: American Management Assn., 1971.

Bass, Bernard M. *Leadership, Psychological and Organizational Behavior.* New York: Harper & Brothers, 1960.

Baxter, Bernice. *Group Experience the Democratic Way.* New York: Harper & Brothers, 1943.

Bell, Arthur D. *How to Get Along with People in the Church.* Grand Rapids: Zondervan, 1960.

Bell, Gerald D. *Leadership, The Achievers: Six Styles of Personality and Leadership.* Chapel Hill, N.C.: Preston-Hill, 1973.

Bello, José M. *A History of Modern Brazil, 1889-1964.* Trans. James L. Taylor. Stanford, Calif.: Stanford University Press, 1966.

Bellows, Roger M. *Creative Leadership.* Englewood Cliffs, N.J.: Prentice-Hall, 1956.

Bennis, Warren. *The Unconscious Conspiracy: Why Leaders Can't Lead.* New York: AMACOM, 1976.

Berne, Eric. *The Structure and Dynamics of Organizations and Groups.* Philadelphia: Lippincott, 1963.

Bertalanffy, Ludwig von. *General System Theory.* New York: Braziller, 1968.

Blake, Robert R. *Corporate Excellence Through Grid Organization Development.* Houston, Tex.: Gulf, 1968.

Bland, Glenn. *Success: The Glenn Bland Method.* Wheaton, Ill.: Tyndale House, 1972.

Blau, P. M. *The Dynamics of Bureaucracy.* Chicago: University of Chicago Press, 1955.

Blau, P. M., and W. R. Scott. *Formal Organizations.* San Francisco: Chandler, 1962.

Bogardus, Emory S. *Leaders and Leadership.* New York: Appleton-Century, 1934.

Bottomore, T. B. *Elites and Society.* New York: Basic Books, 1964.

Bowie, Walter Russell. *Men of Fire.* New York: Harper & Row, 1961.

Brandes, George. *Michelangelo: His Life, His Times, His Era.* New York: Ungar, 1963.

Breen, T. H. *The Character of the Good Ruler.* New Haven, Conn.: Yale University Press, 1970.

Brent, Charles H. *Leadership.* New York: Longmans, Green, 1908.

Brion, Marcel. *Michelangelo.* New York: Crown, 1940.

Brown, James D. *The Human Nature of Organizations.* New York: AMACOM, 1973.

Browne, C. G., and Thomas S. Cohn, eds. *The Study of Leadership.* Danville, Ill.: The Interstate, 1958.

Bryan, George S. *Edison: The Man and His Work*. New York: Garden City, 1926.

Buckley, Walter, ed. *Modern Systems Research for the Behavioral Sciences*. Chicago: Aldine, 1968.

_____. *Sociology and Modern Systems Theory*. Englewood Cliffs, N.J.: Prentice-Hall, 1967.

Burke, James. *Connections*. Boston: Little, Brown, 1978.

Burns, E. Bradford. *Nationalism in Brazil: A Historical Survey*. New York: Frederick A. Praeger, 1968.

Burns, James MacGregor. *Leadership*. New York: Harper & Row, 1978.

Burns, Tom, and G. M. Stalker. *The Management of Innovation*. London: Tavistock, 1961.

Carlisle, Howard M. *Situational Management: A Contingency Approach to Leadership*. New York: American Management Assn., 1973.

Carlyle, Thomas. *Heroes and Hero Worship: The Heroic in History*. New York: Rand, McNally, 1925.

Carter, Peter. *Mao*. London: Oxford University Press, 1976.

Cartwright, Dorwin, ed. *Group Dynamics: Research and Theory*. Evanston, Ill.: Row, Peterson, 1960.

Ch'en, Jerome. *Mao and the Chinese Revolution*. London: Oxford University Press, 1965.

Clark, Burton R. *The Open Door College*. New York: McGraw-Hill, 1960.

Clark, Kenneth. *Civilization, A Personal View*. New York: Harper & Row, 1969.

Clements, Robert J. *Michelangelo: A Self Portrait*. New York: New York University Press, 1968.

Cleveland, Harlan. *The Future Executive*. New York: Harper & Row, 1972.

Cobb, Stanwood. *The Importance of Creativity*. Metuchen, N.J.: Scarecrow Press, 1967.

Cohen, Michael D. *Leadership and Ambiguity: The American College President*. New York: McGraw-Hill, 1974.

Colman, James S. *Community Conflict*. New York: Free Press, 1957.

Conot, Robert. *A Streak of Luck*. New York: Seaview, 1979.

Cooper, Joseph D. *The Art of Decision Making*. Garden City, N.Y.: Doubleday, 1961.

Coray, Henry W. *Son of Tears: Saint Augustine*. New York: Putnam's, 1957.

Cousins, Norman. *Dr. Schweitzer of Lambarene.* New York: Harper & Brothers, 1960.

Crawford, Robert P. *The Techniques of Creative Thinking.* New York: Hawthorn, 1954.

Crossland, Weldon F. *Better Leaders for Your Church.* Nashville: Abingdon Press, 1955.

Cyert, Richard M., and James C. March. *A Behavioral Theory of the Firm.* Englewood Cliffs, N.J.: Prentice-Hall, 1963.

Dahl, Robert A. *Who Governs?* New Haven, Conn.: Yale University Press, 1961.

Davis, Jerome. *Contemporary Social Movements.* New York: Century Co., 1930.

De Tolnay, Charles. *The Art and Thought of Michelangelo.* New York: Pantheon, 1964.

Dos Passos, John. *Brazil on the Move.* Garden City, N.Y.: Doubleday, 1963.

Douglas, Mack R. *How to Make a Habit of Succeeding.* Grand Rapids: Zondervan, 1966.

_____. *Success Can Be Yours.* Grand Rapids: Zondervan, 1968.

Dressel, Paul L. *Administrative Leadership.* San Francisco: Jossey-Bass, 1981.

Drucker, Peter F. *The Effective Executive.* New York: Harper & Row, 1966.

_____. *Men, Ideas & Politics.* New York: Harper & Row, 1971.

_____. *The Practice of Management.* New York: Harper & Brothers, 1954.

Dubin, Robert, et al. *Leadership and Productivity.* San Francisco: Chandler, 1965.

Eaton, Jeanette. *Leader by Destiny.* New York: Harcourt, Brace, 1938.

Edwards, Mary. *Leadership Development and the Workers Conference.* Nashville: Abingdon Press, 1967.

Egan, E. W. *Brazil in Pictures.* New York: Sterling, 1967.

Eisenhower, Julie Nixon. *Special People.* New York: Simon & Schuster, 1977.

Engstrom, Ted W. *The Making of a Christian Leader.* Grand Rapids: Zondervan, 1976.

Etzioni, Amitai. *A Comparative Analysis of Complex Organizations.* Glencoe, Ill.: Free Press, 1961.

_____. *Complex Organizations.* New York: Holt, Rinehart & Winston, 1964.

Ferrell, Robert H. *The Eisenhower Diaries.* New York: W. W. Norton, 1981.

Fiedler, Fred E. *A Theory of Leadership Effectiveness.* New York: McGraw-Hill, 1967.

Fisher, R. "Fractionating Conflict," *International Conflict and Behavioral Science: The Craigville Papers.* New York: Basic Books, 1964.

Fitzgerald, Gerald B. *Leadership in Recreation.* New York: Ronald Press, 1951.

Formagio, Dino. *Michelangelo.* Milan: Uffici Press, 1955.

Franck, Frederick. *Days with Albert Schweitzer.* New York: Henry Holt, 1959.

Fraser, Antonia. *Heros & Heroines.* New York: A & W, 1980.

Friedman, Milton, and Rose Friedman. *Free to Choose: A Personal Statement.* New York: Harcourt Brace Jovanovich, 1980.

Freeman, Graydon. *How to Pick Leaders.* New York: Funk & Wagnalls, 1950.

Galbraith, Jay. "Environmental and Technological Determinants of Organizational Design," *Studies in Organizational Design.* Ed. Jay W. Lorsch and Paul R. Lawrence. Homewood, Ill.: Irwin, Dorsey Press, 1970.

Galbraith, John Kenneth. *The Age of Uncertainty.* Boston: Houghton Mifflin, 1977.

Gangel, Kenneth. *Leadership for Church Education.* Chicago: Moody Press, 1970.

Gardner, John W. *Excellence: Can We Be Equal and Excellent, Too?* New York: Harper & Row, 1961.

_____. *Self-Renewal.* New York: Harper & Row, 1964.

Gerlach, L. P., and V. H. Hine. *People, Power, Change: Movements of Social Transformation.* Indianapolis: Bobbs-Merrill, 1970.

Gerth, H. H., and C. Wright Mills. *From Max Weber: Essays in Sociology.* New York: Oxford University Press, 1969.

Getty, J. Paul. *As I See It: Autobiography of J. Paul Getty.* Englewood Cliffs, N.J.: Prentice-Hall, 1976.

_____. *How to Be a Successful Executive.* Chicago: HMH, 1971.

_____. *How to Be Rich.* Chicago: HMH, 1961.

Gordon, Thomas. *Group-centered Leadership.* Boston: Houghton Mifflin, 1955.

————. *L. E. T.: Leader Effectiveness Training.* Ridgefield, Conn.: Wyden, 1977.

Gouldner, Alvin Ward. *Studies in Leadership.* New York: Russell, 1965.

Grimm, Herman. *Life of Michael Angelo,* vol. II. Trans. Fanny E. Bunnett. Boston: Little, Brown, 1896.

Gunther, Max. *The Luck Factor.* New York: Macmillan, 1977.

Hagedorn, Herman. *Prophet in the Wilderness.* New York: Macmillan, 1954.

Haiman, Franklyn S. *Group Leadership and Democratic Action.* Boston: Houghton Mifflin, 1959.

Hall, D. M. *Dynamics of Group Action.* Danville, Ill.: The Interstate, 1960.

Harford, John A. *Life of Michael Angelo Buonarroti,* vol. I. New York: Longman, Brown, 1858.

Harrison, Raymond H. *Supervisory Leadership in Education.* New York: American Book Co., 1968.

Hawley, Willis D., and Frederick M. Wirt, eds. *The Search for Community Power.* Englewood Cliffs, N.J.: Prentice-Hall, 1968.

Hermann, Charles. *Crisis in Foreign Policy.* Indianapolis: Bobbs-Merrill, 1969.

Hersey, John. *The Writer's Craft.* New York: Knopf, 1974.

Hersey, Paul, and K. H. Blanchard. *Management of Organizational Behavior: Utilizing Human Resources.* Englewood Cliffs, N.J.: Prentice-Hall, 1969.

Holsten, Roy W., ed. *Symposium on the Requirements for Leadership in the 1980's.* Chapel Hill: University of North Carolina, 1967.

Hoyt, Edwin P. *The Supersalesmen.* Cleveland: World, 1962.

Hunt, James G., and Lars L. Larson. *Leadership: the Cutting Edge.* Symposium held at Southern Illinois University, Oct. 27-28, 1976. Carbondale, Illinois: Southern Illinois University Press, 1977.

Hunter, Floyd. *Community Power Structure: A Study of Decision Makers.* Chapel Hill: University of North Carolina Press, 1953.

————. *Top Leadership, USA.* Chapel Hill: University of North Carolina Press, 1959.

Hutchinson, Eliot D. *How to Think Creatively.* New York: Abingdon Press, 1949.

Hyde, Douglas A. *Dedication and Leadership: Learning From the Communists.* Notre Dame, Ind.: University of Notre Dame Press, 1966.

Jacobs, James V. *Ten Steps to Leadership.* Cincinnati: Standard Publishing, 1956.

Jennings, Eugene E. *An Anatomy of Leadership: Princes, Heroes and Supermen.* New York: Harper & Brothers, 1960.

_____. *Routes to the Executive Suite.* New York: McGraw-Hill, 1971.

Jones, Charles E. *Life Is Tremendous!* Wheaton, Ill.: Tyndale House, 1968.

Keller, Frank A. *Managerial Decision Making: A Study of Leadership Styles.* Chicago: Barnes & Noble, 1971.

Keller, Helen. *My Key to Life: Optimism.* New York: Crowell, 1926.

Kemp, Clarence G. *Perspectives on the Group Process: A Foundation for Counseling With Groups.* Boston: Houghton Mifflin, 1964.

Kennedy, Robert F. *Thirteen Days.* New York: W. W. Norton, 1969.

King, Guy H. *A Leader Led.* Fort Washington, Pa.: Christian Literature Crusade, 1957.

Klein, Alan F. *How to Use Role Playing Effectively.* New York: Association Press, 1959.

Knapp, Forrest L. *Leadership Education in the Church.* New York: Abingdon Press, 1933.

Knowles, David. *Leaders of Religion.* Stanford, Calif.: Stanford University Press, 1971.

Knowles, Henry P. *Personality and Leadership Behavior.* Reading, Mass.: Addison-Wesley, 1971.

Koestler, Arthur. *The Act of Creation.* New York: Macmillan, 1964.

Komori, Paul K. *Principles for the Leader* (written in Japanese). Tokyo, Japan: 1960.

Kuhn, Thomas S. *The Structure of Scientific Revolutions.* Chicago: University of Chicago Press, 1962.

Laird, Donald A. *The Technique of Building Personal Leadership.* New York: McGraw-Hill, 1944.

Larned, Joseph N. *A Study of Greatness in Men.* New York: Libraries Press, 1911.

Lasswell, Harold D. *Power and Personality.* New York: Viking Press, 1966.

Lawrence, Paul R., and Jay W. Lorsch. *Organization and Environment.* Boston: Harvard Business School, Division of Research, 1967.

Lehrer, Stanley. *Leaders, Teachers and Learners in Academe: Partners in the Educational Process.* New York: Appleton-Century-Crofts, 1970.

LeTourneau, Richard. *Management Plus: The Spiritual Dimension in Leadership.* Grand Rapids: Zondervan, 1973.

Linderman, Carl W. *Invitations to Vision.* Dubuque, Ia.: W. C. Brown, 1967.

Linkletter, Art. *Yes, You Can!* New York: Simon and Schuster, 1979.

Linscott, Robert N., ed. *Lives of the Most Eminent Painters, Sculptors and Architects.* New York: Modern Library, 1959.

Litterer, Joseph A. *Organizations: Structure and Behavior.* New York: Wiley, 1963.

Lorsch, Jay W., and Paul R. Lawrence, eds. *Studies in Organizational Design.* Homewood, Ill.: Irwin, Dorsey Press, 1970.

Ludwig, Emil. *Napoleon.* New York: Random House, 1953.

Lundborg, Louis B. *The Art of Being an Executive.* New York: Free Press, 1981.

MacArthur, Douglas. *Representative Speeches.* Washington: U.S. Government Printing Office, 1964.

_____. *A Soldier Speaks.* New York: Frederick A. Praeger, 1965.

Maccoby, Michael. *The Gamesman, The New Corporate Leaders.* New York: Simon & Schuster, 1976.

_____. *The Leader.* New York: Simon & Schuster, 1981.

Machiavelli, Niccolo. *The Prince.* Trans. James B. Atkinson. Indianapolis: Bobbs-Merrill, 1976.

Madison, Charles A. *Leaders and Liberals in 20th Century America.* New York: Ungar, 1961.

Madsen, Paul O. *The Person Who Chairs the Meeting.* Valley Forge, Pa.: Judson Press, 1973.

Maier, Norman. *Problem-solving Discussions and Conferences: Leadership Methods and Skills.* New York: McGraw-Hill, 1963.

Manchester, William. *American Caesar: Douglas MacArthur.* Boston: Little, Brown, 1978.

Mann, Peggy. *Golda: The Life of Israel's Prime Minister.* New York: Coward, McCann & Geoghegan, 1971.

March, James C., and Herbert A. Simon. *Organizations.* New York: Wiley, 1958.

McCall, Morgan W., Jr., and Michael M. Lombardo, eds. *Leadership: Where Else Can We Go?* Durham, N.C.: Duke University Press, 1978.

McDonald, J. G. *Rhodes: A Life.* Bulawayo: Books of Rhodesia, 1971.

Meir, Golda. *My Life.* New York: Putnam's, 1975.

Merrifield, Charles W. *Leadership in Voluntary Enterprise.* New York: Oceana, 1961.

Milson, Frederick W. *His Leadership and Ours*. London: Epworth Press, 1969.

Miner, John B. *Theories of Organizational Behavior*. Hinsdale, Ill.: Dryden Press, 1980.

Momsen, Richard P., Jr. *Brazil: A Giant Stirs*. Princeton, N.J.: Van Nostrand, 1968.

Montapert, Alfred A. *Success Planning Manual*. Englewood Cliffs, N.J.: Prentice-Hall, 1967.

Morgan, Charles H. *The Life of Michelangelo*. New York: Reynal, 1960.

Morris, Edmund. *The Rise of Theodore Roosevelt*. New York: Coward, McCann & Geoghegan, 1979.

Morris, Terry. *Shalom, Golda*. New York: Hawthorn, 1971.

Musashi, Miyamoto. *A Book of Five Rings*. New York: Overlook Press, 1974.

National Cyclopedia of American Biography, The, vol. XXV. New York: James T. White, 1936.

Nelson, Charles A. *Developing Responsible Public Leaders*. New York: Oceana, 1963.

Overstreet, Harry A. *Leaders for Adult Education*. Washington, D.C.: American Assn. for Adult Education, 1941.

Pahlavi, Mohammad Reza, The Shah. *Answer to History*. New York: Stein & Day, Scarborough House, 1980.

Pascale, R. T., and A. G. Athos. *The Art of Japanese Management*. New York: Simon & Schuster, 1981.

Patter, Magnus C. *Albert Schweitzer: Life and Message*. Boston: Beacon Press, 1950.

Payne, Robert. *The Life and Death of Adolph Hitler*. New York: Praeger, 1973.

Peale, Norman Vincent. *Enthusiasm Makes the Difference*. Englewood Cliffs, N.J.: Prentice-Hall, 1967.

_____. *The Power of Positive Thinking*. Englewood Cliffs, N.J.: Prentice-Hall, 1956.

Penland, Patrick R. *Group Dynamics and Individual Development*. New York: Dekker, 1974.

Peter, Laurence J., and Raymond Hull. *The Peter Principle*. New York: Morrow, 1969.

Petrullo, Luigi, and Bernard M. Bass, eds. *Leadership and Interpersonal Behavior*. New York: Holt, Rinehart & Winston, 1961.

Pierson, George W. *The Education of American Leaders: Comparative Contributions of U.S. Colleges and Universities.* New York: Praeger, 1969.

Pigors, Paul. *Leadership or Domination.* Boston: Houghton Mifflin, 1935.

Polsby, Nelson W. *Community Power and Political Theory.* New Haven, Conn.: Yale University Press, 1963.

Preston, Mary. *Christian Leadership.* Nashville: Sunday School Board of the Southern Baptist Convention, 1934.

Purcell, Hugh. *Mao Tse-tung.* New York: St. Martin's Press, 1977.

Ranesden, E. H. *The Letters of Michelangelo,* vol. I, 1496-1534. Ed. & annot. E. H. Ranesden. Stanford, Calif.: Stanford University Press, 1963.

Reed, Harold W. "The Thrust of Dedicated Personality," *Committed to Christ.* Grand Rapids: Baker Book, 1960.

Reeves, Elton T. *The Dynamics of Group Behavior.* New York: American Management Assn., 1970.

Rhodes, H. T. F., and C. J. Smith, eds. "Kubitschek, Juscilino," *The International Year Book and Statesman's Who's Who.* London: Burke's Peerage Limited, 1961.

Ringer, Robert J. *Winning Through Intimidation.* Beverly Hills, Calif.: Los Angeles Book Pub., 1973.

Roberts, Dorothy M. *Leadership of Teen-Age Groups.* New York: Association Press, 1950.

Robinson, George L. *Leaders of Israel.* Grand Rapids: Baker Book, 1955.

Rothenberg and Hansman, eds. *The Creative Question.* Durham, N.C.: Duke University Press, 1976.

Rubin, Louis J., ed. *Frontiers in School Leadership.* Chicago: Rand McNally, 1970.

Schmidt, Warren H., and Paul C. Buchanan. *Techniques That Produce Teamwork.* New London, Conn.: Croft, 1954.

Schott, Rolf. *Michelangelo.* London: Thames & Hudson, 1963.

Schuller, Robert H. *Move Ahead With Possibility Thinking.* Garden City, N.Y.: Doubleday, 1967.

_____. *Reach Out for New Life.* New York: Hawthorn, 1977.

Schwab, Charles. *Leadership on the Job.* New York: Holt, Rinehart & Winston, 1957.

Schweitzer, Albert. *Memoirs of Childhood and Youth.* New York: Macmillan, 1963.

_____. *Out of My Life and Thought.* New York: Henry Holt, 1949.

_____. *The Teaching of Reverence for Life.* New York: Holt, Rinehart & Winston, 1965.

Seeman, Melvin. *Social Status and Leadership: The Case of the School Executive.* Columbus, Ohio: Ohio State University Press, 1960.

Selligman, Edwin R. A., Ed.-in-Chief. *Encyclopedia of the Social Sciences,* vol. 9. New York: Macmillan, 1933.

Selvin, Hanan C. *The Effects of Leadership.* Glencoe, Ill.: Free Press, 1960.

Selznick, Philip. *Leadership in Administration: A Sociological Interpretation.* Evanston, Ill.: Row, Peterson, 1957.

_____. *TVA and the Grass Roots.* New York: Harper & Row, 1949.

Simon, William E. *A Time for Truth.* New York: McGraw-Hill, 1978.

Siu, R. G. H. *The Craft of Power.* New York: Wiley, 1979.

Snow, Edgar. *Red Star over China.* New York: Garden City, 1939.

Solzhenitsyn, Aleksander I. *The First Circle.* New York: Harper & Row, 1968.

Spruce, Fletcher. *Of Grasshoppers and Giants: A Formula for Achieving Ministers.* Kansas City, Mo.: Beacon Hill Press, 1975.

Stahl, LeRoy. *How to be a Successful Emcee.* Minneapolis: Denison, 1953.

Stock, Harry T. *Young People and Their Leaders.* Chicago: Pilgrim Press, 1933.

Stogdill, Ralph M. *Handbook of Leadership: A Survey of Theory and Research.* New York: Free Press, 1974.

Stone, Irving. *The Agony and the Ecstasy.* Garden City, N.Y.: Doubleday, 1961.

Stroup, Herbert. *Bureaucracy in Higher Education.* New York: Free Press, 1966.

Swanberg, W. A. *Citizen Hearst: A Biography of William Randolph Hearst.* New York: Scribner's, 1961.

Swearengen, Rodger, ed. *Leaders of the Communist World.* New York: Free Press, 1971.

Tannenbaum, Arnold S. *Control in Organization.* New York: McGraw-Hill, 1968.

Tannenbaum, Arnold S., et al. *Hierarchy in Organizations.* San Francisco: Jossey-Bass, 1974.

_____. *Leadership and Organization.* New York: McGraw-Hill, 1961.

Tead, Ordway. *The Art of Leadership.* New York: McGraw-Hill, 1935.

Teggart, Fredrick J. *Theory of History*. New Haven, Conn.: Yale University Press, 1925.

Terrill, Ross. *800,000,000: The Real China*. Boston: Little, Brown, 1971.

Terry, George R., and Roger H. Hermanson. *Principles of Management*. Homewood, Ill.: Learning Systems, 1968.

Thomas, Lowell. *The Vital Spark*. New York: Doubleday, 1959.

Thompson, J. D. *Organizations in Action*. New York: McGraw-Hill, 1967.

Thorndike, Joseph J., Jr. *The Magnificent Builders*. New York: Simon & Schuster, 1978.

Titus, Charles H. *The Process of Leadership: Human Relations in the Making*. Dubuque, Ia.: W. C. Brown, 1950.

Tolstoy, Leo. *War and Peace*, The Inner Sanctum Ed. Trans. Louise & Aylmer Maude. New York: Simon & Schuster, 1954.

Townsend, Robert. *Up the Organization*. New York: Knopf, 1970.

Uris, Auren. *How to Be a Successful Leader*. New York: McGraw-Hill, 1953.

Van Aaken, Ernst. *Van Aaken Method*. Mountain View, Calif.: World, 1976.

Vasari, Giorgio. *Lives of the Most Eminent Painters, Sculptors and Architects*, vol. IV. Ed. Blashfield & Hopkins. London: George Bell.

Verba, Sidney. *Small Groups and Political Behavior: A Study of Leadership*. Princeton, N.J.: Princeton University Press, 1961.

Verkuyl, Gerrit. *Qualifying Men for Church Work*. Chicago: Revell, 1927.

Von Einem, Herbert. *Michaelangelo*. Trans. Ronald Taylor. London: Methuen, 1959.

Wagner, Joseph A. *Successful Leadership in Group and Organization*. San Francisco: Chandler, 1959.

Weber, Clarence A. *Leadership in Personnel Management in Public Schools*. St. Louis: W. H. Green, 1970.

White, Theodore H. *China: The Roots of Madness*. New York: W. W. Norton, 1968.

White, William R. *Leadership*. Boston: Meador, 1951.

Wizeyewardene, Gehan, ed. *Leadership and Authority: A Symposium*. Singapore: University of Malaya Press, 1968.

Wolff, Richard. *Man at the Top: Creative Leadership*. Wheaton, Ill.: Tyndale House, 1969.

Zaleznik, Abraham. *Human Dilemmas of Leadership*. New York: Harper & Row, 1966.

Zaleznik, Abraham, and Manfred E. Kets De Vries. *Power and the Corporate Mind*. Boston: Houghton Mifflin, 1975.

Ziglar, Zig. *See You at the Top*. Gretna, La.: Pelican, 1976.

Periodicals

Case, Clarence Marsh. "Leadership and Conjuncture: A Sociological Hypothesis." *Sociology and Social Research Journal*, July-August 1933.

Devoss, Richard M. "Success Is Not Sinful." *Saturday Evening Post*, March 1980.

Fixx, James E. "The Fine Art of Making Up Your Mind." *Sky Magazine*, September 1977.

Hass, Henry B. "Stimulating Creative Minds." *The Chemist*, vol. 32, no. 12, June 1955.

Latham, Gary P., and Edwin A. Locke. "Goal Setting: A Motivational Technique That Works." *Organizational Dynamics Quarterly*, vol. 8, no. 2, Autumn 1979.

Mockler, Robert J. "Situational Theory of Management." *Harvard Business Review*, May-June 1971.

Organizational Dynamics Quarterly, vol. 9, no. 2, Autumn 1980.

Planning for Higher Education, vol. 4, no. 6, December 1975.

"People of the Week." *U.S. News and World Report*, Jan. 6, 1956.

Woodward, Joan. "Management and Technology." *Problems of Progress in Industry*, no. 3, 1958.

Miscellaneous

Gardner, John W. *The Anti-Leadership Vaccine*. The Carnegie Corporation, 1965.

Johnson, Howard W. "Education for Leadership." Address given to the symposium, "Requirements for Leadership in the 1980's," at the University of North Carolina, Chapel Hill, 1967.

Peale, Norman Vincent. *Keep Enthusiasm Going for You*. Pawling, N.Y.: Foundation for Christian Living, vol. 21, no. 24.

Pesqueira, Richard E. *Equal Opportunity in Higher Education: Choice as Well as Access*. Pamphlet 97. College Board of Review, 1975.

Reed, Hal. "The Artist as a Leader." Address given to a leadership symposium at Kankakee, Ill., November 1979.